SISTER
FAUSTINA KOWALSKA
HER LIFE AND MISSION

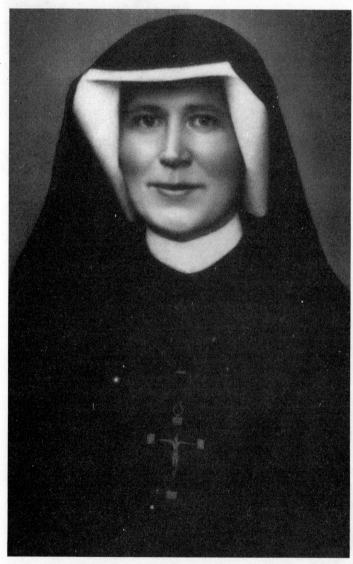

1. Sister Faustina Kowalska, Servant of God

Maria Tarnawska

SISTER FAUSTINA KOWALSKA — her life and mission

Foreword by
Bishop Szczepan Wesoły

Translated by Anne Hargest-Gorzelak

Marians of the Immaculate Conception
MARIAN HELPERS
STOCKBRIDGE, MA 01263

DECLARATION

Until such time as the Church formally decrees its approval, only
private and human faith is attributed to the revelations, extraordinary
graces and events described in this booklet. There is no intention, in
relating them, to anticipate a decree of the Holy See. The devotion is thus
for private use.

ISBN 0-944203-09-4
(previously published by *Veritas Foundation Publication Centre*
under ISBN 0-948202-43-2)

First published: 1989
Second edition with revisions (2nd printing): 1990

Available for North American Distribution only from
Marian Helpers, Stockbridge, MA 01263
1-800-462-7426 U.S.A. — 1-800-344-2836 CANADA

FOREWORD

St. John teaches us that *"No one has ever seen God; the only Son who is in the bosom of the father, He has made Him known".*(John I, v. 18).

Christ came into the world so that, by His humanity, He could pass on His divine mission, tell us the truth about His Father, and through His death and resurrection unite us once again with His Father.

His mission is constantly passed on to the world by people who, because of their special vocation, voice it down the generations. It is also passed on by all who, living with Christ, witness to Him in their lives according to the last commandment of Christ, *"that repentance and forgiveness of sins should be preached in His Name to all nations... You are witnesses of these things"* (Luke 24, v. 47-48).

From everyday experience we know that a witness is one who shares with others what he has seen and heard, someone who shares with us his experiences. Christ commanded His disciples so to do, and also all who believe in Him.

An apostle is, above all, a man of God, a man who lives by Christ. An apostle is not a man who propagandizes, seeking successes and followers, but a man living by Christ and revealing the Name of Christ to the world. In a farewell address at the Last Supper, He asked that as He was with the Father, so those who believed should be one with Him. *"I in them, and Thou in me, that they may become perfectly one, so that the*

5

world may know that Thou hast sent me... I have made known to them Thy Name, and I will make It known, that the love with which Thou hast loved me may be in them, and I in them" (John 17, v. 23, v. 26).This is the real meaning of apostolate, to live with Christ so as to make His Name known.

When this truth seems to be vanishing or forgotten, Christ reminds us of it again through His intervention in the souls of those of the faithful who live united with Him in a special way.

Such interventions have been various. One of them is the message of Divine Mercy which Sister Faustina, a Polish nun, passes on to the world of today.

This book gives us a picture of Sister Faustina, an account of her life, her spiritual formation and her life in Christ. In learning about her life, we shall more fully understand the message, *"God, Who is rich in mercy, out of the great love with which He loved us..."* (Epistle to the Ephesians, 2, v.4). She herself in her own life experienced particular Divine Mercy and was an authentic apostle of the Mercy. She passed on to the world what she had herself known. Christ made use of her so that she could teach us and remind us of the greatness of Divine Merciful Love. This reminder is today most contemporary and greatly necessary.

In his Encyclical on Divine Mercy, the Holy Father Pope John Paul II writes, *"The modern intellect, perhaps more so than the mind of past generations, appears to oppose a God of mercy, and also aspires to push the very idea of mercy to the periphery of life and cut it off from the human heart. The very word and concept of "mercy" seems to hinder man, who, through the previously unknown development of science and technology has, more than at any time in the past, become a ruler: he has made the earth subject to him."* This "rule over the earth", often understood in a partial and superficial way, seems not to have left room for mercy.

This, then, is why the truth about Mercy is so necessary to today's generation. The Pope says, *"The truth revealed in Christ concerning God, that He is "the Father of Mercy", allows us to "see" Him specially near to man when man suffers, when he is threatened at the very root of his human dignity and existence. Therefore many people and many communities, directed by a lively sense of faith, turn almost spontaneously to the Divine Mercy in the present situation of the Church and the world. It is Christ Himself who doubtless causes this, acting through His Spirit in the depths of the human heart. For the divine mystery revealed by Him, that He is "the Father of mercy", becomes, in the context of the threats to humanity in our times, a particular challenge to the Church."*

In following the life of Sister Faustina, we shall more easily understand that truth of which Christ reminds us through her, that He Himself is strength in overcoming difficulty and that He is our hope. He says, *"Come to Me, all who labour and are heavy laden, and I will give you rest."* (Matthew 11, v. 28).

Bishop Szczepan Wesoły

INTRODUCTION

In writing the story of the life of Sister Faustina Kowalska of the Congregation of the Sisters of Our Lady of Mercy, the apostle of Divine Mercy, certain difficulties are met at the beginning. We do not have accurate and first-hand knowledge of her life. The chief source is her "Diary", which she wrote during the last four years of her life at the command of her confessor. However, there is little in it on the subject of her childhood and early youth, i.e. the period before she entered the religious life. It is true that in the first version of her diary there was a much more exact discussion of those years, but unfortunately in the absence of her spiritual director, Rev. Prof. Michael Sopoćko, Sister Faustina burnt her diary, misled by an evil spirit. Fr. Sopoćko ordered her to rewrite the part that was destroyed, but she did so in an abbreviated form, incomplete and chaotic.

Thus, she has left us no information from that time in which the principal aspects of the human character and personality are formed, and we cannot learn from her (apart from a mention in a single sentence) when her sense of vocation first arose and how it developed, later so beautifully to be realized in all its fullness. Only the memories of her family and all those who kept her in faithful remembrance, collected in many cases many years after her death, can throw some light upon the childhood and early youth of Helenka, who became Sister Faustina Kowalska. These memories are, however, scanty, partial and monotonously repetitive. We have full biographical details only after she had entered religion. From this time on, we have a rich and exhaustive description of Sister Faustina's inner life, given by herself in her diary, and also in the copious memories of her superiors and numerous companions in the Community, as well as those of the convent employees and wards. There is also the recollection of her confessor, in this case particularly significant.

Of course, one might observe that these gaps in our information should not perturb us, since we are not principally concerned with her but with her mission received from Jesus. Naturally, the latter is our chief concern. Nevertheless, her mission was so closely connected with her personality that it would be impossible to omit details of her. She was not merely a passive instrument. Jesus assured her of an active role in passing on that message He wished us to know.

Additionally, the paths He led her along on the way to greater perfection and closer union with Himself are instructive - they show how He formed her so that she might properly and effectively remind the world of that greatest truth of the Gospels, Mercy; and of the constantly pulsing fountain and source of that Mercy: Jesus hidden in the Most Holy Sacrament. This preparation by Jesus, by mystical maturing until she could be His bride, and later His apostle, can be followed in her case in the most minute detail. It was thus important to be able to begin our account in her childhood, when the first memories of her family and those who knew her at this time are some help to us.

The material we have on Sister Faustina shows her from two aspects: the interior and the exterior. We learn of the interior side, her experiences and spiritual development, and her attitude to those about her, which she reveals in her own words with astonishing and disarming frankness, directly and without inhibitions, concealing neither her failings, nor the hesitations or the difficulty she often had in understanding the will of God. What Jesus asked of her did not come easily to her. She gave in gradually, and even reluctantly, although she always most fervently wished to be totally obedient to His will. In practice this posed problems difficult to resolve.

As far as the picture of Sister Faustina's spirituality seen from the exterior is concerned, the gamut of accounts from various people concerning her is wide: it ranges from those who were in permanent contact with her, through those who knew her well to those who met her once or twice, and from the purely external to those who knew her intimately and personally. In total, all these reminiscences provide a rich and interesting picture, not only of Sister Faustina's mission and how it came to maturity within her, but also how those among whom she lived and worked received it.

A superficial glance at the manuscripts lying before us will show the clear outline of the divine action, just as how a magnificent fruit arises from a little seed. The seed of vocation was sown by Christ in her soul in early childhood, and the crucial point appears to have been her first Holy Communion. The earliness of her vocation had the effect that, although the child Helenka Kowalska got on with everyone, personally committed and frank in her dealings with others, she never fell in love in an earthly sense, nor ever enjoyed a true, deep friendship. Everything was directed towards God. From a very early age she had her secrets with God, but revealed them with greater and greater caution when experience quickly showed her that her own interior life differed from those of others in her environment and was interpreted incorrectly. This explains why, even in the reminiscences of her family, details concerning her personal life are few. The reminiscences concentrate chiefly upon family relationships and the visible signs of piety. Helenka's heart was full of love for God from the time she was a tiny girl, and her loving filled her life to the point that she did not feel the need for other emotional outlets, nor did she even feel the need to be understood or to confide. She told everything to God, and expected an answer and an explanation for the problems besetting her. This can be clearly shown: all reminiscences uniformly declare that Helenka, later to become Sister Faustina, did not recall injury done to her by others and remained calm even with those who annoyed her greatly. At the same time, as her diary shows, she had grudges against them, but she took these to Jesus in her pain, only to Him, and He gradually erased a grudging memory from her soul transforming it into magnanimity, while He taught her to treat trials as of positive value, from which she was to learn love of one's neighbour by experience, a true disinterested and self-sacrificing love.

This close communion with God is the core of her life. There is, it is true, a certain hesitation on the question of the choice of her path in life: whether to enter a convent or to remain in the world. This however was caused only by external factors: the lack of permission from her parents, and it does not change the fact that God remained her one great love.

Nevertheless she loved her family too, and was openheartedly kind to all whom she knew. It appears even that she longed for closer contact with people. That singular experience which totally absorbed her, love which by its nature cannot be selfish nor even selfcentred, overflowed in her into a natural wish to embrace her whole environment. This was hidden in the discreet silence she in fact imposed on herself, but it shone through her whole being, emerging indirectly: from her deportment, from facial expressions, from her behaviour and from her interests and what she focused her attention upon. *"There was something intangible in her which radiated from her person, which sometimes other sisters felt. It was something positive, which, however, did not always meet with comprehension,"* said her superior in Vilnius.

The mission of Sister Faustina, reminding the world of the Divine Mercy, is a universal mission, and yet the framework within which it was to develop and radiate out beyond her life was so extremely modest and limited! She was a simple country girl, and in her convent she was a co-adjutrix, as her Congregation called such nuns, performing manual labour, since she had no professional qualifications. She had, however, a good deal of innate intelligence, and during the course of her work she amassed an extraordinary knowledge of human beings and their complicated spiritual problems. Above all, she understood what faith is in human life and what are its needs if it is develop fully and embrace the whole human soul. This had a crucial significance for her apostolic mission.

Sister Faustina's mental development was greatly affected by the fact that, in her religious community, she was several times moved to different houses and to different types of work: to the kitchen, the bakery, the garden and the work of portress. It certainly cannot have been easy or pleasant to get used to new conditions and a new place so frequently, but it did widen her outlook and made it easy to cut herself off from earthly ties and habits. In addition, work as portress and her contact with the convent wards, as also her occasional stays in hospital because of her increasingly severe lung disease, opened her eyes to problems of which she might otherwise have remained unconscious. Wherever she was, she quickly absorbed an elementary knowledge of the work and could work independently with a great sense of responsibility. Her knowledge was considerable, not only on practical matters, but extended to bringing up young people. She had brought with her all she had learned in her family home, where she had looked after her younger brothers and sisters, and what she learned when employed, caring for her employers' children. She was no pedagogue, but her influence was considerable, sometimes greater than that of professional teachers, even in her own environment.

Naturally, this did not make her life any easier, and sometimes caused conflicts. Observant by nature, she could perceive in another what is usually hidden from the too curious or intrusive. Her natural gift was supplemented by grace. Submitting herself to the action of grace, Sister Faustina obtained a supernatural gift, the charism of being able to read the human soul. She learned to see through human beings to their interior difficulties, sufferings and struggles. As time went on and as she gained experience, she became a marvellous counsellor, finding the appropriate solution to spiritual conflicts even when she had not been told of them. It is not surprising then, that although formally speaking she occupied a humble role in her religious community, this particular wisdom in observing human affairs from the standpoint of God's plan caused her more than once to rise beyond her social position, and it astounded those who were better educated than herself and sometimes occupying highly responsible posts. This trait drew attention to itself, in some cases attracting others to her, and in others repelling sharply. In general, however, dislike softened with the passage of time. Perhaps her gentle and peaceable approach, and the unchanging kindness and naturalness with which she treated those who disliked her, had their effect. Perhaps a longer contact with her simply caused the first ruffled feelings to subside.

The fact that she had her opponents is by no means a negative element in an appraisal of Sister Faustina. Every active person causes reaction, and a measure of a person's worth is not only his positive achievements and the appreciative reaction of those around him, but also the type of opposition he provokes and the method of coming to terms with it.

Let us try to imagine her. What was Helenka Kowalska like, when, as a nineteen-year-old she entered the convent? On the exterior, she was nothing special, small and slim. *"A skinny little thing, thin and poor looking, with not much expression, unpromising"*, was the description of the sister who received her when she first knocked at the door of her Congregation. This picture can be contrasted with another, more favourable, from the same period. It is not based upon a first impression, but arises from having frequently met her: *"Helenka gave me the impression that she was a good, discreet girl, with some great inner authority which I could not explain"*, writes Dr Katharine Steinberg, later to become a Franciscan nun at Laski. She had often seen Helenka at the house of her friend Mrs Lipszyc, where Helenka was employed for a year as a maid. This was Helenka's last post. She went straight from there into the convent.

Others confirm that some time had to elapse before one noticed Helenka, but then she drew one to her by her trusting and open attitude, and even made people curious by her seriousness and maturity, both above average.

The first impression was of her beautiful copper-sheened hair, gathered into a thick plait. From a fairly regular face with a strong chin, all rather pale and freckled, grey-green eyes with enormous pupils that reflected warmth and interest looked out. Hers was a cheerful open face, lightened even more by frequent smiles. Closer observation showed the liveliness and changeability of expression in her eyes, which eloquently revealed her feelings. By nature lively, joyous, and even impulsive in her reactions, whether of laughter or tears, she was, nevertheless, controlled and quiet in her movements to the point where someone even called her "phlegmatic". She was above average in her behaviour, reactions and personality, so that first indifferent impressions of her quickly gave way to a friendly interest.

2. Family home of Sister Faustina, Servant of God

THE FAMILY HOME

When, on 28th October 1892, Stanislaus Kowalski and Marianna Babel were married, it never entered their wildest dreams that God would so bless their union. He was 25 and she 18, and their life was to be by no means a bed of roses. They were both poor country people from smallholdings, but he was a carpenter and that was his chief livelihood. Their dreams were modest: to lead an honest and godly life with a roof over their heads and without going hungry.

The wedding was in the village of Dąbie in the Turek district of Łódź voivodship*, where the bride's parents lived. The bridegroom was a "local", living in Głogowiec, a few kilometres away. There he had a small cottage built half of stone and half of brick, and just over 407 ares of arable land (ten acres) and 132 and a half ares (three and a quarter acres) of pasture for his three cows. He farmed this in the evening and in the early morning before leaving to earn his bread in the sweat of his brow. When he married, he hoped that life would become a little easier, as his wife would take on the farm and look after the small number of livestock. She did not disappoint him. She was a faithful and loyal companion who kept the homestead in perfect order, looked after him and helped him in all she could. She even brought him his lunch to work, summer and winter, daily throughout their married life.

---

* A voivodship corresponds to a British county or French department - Translator

Although they lived a godly, harmonious, honest and hard-working life, for a long time they were not blessed with children. Were they to spend a lonely old age, just when strength fails, without any help? Would there be no one to mourn their deaths, close their eyes and bury them in consecrated ground? They dreamed their simple dreams, hoping anxiously for children. What happiness, when, after ten years of marriage, Marianna bore a daughter! From then on, it was as if a magician had waved his wand.

Everything changed, for child after child arrived. Altogether they had ten, of whom eight survived: six daughters and two sons. Two little girls died in infancy. At first there were only daughters. Their sons arrived later, one after the other. The first son was their seventh child, and the second son was the eighth. Stanislaus was well over forty then, and his wife nearly forty.

But their sons were not to be their chief pride, a treasure to be marked by God's special election. This was to be their third daughter, Helena, born on 25th August 1905. Through her the blessings of God were poured out on the whole house.

She inherited from her parents their best qualities: their simple honest piety, their hard-working natures, their integrity and perseverance. Their faults seem to have passed her by. All reminiscences, both from the family and their friends, agree that little Helenka differed from the rest of her brothers and sisters from an early age: *"She was quite different from them".* Especially loved by her parents, she was always their chief prop and therefore had a special place in the home. She was the only one of their children who could be completely and absolutely trusted.

So, then, after the "lean" years when the Kowalskis sadly dreamed of children, came the good years when their cottage quickly filled with children. As the babies arrived, so the family needs rose, and difficult times were upon them. The first world war devastated

Poland, and their father had to redouble his efforts to fulfil his family obligations. It was not easy, but he worked conscientiously, sparing neither strength nor effort, never getting enough sleep and sometimes working without rest, for the earth will not wait and gives a harvest only when work is completed in the right season. Stanislaus knew his duty, was conscientious and responsible both at work and in the upbringing of his children, and looked after the bodily needs of his numerous family, but even more after their spiritual needs. He treated these duties with equal weight and demanded the same from the family. He was heavy-handed with his children and nothing escaped his eagle eye. His belt was brought out for the slightest offence and went into action on the offender. By nature he was severe and exacting, and life had reinforced these traits. Only their mother was able to temper their father's ruthless justice, but even she did not always succeed.

The Kowalski family was very obviously patriarchal in character. The father kept most of the authority in his hands and there was no appeal against his decisions. He was the one who designated the children's chores at home, and their mother saw that they did them. Both parents agreed in training the children to be conscientious, exact and systematic, but their mother had a gentler way with her. Their father was not indulgent though he loved his children in his way. Completely taken up with the needs of his home, he demanded the same from others as he did from himself. He wanted to train them in strict morality and to being dependable in any work entrusted to them.

What was the role of their mother? The children were at home all day under her care. Despite the peremptory nature of their father, she had her own part to play in the upbringing of her children. She was emotional and sensitive, mild and understanding, and, like her husband, hard-working and persevering. She taught them the same principles, but by other methods. It was

3. St. Casimir's church at Świnice, parish Church of the Servant of God

their mother who taught the children the Lord's Prayer and the elements of their religion. She did it so well and systematically that when the children went to school, they already knew a lot of what is contained in the catechism, and lessons in religious knowledge presented them with no difficulty. Such lessons were a natural supplement to what they had learned at home.

Their mother taught the children to keep everything tidy and clean. The cottage interior was always perfectly neat, and the children's clothing, though poor, kept clean and carefully mended. This love of order and cleanliness, learned in the family home, remained with Sister Faustina throughout her life. She never neglected it, even when exhausted by years of strength-sapping illness. Her religious habit, though old and darned, was always carefully maintained. In Sister Faustina's eyes, taking pains over one's dress was a mark of respect for those around one, and it was, of course, out of the question to "pay a visit" to God in church without being neatly dressed.

In this family religion was the principal element in their lives. Faith gave them the model for their daily lives, and gave it a clear and personal style. Everything was saturated by faith. Both parents took care that religious duties were performed, such as the obligation of hearing Sunday Mass, and daily prayer. At least twice yearly, at Christmas and Easter, they went to Confession and Holy Communion.

The most difficult problem to solve was Sunday Mass. The parish church at Swinice, two kilometres away, had only one Mass, so the whole family had to go at the same time. This conflicted with certain domestic duties, which had to be done whether or not it was Sunday; for example, taking the cows out to pasture. How was this to be reconciled with the obligation to attend Mass? Only Helenka found the answer. In the evening, before going to bed, she opened the window, and, before dawn, slipped out of it. Before the whole family assembled for breakfast, the cows were returning fed from their grazing.At the beginning of her plans, there was very nearly a serious misapprehension. Their father, knowing nothing of his daughter's plan, on Sunday morning found the byre empty with wide-open doors. He was terrified that thieves had stolen his cattle. He ran out of the farmyard and was surprised to see Helenka bringing the cows back from grazing. The animals walked between two fields of wheat slowly, along the path, stopping to graze the grass growing beside the track, without - strangely - reaching for the ears of wheat. Kowalski was struck dumb - he had been sure that the animals would have damaged the crop - and the belt he had intended to use on Helenka fell from his hand.

For a long time afterwards the story went around in the family as "miraculous", because the cows, as if in the grip of an invisible force, were contented with the poor grass beside the track, and did not reach for the wheat. In their simple naivete it seemed to them like an unmistakable proof that God had helped Helenka in her plans to attend church. Was it naive? What forces could help the child in her stubborn wish to be with God? There was yet another problem in connection with church-going. It was the lack of sufficient Sunday-best clothing. In the Kowalski family there was never enough for everyone. The girls lent each other their dresses, working out the order in which each would wear the best. Helenka well knew her parents' money problems, so, like her sisters and brothers, she did not ask for new clothes. Because she was not selfish, she was often the one to remain at home. She would retreat to a corner in the garden with a large book of devotions and there she prayed the Sunday prayers. This was the only time she did not respond to her mother's calls for help. She did not stir from her place until Mass had finished in the parish church. Then she immediately ran up to her mother apologizing and kissing her hand, explaining why she had been dis-obedient: Jesus would be angry if she did not perform that duty. This is the single example that we know of her disobedience to her mother, which was repeated every time she stayed at home on a Sunday, and it is not without significance. It is the first example of Helenka's establishing a hierarchy of obedience: it is owed first to God, and then to the parents.

In the religious practice of the country folk, by custom a large part was played by hymns and religious song. Devotion to the Blessed Virgin was most fully expressed by the Polish people in hymns. Among these, the most common was The Little Office of the Immaculate Conception, extremely popular and often sung even during housework. In this natural manner, prayer entered directly into their lives and sanctified them.

Stanislaw Kowalski made the singing of the Little Office a family practice. Because he was working away from home during the day, there were only the early mornings. He began to sing the moment he got up, often before dawn, and he woke the whole family with his song, despite the protests of his wife who had to ensure that the babies had enough sleep. The father would not give in. It was he who wanted the children to begin each day with this song. His hymn repertoire was by no means limited to the Little Office, although he sang this year-round. Apart from daily hymns and those for special occasions, the liturgical year brought round the Polish Lenten hymns and Christmas carols. In May there were the May devotions to the Blessed Virgin, and again in October, the month of the Rosary. Because it was some way to the church, and May devotions and the rosary may be said at home, Kowalski made a little shrine and fixed it to the pear tree standing on the track outside his home. The children, especially Helenka, would decorate the holy picture with flowers and the whole family and their neighbours would gather there for communal prayers. For the ease of the adults there were two wooden benches, and if necessary Helenka would bring out some stools.

The main part of every day in the hard life of the Kowalskis was taken up with work. The children had to share their parents' work, so they did not have a lot of time for play. When they reached five years of age, they began to help with the chores. The younger ones gradually took over tasks from the elder, who, when grown up, "went into service", to bring in a little money. The work was divided up according to a plan. The girls had to take the cows to pasture and help their mother at home, and they looked after the younger ones. Helenka helped her father to farm until the boys grew and could take over from her.

Every age in the human being has its own special rights, needs and demands. The most natural and basic right of a child is play. In play the child develops and shows its first individual interests and abilities, which is why the child tries to play, instinctively, in any way open to it. So the Kowalski children would try to avoid the chores they had been given, thinking up all sorts of tricks to get time for play. It was only Helenka - though she too had her favourite games - who treated her responsibilities seriously. Lies and tricks are the weapon of the weak, who are incapable of open opposition. In any case, revolt in the Kowalski family 'was virtually impossible. Their father was too severe and punished disobedience heavily. Nothing was to be gained by defiance. Either you did what he wanted, or you resorted to deceit. Only one child, Helenka, was not cowed by her father. She never learned to lie, or even to cover up embarrassing matters. Quite the opposite. Her father's hard-handed methods made her a stronger character, although she was by nature honest and direct. Very early on, she learned to adapt herself to the will of others, while keeping her inner freedom. She did not avoid the necessity for obedience, but neither did she hide her personal preferences, tastes, and aspirations. She was open and frank, working exactly as her parents had ordered her, and she not only willingly did as she was told, but often went out of her way oblige them. Her sensitive heart was unable to watch unaffected while her parents toiled. With a child's little hands she tried to bring them some help, thereby developing her initiative and inventiveness: of her own will she would tidy up something at home, or feed the pigs or poultry, and happily wait for her parents to find the surprise. Sometimes she was disappointed in this. Despite her expectations, her parents often accepted this gift of voluntary work as something to be expected, only emphasising it when it was a good example to the other children. This was probably her first experience of the hard school of life. Sometimes it must have been painful, but because the lesson was learned at home from her parents, of whose feelings for her she was certain, and whom she very much loved, there was no aftertaste of bitterness. In fact it was very good training for the life she was to choose. She quickly understood that it is no use in life to expect a reward, or even recognition for perfectly performed duties or kindliness. One may be praised, but - and how often it happens! - one may simply be ignored. Only God will make it up to you, her mother explained when teaching the attentive Helenka her faith. One day there will be a reward from God, Who knows everything, sees everything and remembers everything.

Two typical moments from this time in her life may throw more light on Helenka's kind of goodness.

Her eldest sister Josephine says, *"When Helenka was about ten years old, she decided to obtain money for the poor in the same way that they do. She dressed in rags and went around the village from house to house saying a prayer and asking for alms. She came back home very depressed saying, 'The poor have a terrible life. How much they have to bear getting food for themselves.' "*

Helenka's brother Stanley has another story about her. When she was twelve or thirteen, *"she decided to organize a raffle for the poor. She went around our neighbours asking for small gifts, wrote out the lottery tickets and then sold them for pennies... She took the money collected in this way to the parish priest, telling him that it was for the poor."*

Another time she made a little shop for the same purpose. In it she sold gifts she had previously collected and toys made by herself from bits of cloth and paper.

These reminiscences show that Helenka was sensitive to poverty and, more importantly, actively sought ways to help, revealing a good deal of inventiveness and initiative. She was not giving from anything extra that she possessed, because she herself had a number of basic unfilled needs, and she well understood the difficulties of her parents. All this did not harden her heart towards people or her immediate family. Her eyes remained open to poverty. Having perceived it, her immediate reaction was to help.

In a child as sensitive and upright as she, the principal traits of character were quickly strengthened. Her character was formed simply and straightforwardly from the cradle. There were no visible deviations in the formation of a personality at once rich and strong. She had an unusually lively temperament. She was spontaneous, but controlled, equable, not prone to bad moods, happy and trusting. Her natural liveliness was tempered by mild behaviour and controlled movements. She was more dignified than one might expect for her age, probably because so early in life she had to care for her younger brothers and sisters.

These qualities meant that Helenka was her parents' favourite child. They held her up to the children as a model of common sense, hard work and obedience. Sometimes her brothers and sisters teased her because of her privileged position, but such conflicts were minor. There were never any serious arguments because Helenka was *"far too likeable"*, since she was not at all haughty and never took advantage of her privileged place. The other children accepted without argument that she was superior. Even her strict father could be charmed by this child. Since he trusted her, he was much gentler with her than with the other children. A special communion grew up between them, and he let her share his few "secrets". For example, she alone knew where he kept his double-barrelled shotgun or other personal possessions, and she knew his plans and his ideas.

Like all children, Helenka had her favourite games, but they were different from the typical games of the children round about her. One should not call the childish activities of this little girl "games", although the element of fiction, so characteristic of the child's mentality, was clearly present in them. It was, however, secondary. The two features which constantly recur are: God, and alms for the poor. We have already spoken of Helenka's kindliness. Let us look at the early manifestations of her fascination with God. She had an innate tendency to contemplation, which developed over the years unrestricted, making use of what each day brought. All the daily happenings and the beauty or power of nature was, to her, a reflection of the living God, and spoke in His voice as an expression of His greatness and power, His love and protection. Helenka, unlike the other children, rarely joined in games. Rather did she gather them around her when she organized a "service" or singing hymns, and even more frequently for her stories. She liked to tell them what she had read, adding her own thoughts and wishes. She was possessed of a lively imagination, marvellous memory, and the gift of communication, so that she was listened to eagerly.

What were her stories about?

Her father, who liked to read, had a modest collection of books. She would tell, above all, what she had heard from him. He read to them *"from the Bible, or about missionaries teaching wild tribes, or about hermits living on roots and totally absorbed in prayer"*. To her father's readings could be added the Sunday sermons, which she would repeat faithfully and convincingly when she came back from church. When she herself

27

had learned to read, she took over from her father the times of reading aloud to the family. Then her repertoire of stories grew far larger, for she borrowed books wherever she could: from neighbours, the parish priest, her teacher. They were always religious books. Unfortunately, we do not know what books were available to her in her immediate surroundings. We can only guess from the few general remarks about them among the reminiscences of her family and neighbours. Her reading deepened her primary interests, giving them a practical direction: like the hermits of whom her father read, who quickened her imagination, she wished to consecrate herself to God. Sometimes she expressed her dreams aloud, although the other children made sceptical remarks. They were particularly doubtful about living on roots. Her parents, too, laughed at her fantasies, and did not attach much importance to them. But Helenka kept coming back to the same theme. She began, more frequently than before, to seek solitude, prayer became a necessity of life to her, and she began to long for the opportunity to pray with all her being. Her spiritual life had begun to germinate. The love of God had awoken within her, fervent and passionate, though as yet very imprecise.

YOUTH

Helenka remained in the parental home until she was sixteen. Among her loving family her personality and character were formed without trauma, mentally, though not always physically, healthy. Although they were poor, this had no influence on their fundamental life-style. Being poor was no excuse for less than strict observance of the generally accepted moral and religious norms. Insufficiency of food was not an excuse to ignore the church fasts, the desire for money for even the most essential needs could not lead to a departure from morality, and weariness after work was not allowed to mean missing prayers. Their duties were to be supplemented if conditions allowed. When Helenka went into service, she was shocked to see that it was possible not to observe a fast. At home, God's commandments and the Church's were all observed. But let us not run ahead.

Helenka was an able and discerning child. She studied willingly, and, because she had a very good memory, she readily absorbed what the school was able to teach her. Sadly, her entire school career was limited to three classes of elementary education. Why was this?

The school was at Swinice, where stood the parish church, but the distance of two kilometres was no obstacle to a child hungry for knowledge. She went to school daily on foot both ways, and hurried home. She knew she had chores awaiting her. She divided her time easily enough between learning and work. She was certain to be useful at home and her parents were glad to see her back. But this was not the most important reason why Helenka had to break off her school career. Her sister Josephine remembers that Helenka went late to school because previously there was no school at all in the area. This was during the first world war, which had totally disorganized life for people living in the war zone. The Front went by the voivodship of Łódź. The school was only opened when things came back to normal. Unfortunately, Helenka soon passed the age of elementary education and had to leave her school. A few years later, her teacher was still regretting that such a clever child had to finish her education so prematurely.

However, knowledge is gained not only at school during the official learning process. Everyone who wants can supplement his education personally, and such individual and independent efforts reveal the personal interests which propel the individual down one path rather than another. Helenka's personal interests had from an early age been connected with God, so it was in the field of religion that she tried to increase her knowledge. When her schooling was ended, she began to read more, using her free time. She shared what she learned mainly with the other children. She had a gift for story-telling, as we have seen, so she collected around her the village children, girl-friends from school and her family, spreading before them the wonderful world of asceticism and holiness. They listened with interest and she had no shortage of an audience. The young girl was easily fired with enthusiasm and her tales had a note of longing for the life of those who had totally consecrated themselves to God. This longing gradually intensified. Other children were sceptical of her raptures. They were less inclined to offer the small joys of daily life in the difficult process of becoming close to God. Helenka's enthusiasm encountered a vacuum. But this did not discourage her.

4. Interior of the parish church at Świnice

She received the Sacraments of Penance and Holy Communion, as was then the custom, at the age of 9. The parish priest prepared her in the class he held 2 or 3 times a week for children. Her mother also greatly assisted, as she well knew the catechism and supplemented the priest's teaching at home with theory and practice. Fortunately, then, the home, the school and the parish complemented each other's work. There were no contradictions between them - indeed, the reverse, and Helenka's world grew larger in a uniform manner without controversy, concession or lies. Such conflict as there was concerned characters and not their outlook on the world. Holy Communion was a deep experience for Helenka. The mystery of the Divine Presence hidden in the Blessed Sacrament had fascinated her since she was very young. She therefore awaited longingly and with some tension the coming of Jesus to her soul. Two neighbours, Mrs Krzyzanowska and Mrs Stanislawska, give some interesting details about the day of her First Communion. On that day she was returning alone from church, deep in thought.

"Why aren't you going back with the other children?" asked a neighbour, meeting her by the way. *"I'm going with Jesus,"* the child replied seriously. But she was unable to contain her overflowing happiness. She stopped a friend going along at a little distance. *"Are you happy about today?"* she asked with bated breath. *"Yes, of course,"* said the friend. *"Look what a pretty dress I'm wearing."* *"I am happy because Jesus has come to me,"* whispered Helenka, smiling sunnily to the secret of her heart, joined in a new way with God.

It is a pity that we know nothing of the next Sacrament she received, Confirmation. We only know the place, and an approximate date. It was in the first half of the year 1922 at Aleksandrów, but no one remembered any details, which is not surprising, as it took place away from home when Helena was in her first post in service. She herself is silent on the topic.

Knowing her piety and love of God, we may, however, be sure this Sacrament was a key moment in her life. The influence of Confirmation may be observed in the later manner of her life.

Confirmation defines our responsibility as a Christian, placing before us the obligation to live our faith actively and like apostles, witnessing to Christ in our lives. For it to be fruitful, however, an essential condition is that we grow in faith, adding to our knowledge of God and meeting Him in prayer.

Helenka accepted the duties arising from Confirmation as an essential Christian duty. She was obviously putting her life in order, making a list of duties in ascending order of importance and adapting her life around them. She was systematically attempting to fulfil them, and her will was becoming stronger in the wish to serve God. Let us follow more closely the period of her early youth, particularly the years directly before and after she had received Confirmation and before she entered the convent. Her first aim was to solve the problem of attending Sunday Mass. She applied to her parents to allow her to go into service and earn money to buy clothes to attend church. She was allowed to take up a position as maid to friends of her parents, Mr and Mrs Bryszewski, in 1921 when she was 16. Her employers had a bakery in Aleksandrów, not very far from home, between Łódź and Głogowiec.

Helenka's first venture into the world was no great change from the kind of life she had been leading until that date. Her employers treated her like a daughter and the work she was doing was not very different from that she had done at home. Nonetheless, the period at Aleksandrów was an important one in her life, for it was there that in circumstances unknown to us her desire to enter the religious life crystallised into a decision. What could have affected her decision?

As we know, a longing to serve God had been with her for a long time. More than once she had said that she would become a pilgrim like those of whom her father had read to her, and that she would consecrate herself to prayer. She often rose to pray in the middle of the night. When her mother told her to go back to bed, she said that an angel had awoken her and told her to pray. Her then mental state can be described as the slow creation of a spiritual climate in which her soul was becoming habituated to live. How she was to plan her future to be able to give herself to God was not yet clear, at least on the exterior.

In Aleksandrów her vocation crystallised: she would enter a convent. Probably an event, which her sister Josephine recalls, had a decisive influence. One day, Helenka began shouting that there was a fire in the courtyard. The alarm caused some confusion, because bread was being put into the bake-ovens at that moment. It was a false alarm. But the girl was so shaken that she fainted, and her employers called the doctor. At that time it was not the common practice to call a doctor for a trifle, especially not for a home visit. Helenka's condition must have seemed serious. Her employers called it "insanity".

Such a strong psychic shock in an equable and balanced girl leads us to suppose that something unusual mu st have occurred. Josephine was sent by their anxious parents to Aleksandrów to see her sister, and when she asked Helenka what had happened, the latter answered briefly and reluctantly that she had seen a "light". But she immediately added: *"Tell Mummy not to worry. I am not crazy, but I shan't say anything more about it to them. I shall not be staying here long."* In some way the "light" she had seen was linked with Helenka's decision to leave her post, and this in turn was connected with her intention of entering a convent. That is all we know about what happened. The "light" remains a mystery. Only a certain similarity with something that occurred a year later enables us to suppose that Helenka did not reveal the whole truth, that she was silent about part of it. In 1923, during a dance in Łódź, she suddenly saw not just a light, but Jesus himself. The words of bitter reproach He addressed to her are astonishing:

> *'How long shall I put up with you and how long will you keep putting Me off?'*

(Diary, Notebook I para. 9)[*]

They suggest that He must have already called her in a similar way to give herself to Him in the religious life. When did this happen? Probably in Aleksandrów. Heedful of His call, she obediently went home and asked her parents for permission to enter a convent.

Her parents would not agree. The reason that they gave was their inability to pay for the trousseau and dowry then required of novices. It was certainly not the only motive. It was a suitable pretext to hide their real reason. Helenka was the best of all the Kowalski children. Her parents considered her a genuine helpmate. We must remember that Stanislaus was then 53, and Marianna 46. They were weary, and old age was creeping up on them. Village folk, worn out by hard physical labour, aged quickly. They therefore protested energetically. God was asking too great a sacrifice. They would not give up their favourite child. Their opposition was categorical, and both parents were in agreement. Her sister Josephine briefly recalls:

> *"I first learned from Helenka of her desire to enter the convent after she returned home from Aleksandrów. We were all very shocked by this, because at that time people knew very little about the religious*

---

[*] Quotations from her Diary are from Divine Mercy in My Soul, the Diary of Sister M. Faustina Kowalska, Marian Press, Stockbridge U.S.A. 1987. American spellings have been retained.

life. Our parents were very sad, and the children were crying."

(Arch. S.F.)*

Helenka was disappointed. She was helpless to do anything. Was she to obey her parents, or to follow the voice of God in her soul? As she had been brought up to be obedient, she tried to submit to the will of her parents and to lead the life of an average young girl. She began to dress well and two or three times she went to a dance. Her last employer in Łódź, Mrs Sadowska, remembers that at first she hesitated to employ Helenka, because she seemed to be too elegantly dressed when she came to work for the first time.

Just at this time, when she was trying her hardest to be obedient to her parents, Helenka was severely punished by her father. The incident is worth recording, as it is the only time her father lifted his hand to her. It happened that Helenka, persuaded by her elder sister, went to a dance with her. Their father agreed on condition that they were to be back early at home. The dance went on and the two girls, who were having a marvellous time, came back late, accompanied home by a boy they knew. Someone told their father of this next day, and he fell into a passion. *"They have brought shame on me,"* he declared. He was especially annoyed that Helenka had betrayed his trust in her. The girl sheltered behind a bed, and, weeping, she promised that it would not happen again. But the enraged father caught her there and beat her with his belt, refusing to overlook her fault. Helenka was very hurt by her father's accusation. She could not calm down for some time.

---

* The quotation here and others subsequently are from the Archives of Sister Faustina, also abbreviated as Arch. SF Recoll. (Archives of Sister Faustina. Recollections of people who knew her).

"I shall not bring any more shame upon him," she afterwards said firmly to her sister. *"I will make him proud."*

This return of Helenka's to a more worldly life did not mean that she had in fact rejected her vocation. Rather, she was trying to turn it into another channel. It is true that she was trying to ignore the voice in her soul urging her to choose the convent, but at the same time she was carefully organizing her religious life. She went away to Łódź to look for a post, but wanted to choose her employers herself and with care. She first stayed with a cousin of her father's who lived in Łódź with his family. He was called "Uncle" Rapacki, and while she was with them she looked for a household where the faith was practised. She found a post with two Tertiaries. In her contract of work she required the right to attend Mass daily, the possibility of an annual retreat, and the right to visit the sick and those needing help.

The idea of entering a convent persisted, so without haste she began to collect information and weigh up the possibilities. She asked for the advice of her confessor, and also trustingly told her secret to her uncle, requesting his help. Her uncle, however, knowing the views of her parents, tried to dissuade her. There seemed nothing but difficulties in her path. Helenka appeared resigned to this and expected to live in the world, though with an interior reservation about doing so. The Helenka of the Łódź period is well described in the brief recollections of one of her employers, Mrs Sadowska:

"Pleasant, polite, hard-working. I cannot say anything against her, because she was almost too good. She was so good there are no words to describe it. When she and I went shopping in town, she would take the shopping bag from me, but I wouldn't give it to her to carry because she was weak - she was always fasting. I would snatch the bag from her, and

5. St. Stanislaus Kostka Cathedral, Łódź

she from me. I was very happy with her because whatever I intended to do, she had already done for me. She was agreeable and amusing. In the evening, when she sat on her stool, my three children would gather round her at once. They liked her because she told them stories and laughed, and they with her. If I had to leave home, I could be free of anxiety, because she did everything at home better than I myself. When she left I don't know where she went. She was to have gone earlier, but she waited until my baby was born. She was so obliging."

This simple account gives a good picture of Helenka as she then was, and throws additional light on her goodness. She was in a hurry to go because she was going to leave town to enter the convent. But even when she was fulfilling her heart's desire, she considered the needs of others. She left everything perfectly organized and able to run without her.

Helenka's departure from Łódź took place suddenly in dramatic circumstances. Jesus had other plans for her than she thought. When the voice in her soul proved too weak to overcome her inner misgivings, God intervened. As she herself relates, during a dance she had gone to with her sister,

"While everybody was having a good time, my soul was experiencing deep torments. As I began to dance, I suddenly saw Jesus at my side, Jesus racked with pain, stripped of His clothing, all covered with wounds, who spoke these words to me: How long shall I put up with you and how long will you keep putting Me off? At that moment the charming music stopped, [and] the company I was with vanished from my sight; there remained Jesus and I. I took a seat by my dear sister, pretending to have a headache in order to cover up what

39

took place in my soul. After a while I slipped out unnoticed, leaving my sister and all my companions behind and made my way to the Cathedral of Saint Stanislaus Kostka. It was already beginning to grow light; there were only a few people in the Cathedral. Paying no attention to what was happening around me, I fell prostrate before the Blessed Sacrament and begged the Lord to be good enough to give me to understand what I should do next. Then I heard these words: Go at once to Warsaw; you will enter a convent there."

(Diary, Notebook I, paras. 9,10)

Jesus' direct appeal overcame all Helenka's interior opposition. She did not know, indeed, how she was to accomplish His Will, where and to which convent she was to go, but she trusted in Him. She trusted without reservations that if Jesus had called her, He would tell her what to do next. In any case, on the way to Him, there is an unfailing help - the Holy Mother Mary. She would ask her.

Thus began Helenka's arduous path to the convent.

THE PATH TO THE CONVENT

Helenka hesitated no longer. The very thought that Jesus might suffer through her was unbearable. Her decision was made: from now on, everything was to be subordinated to her main aim - the giving of herself to the service of God.

In her situation, this decision was an act not only of heroic courage, but of heroic trust in God. There were so man difficulties and of such a kind that, humanly speaking, there were no chances of overcoming them. Wherever she turned, there was only darkness. Only the voice of the Lord, calling her to Himself, was the Star of Bethlehem to Helenka, lighting her path sufficiently brightly to give her the courage to take the decisive step.

Nevertheless the question she had been asking herself over the last few years - how to go about entering a convent - by no means suddenly became easier and simpler to answer. Rather the reverse - it took on dramatic urgency. According to the previously offered advice of her confessor, and the Divine call, Helenka ought to go to Warsaw and there apply to one of the many religious Congregations to be admitted. But where was she to stay after arriving? With whom? What was to be her base while she applied? She did not know the city, or anyone in it. The only city she had known so far was Łódź - it was not so far from home, known to her, and many threads of her life were bound up with it. How was such an inexperienced girl as herself to travel alone into the distant, unknown world of the capital? This was the first problem and the most important. Another was just as difficult, and far more emotionally loaded. What was she to do about her parents? Helenka was 19, and still a minor. Her parents had refused their consent. She well knew that her behaviour would grieve and disappoint them, but she understood that no matter how she might wish not to cause them pain, it was unavoidable. She would, unfortunately, have to present them with a fait accompli, otherwise they would never agree.

She knew all the reasons her parents had for wishing to keep her with them in the world, and she did not delude herself that they would not do all they could to prevent her. With all her heart she wanted to be obedient and to help them in their approaching old age, but her two duties - to God and to her parents - could not be reconciled: indeed, they were in sharp conflict. She must choose, and she had done so: she would disobey her earthly parents, and obey her Heavenly Father.

She decided to act courageously and quietly, though such a decision made it impossible to continue collecting information about the various religious communities and their requirements. From necessity her knowledge was limited to that she had obtained from her confessor. But he was her confessor and through him God was speaking to her. Her confessor had told her to go to Warsaw. There was thus no choice - to Warsaw she must go.

She gave up her job without giving a reason, nor saying where she was going. She packed her things - the few clothes she had - and took the little bundle to her uncle's house, asking that it should be given to her parents and sisters after her departure. She remembered every member of her family, designating some trifle for each from her modest possessions. She took nothing with her. She thought worldly clothes would no longer be of use to her. Whatever she did need, Jesus would give her at the right time and in the right manner. Years later, her uncle's wife spoke of the following scene to one of the Sisters of the Congregation:

"When Helenka was about to go to Warsaw, she brought her things to her uncle, weeping so much that she shook. But she did not complain, or say one word about why she was weeping. She asked her uncle to take her to the railway station. He afterwards told me that when she was seated in a carriage, she wept so that it was pitiful to see. She was obviously missing her family and saying farewell to them in this way. Her uncle declared, "If the train had remained standing, I would probably have taken her from it. But it did not.""

(Archives S.F., Recollections of Mrs S. Rapacka, wife of H.'s uncle).

It is not easy to break the bonds with those close and dear to our hearts and to go alone "into the unknown" to which God's voice directs us. It is a moment of complete inner nakedness. The past has been cut off, the future is not even dimly visible. Which of the religious Houses in the capital would wish to open its doors to her? She knew little of their variety, their aims and their activities. The only signpost she had - surely unmistakable - was that Jesus was calling her. Yet how difficult it was to follow. Helenka did not question the authenticity of her vocation, God's calling in her soul. Of that she had no doubt. She would have in the future, but at that moment her faith was open and trusting like that of a child, and, like a child's, uninhibited. Her understanding was simple and logical: if she wanted to do the will of God - and that is what it was all about - she had to keep in constant contact with God. She therefore concentrated all the strength of her soul on this one problem - to understand the will of God properly, and to do it. She prayed intensively

6. St. James' Church, Warsaw

and fervently. Her soul tensed itself to the maximum effort to understand God's wishes, so she reacted to every touch of His grace.

Let us follow her.

The train arrived at Warsaw. She had to get out. What to do next? Where should she go from here? She turned confidently in prayer to the Blessed Mother, with the request for some indication. Obedient to the voice in her soul, and led, too, by her right instincts, she left the capital's possible distractions, and spent the first night in some village on the southern outskirts of Warsaw.

Early the next morning we find her kneeling in St. James' Church in the Ochota district, a southern suburb of the metropolis.

One Holy Mass followed another. Helenka remained in prayer and persistently asked Divine Providence for further illumination. Her inner voice directed her to speak to the parish priest of St. James', Rev. James Dabrowski. When he entered the sacristy after Mass, she followed him, asking to be directed to a suitable convent.

He was clearly surprised. He did not refuse help, but told her to find a post until she could be received into a convent. With this in mind, he gave her a letter of introduction to his friends, Mr and Mrs Lipszyc, who lived very near to Warsaw in Ostrowek near Wolomin. With a little bundle of all her possessions in her hand, the girl went to the address she had been given and was accepted on the spot. She by no means concealed her plans, so Mrs Lipszyc realised she was only to have temporary help, but with several small children she needed it immediately. Mr and Mrs Lipszyc were not to regret their decision. In a short time she won not only their complete trust, but their hearty kindness.

In this house, as in all the others she had worked, she was treated almost as a member of the family. She repaid them with obliging affection. Perhaps nowhere she had worked before was she to be so emotionally committed as there. In her last post before entering the convent, she had found a second family, to which she gave her heart, with her own brand of directness and devotion.

She remained with them a whole year, and the time repaid her for the previous torment, for it was a period of mental relaxation, of happy preparation for the day when she would pass through the gates of "her" convent. Her preparations were easy, without special effort. She had only to save a certain sum of money, required by the Congregation of an entrant.

At last Helenka found "her" convent. It is true that the search began with some disappointments, for a couple of convents she approached refused her. But one day she knocked at the door of the Congregation of Sisters of Our Lady of Mercy on Żytnia Street. In Sister Faustina's Diary the details of the scene are noted. The then Superior, Mother Michael, came out to her and after a short conversation told her to go to the chapel and ask "the Lord of the House", i.e. the Lord Jesus, if He would accept her into the Congregation. Without hesitation Helenka went to the chapel as she had been told. In answer she heard a voice in her soul: **"Yes, I accept you."** Rejoicing, she quickly returned with the news of the Lord's answer, and the Superior replied, "If the Lord accepts you, so do I."

But despite this positive reply, matters were still delayed and Helenka had to be patient. She had no money, and the Congregation asked each new entrant for a certain minimal dowry to cover the most essential expenses. The time during which she was to collect the money was agreed as a year, and the certainty which now arose filled the girl's heart with overwhelming happiness. The first, probably most difficult step had been taken. Her dreams were on the way to being realised. With God's help she would fulfil the necessary conditions, and in a year, without obstacles, she would cross the convent threshold at last. Both Mrs Lipszyc and her friend Dr Katharine Steinberg, who was then a frequent guest at their house, and who paid particular attention to Helenka, are agreed that she was a happy girl, full of good humour, equable although she had a lively temperament, and well able to cope with the children, who made friends with her in perfect trust; they were fascinated by her inventiveness in thinking up games, and never weary of her colourful tales. Apart from her talkativeness, the characteristic of Helenka that they most recall was that she liked to sing while she worked. Mrs Lipszyc states that they were always religious songs and hymns, and the most frequent was one to Jesus in the Most Holy Sacrament, commencing, "I worship Jesus hidden in the Blessed Sacrament". This hymn is forever associated in her mind with the image of the girl.

Helenka went into the convent on 1st August 1925, and the whole family said goodbye to her with regret. Mrs Lipszyc, who was only nine years older than Helenka, equipped her to leave home like a daughter, and assured the girl that if her attempt to stay in the convent proved unsuccessful, she could always return to them. Helenka reacted positively to the understanding and friendship offered to her. Mrs Lipszyc was the only person whom she told of her first experience of convent life, of her difficulties and even of her doubts as to whether she should stay in that convent. Mrs Lipszyc saw Helenka twice more; once in the convent, when she came at the request of the Sisters to give a reference for Helenka's character, and a second time at home. Aldona Lipszyc, although knowing nothing of convent life or its requirements, showed great understanding about the difficulties that Helenka, with her lively temperament, might encounter. She expected that the girl would not be able to bear the necessity of constantly controlling her natural liveliness and would give up her plans. But she had not understood the essence of the matter. The principal problem lay elsewhere.

7. Mother House of the congregation of Sisters of Our Lady of Mercy, 3 - 9 Zytnia Street, Warsaw, to which Sister Faustina applied for admissions

HELENKA'S SPIRITUAL BOUQUET

A person does not give him or herself to the service of God as a blank piece of paper, for God to write on for the first time. One brings to such a life one's own personality, one's whole inner world, a character formed in this or that way, one's own clearly - formulated interests, and one's knowledge - both the officially taught and the practically acquired. One brings in one's experience, and with it the features imprinted upon the psyche by the years and conditions of one's past existence: good features, and blemishes which might have affected the young character. In giving the self to God, then, a person offers Him not only what has been collected of the good, but also certain remnants saved from the conscious or unconscious wastage of our heritage. Everyone has this double entry of profits and losses in his account, and brings to God both the straight and crooked paths of his life for further entries. God receives them both, because He receives the whole person and He is able to straighten even the most twisting paths of our personalities. But grace always builds upon nature and it is important not to forget this when we are considering someone's road to sanctity.

It is thus not without significance what psychological baggage a candidate to a religious community brings across the convent threshold. It is sometimes emphasised that it is necessary to bring a dowry, in order to be accepted into a convent, but money is all that is thought of. (This concerns the times of Sister Faustina. Nowadays the question of a dowry has no importance). Certainly, dowries were necessary, and an insufficiency might greatly hinder the realization of a religious vocation. Nevertheless money does not decide the achievement of the aim, but perseverance and patience in the attainment; in other words, suitable traits in the character. Thus the most important element in a proper dowry is the person herself. In her is the bouquet which the candidate for religious life offers the community, to gain the grace within it to become the bride of Christ. Money plays a secondary role and concerns only the exterior matters. But every community grows and develops by using the spiritual dowry of its members, as God multiplies it by His grace, and the human being responds by a total self-giving without reserve. Thus saints are born into the community.

To trace the path of someone's sanctity in the religious life, one cannot start research from the moment that person crossed the convent threshold. One must look back and seek the evangelical treasure, or, rather, the "grain of mustard seed", the growth and blossoming of which occurs in the years of religious life.

Let us come to the subject in which we are directly interested - the life of Helena Kowalska, known in her Congregation as Sister Faustina of the Blessed Sacrament. Although we have accompanied her in the preceding chapters, now that she is at the threshold of her religious life we can recapitulate what she had to offer to God, and with what spiritual capital she began the last stage of her life - thirteen years in the Congregation of Sisters of Our Lady of Mercy - during which God developed her in such a way that she was capable of understanding, in a new way, the great Christian mission of Divine Mercy and of becoming its apostle.

Her general education stopped short at three classes of elementary school. But her spiritual capital was considerable.

For her station in life, she was well-read in religion. However, we should be more precise here, for a misunderstanding is possible. Helenka had access to popular religious literature, but she obviously had chosen suitably, since she had formed a clearly defined Christian outlook on life. In her religious education no small part was played by sermons, church missions and retreats, which she had followed from childhood with great attention. By nature a capable girl, with considerable initiative and her commonsensical way of reasoning, she had learned how to take advantage of all the ways available to her to obtain a basic knowledge of the Christian faith, in order independently to think it over and apply it to her life. She knew the catechism and the commandments well and tried to follow them. But, unfortunately, she was obliged to decide quite independently the measure and manner of their application, especially from the time she left home at the age of sixteen to go into service. We may therefore have doubts whether she invariably found the correct solution or kept things in proper proportion. In particular, she undertook fasting so often and so rigorously that it soon affected her health. She left home a sturdy girl, yet three years later when she applied to the convent, Mothers Michael Moraczewska and Margaret Gimbutt, who spoke to her at that time, both called her "skinny little thing" and "thin".

Up to the time of her entry into the religious community there had never been, most probably, in her life any more remarkable priest in whose experience and wisdom she had felt able to trust. It does not seem that she had understood at all the need for a permanent confessor, who might have enabled her to understand the reefs and difficulties of the religious life. In her as yet semi-childish reasoning, everything seemed simple and straightforward. Because her inner religious life was far more intense than that of those around her, she very early learned to be independent in her interior life and formed her own judgment, together with the courage to do what she thought was right. Although she was easy to get along with and obliging by nature, she was neither timid nor shy, and she did not admit of compromise. She had loved prayer since she was a child. She knew all the paraliturgical devotions - which were very popular among country folk - and she was pleased to take part in them, but at the same time she made her own personal prayers, which became more important to her as she grew older. Her silent prayer was not only Christocentric, but had a sacramental character: it was composed of two parts; on the one hand there was adoration, and on the other there was a form of permanent contact on everyday matters with Jesus hidden in the Blessed Sacrament. In seeking God, Helenka, led by sure spiritual instinct, did not find Him in Nature - though that delighted her - but in His home, the tabernacle. When once she had found Him, she stayed with Him always. This had probably begun with her first Holy Communion, and it is why, at the beginning of her spiritual life, we find no trace of uncertainty or hesitation.There could be no misunderstanding about the Eucharist. Here God, though concealed under the appearance of bread, was real and comprehensible. The Eucharist was the essential element around which, for Helenka, everything else revolved. In it, she was quietly confident of Christ's presence It was a personal union, an embrace of the person of Jesus Christ, and from it the wide perspective of the incomprehensible mystery of the Holy Trinity could be glimpsed. When Helenka entered the convent, she already had a well-formed devotion to God in the One Blessed Trinity. God was the pole which attracted her, and Jesus was the Way which led her to Him.

The Communion of Saints was not of great significance to her. The number of saints she knew was not large and was of secondary importance. But she always prayed to her Guardian Angel, and above all to Our Lady, who alone, after God, took up much place in her prayers and whose help she always sought whenever direct access to God, for whatever reason, became difficult. So, for example, she asked Our Lady for help in finding a suitable convent for her, sensibly reasoning that only she could guide her to the right place.

One of the main elements in Helenka's prayer was praise. Sensitive to beauty - particularly the beauty of Nature - she treated it as the gift of a loving God. A starry night, the quiet sleep of the whole of Nature, the shining morning dew and birdsong, and flowers, all spoke to her in the language of adoration of the Creator. She kept this sensitivity to the beauties of Nature to the end of her life. It fascinated her as a revelation of the beauty of the Divine world. She paid little attention to beauty as created by man. She was not particularly interested even in the appearance or the interior decoration of a church, because she was totally absorbed in the presence of God within it. Her attention in church was focused upon the Blessed Sacrament. Prayerfully she knelt before the tabernacle. It is from this, most probably, that the undeserved charge that she was practically illiterate and primitive arose. Indeed, she prayed little from prayerbooks when she was in church, but this was by no means due to illiteracy. When she was still at home, she would go to church with a large prayerbook. Most frequently, however, it lay unopened while Helenka knelt sunk in adoration. But, according to her family and neighbours, whenever it happened that she had to stay at home on a Sunday, that prayerbook accompanied her to some quiet corner of the garden, where she said all the prescribed prayers. For a country girl, she read a great deal, taking advantage of every opportunity to do so.

The five years she spent away from home had no basic influence on the development of her character. They were years which prolonged the style of life in her family circle, although she was in different surroundings. She was still within the closed circle of family life, though the families were not her own.

Though she had entered these households as paid help, because she was so easy to get along with and because she was so young, she was treated as one of the family and her work did not make for changed circumstances. She was still concerned with childcare and housework, and the only new element for her was cooking on a far grander scale than had been possible at home. She had no close personal contact with the city world of factories and service industries. The problems of employment and the city proletariat were unknown to her, so that when she arrived at the convent doors, she was a pure product of Poland's countryside.

In order to make clear what I understand by that culture of country folk, it is worth making a small digression, to define more closely the nature of the peasant or small farmer who has been produced by this set of values. I quote from Professor Stanislaus Pigon, the prominent scholar who, being himself of peasant origin, has analysed the conditions and lifestyle in the Polish countryside, and who presents the following picture of the mentality of the small farmer and peasant:

> "It is to his type of work that the small farmer owes his natural instinct for the harmony and order of farm life, an instinct of duty and sense of responsibility for the whole of life. He finds within himself, compelled by the necessities of daily life, the whole gamut of human abilities. He cannot, of course, limit himself to ploughing and sowing, but must know how to mow and reap, thresh and clean grain, and mill it. Nor can he limit himself to the fields and the care of livestock. He must be able to undertake carpentry, weaving, any kind of craft for his own use, if he wishes to be a thrifty and capable farmer... This variety of practised capabilities must give the small farmer's mentality a richness of growth and fulfilment unattainable in that system of specialization found in the town."

Helenka, inheriting that folk culture, was too young when she left home to be able herself to have all the qualities and skills enumerated by Professor Pigon. But she was brought up surrounded by them, and, like every child, she absorbed the lifestyle of her environment. This lifestyle formed her, firstly by its own atmosphere, and only later, and gradually, in various skills. There is no doubt that, helping her father in the farm work and her mother in housework and with the livestock, she already had a store of general knowledge. Most importantly however, she had absorbed those mental characteristics of the small farmer that Professor Pigon lists:

"a sense of duty, an inner seriousness, strict moral rigour and a range of interests and skills which together make up a specific philosophy of life."

All these traits are clearly visible in Helenka. This formative influence of country life remained so strongly with her that the character delineated by it was the elementary framework upon which, to the end of her life, she was to build her special virtues or skills. When she entered religious life she was a distinctive individual: strong, hardy and independent. Her character was upright and direct. Two special traits may be emphasized, as they had a basic significance for the religious life awaiting her: a disciplined obedience, and asceticism. She had been brought up to obedience as a little child. She well understood its worth and the need of it, and submitted to its rigours without interior revolt. She fulfilled commands given to her responsibly and without evasions. The factor which strengthened her innate tendency to be obedient was her kindliness for those around her, which was expressed not so much in seeking an occasion to give someone pleasure as in filling that person's daily needs and wishes. Thus, obedience on the one hand formed within her a sense of authority, and on the other developed her ability to see the point of view of another human being.

Helenka's daily ascetic practices were also an important trait for her future religious life. She conscientiously carried out those mortifications required by the Church, especially fasts, differentiating them well and often multiplying them excessively, which became limited in the community because of the duty of obedience. She liked to offer Jesus the little sacrifices of daily mortifications. They were "flowers laid at His feet". Through the obedience she had practised and her mortifications, Helenka had thus attained the basic ability to control herself, which could be observed in her quiet equable behaviour but, which, however, did not inhibit her liveliness. She laughed aloud a good deal, sang, and when she was hurt she wept loudly and pitifully. The latter happened rarely, and only over matters that were vital to her. She was not tearful. Lively, active and very talkative, she entered the convent as an embryo apostle by free choice and temperament. She liked to instruct and knew how to do it, to draw others when the opportunity arose. Her innate discretion kept this in the proper proportions and to suitable occasions. She was, in this, neither intrusive nor did she thrust herself on others, and perhaps therefore the more convincing. What she said came from the fullness of her heart.

A DREAM COME TRUE

Her dream had come true: Helena* had obtained what she had wanted, and was now in the convent. After all the obstacles, we have at last a typical happy ending. The path to the service of God was now open before her and nothing separated her from Him. Is it therefore possible to draw a veil over her self, and concern ourselves solely with her mission from Jesus which she received to pass on to us? It certainly is not.

That kind of happy ending in which marriage crowns the love of two young people and ends their story, happens only in novels. In reality the wedding is only the crossing of the first threshold in their new life together. Their whole life lies before them. Whether their marriage is a happy ending for the two of them, only the future will show.

It is similar with entry into a convent. This is just the first step. The new candidate stands before a great Unknown. The lifestyle in a religious community is quite different from that in the world, and has its own specific requirements and customs. Now it has to be learned, adopted, and come to be loved. It needs preparation and teaching. This is why every candidate for the religious life begins with the postulancy in which he or she learns of first duties in religion. This

---

*Translator's footnote: It now seems time to stop calling Sister Faustina by her childhood name of Helenka, and to use Helena. The American edition of her Diary calls her Helen.

is a time in which both sides observe each other intently: the community checks whether the candidate is suitable, and the candidate whether life in that particular community is what he or she wants. The true religious formation begins only after these first attempts, in the novitiate. This is even emphasized externally, by the putting on of the religious habit.

Helena was accepted into the Congregation of the Sisters of Our Lady of Mercy as a sister of the second choir, i.e. to the company of the sisters-coadjutrices who do manual work such as cleaning, cooking, gardening, etc.

The candidates to the Congregation divided their time between lessons preparing them for the religious life, and performing some introductory duties in that field of work appropriate to the choir to which each was assigned. The two types of occupation were so arranged that one type of occupation should not interfere with the other. The postulancy, like the novitiate, was basically the same for each of the two choirs; the first lessons and the recreation periods were held in common. Thus, the convent formation was more or less identical for all the religious. The difference between the two choirs was a matter of education, of the mental preparation for the filling of appropriate functions within the Congregation. They were thus divided for lessons and practical experience in the sphere of craft or profession, which was different for the two choirs.

Helena began her first introduction to the religious life and its religious duties while also helping in the kitchen. Up to this point, she knew nothing of convent life; everything was new, sometimes surprising and not easy to accept. She had mixed feelings. The convent of her dreams and the convent of reality seemed like two totally different worlds, which had nothing in common. The confrontation of the reality with the imagined ideal that Helena treasured and brought with her must have been a painful shock, so that a crisis began to form for her. We find traces within her Diary, but the best picture of those days is given us by Mrs Lipszyc, whom Helena saw, as we have already mentioned, twice after entering the convent, and to whom she frankly confided her new impressions.

Helena had come to the convent without the permission of her parents. She informed them of her intention only when she had been provisionally accepted, and she requested the necessary documents. In answer, her parents sent her elder sister Eugenie with instructions to dissuade her.

Her sister's visit did not have the desired effect. Helena wrote direct to her former parish priest and obtained the necessary certificates within the stipulated time, and having collected the required sum of money, entered the convent without further contact with her parents. For the necessary reference on her character and behaviour, she turned to her most recent employer, Mrs Lipszyc. This lady did not refuse, and shortly betook herself to the convent.

The visit turned out well. Mrs Lipszyc gave a most favourable reference for Helena. As a digression, it is worth mentioning the following adventure which befell Mrs Lipszyc when she was looking for the right convent, for no reference could better indicate the opinion she had of Helena:

"I knew that Helena had entered a convent on Żytnia Street in Warsaw, but I did not know the name of the Congregation. While looking for it on that street, I went inside the convent of some Congregation. I mentioned that I was there to provide an opinion of a girl who had worked as a maid for me for a year, and had now entered the Congregation. The Sister who was talking to me became annoyed that the candidate had deceived her in not admitting that she had been a servant, for their Rule, that of a single-choir community, did not permit them to accept servants. I at first began to explain that Helena was not a domestic by trade, but just a country girl, who

had been working as a domestic for that time in order to earn her dowry. But when I heard the accusation that Helena had deceived them, I became angry and hotly denied it, saying, "Helena is not capable of lying. I have probably come to the wrong place and she is not here." I asked if there were another convent nearby, and they directed me to the Convent of Sisters of Our Lady of Mercy. Helena was indeed with them."

From the rest of Mrs Lipszyc's account, we learn that after seeing the Mother Superior she saw Helena herself.

"Helena obviously wanted to speak to me alone. Taking advantage of the temporary absence of her companion, while showing me to the door, she said that she was in difficulties, that she found the Rule with its insistence on silence and walking slowly to be burdensome, that she could not defend herself when unjustly accused of anything... She did not feel right, there, and did know if she could persevere in that Congregation, for she had to suppress her temperament and speak quietly, and this was very hard for her. She also spoke of humiliations she had to undergo."

In telling her daughter what had transpired on her visit to the convent Mrs Lipszyc was unable to control her anger at anyone accusing such a truthful girl as Helena of lying.

"If I were deceived in her, I could trust nobody," she said. Although saddened by the girl's problems in the convent, she was not surprised. *"I understood her, knowing her lively personality, and I knew,"* she said, *"that she might experience some difficulties from her superior."*

(Archives of S.F., Recoll.)

Helena's experiences should not surprise us. Despite the young woman's sincere piety and upright character they were unavoidable. A conflict had arisen between the conventual and the lay style of Christian life.

In lay life, our lifestyle is dictated by our earthly conditions, and within their limit the individual establishes his Christian principles. In conventual life, those conditions are subordinated to religious goals, which take precedence. This, of course, essentially changes the whole behaviour of a person and affects his or her character and mental formation. Since the whole religious life is based upon strict obedience, which is the keystone, an understanding and acceptance of this is one of the most basic indices of a true religious vocation.

It becomes necessary to explain this type of obedience.

In the world, the norms regulating obedience are utilitarian: the ensuring of order in personal and social life. In the convent, obedience has a sacral character. One has to obey, for different reasons. A nun has to obey not for the logical and utilitarian reasons known to us, but for the love of God. Natural reasons give way to supernatural reasons. Through obedience to superiors and the Congregation's Constitutions, obedience to God Himself is expressed. Because of its strictly religious nature, obedience in a religious house is unconditional and not open to discussion. In the Congregation of Sisters of Our Lady of Mercy the whole day was filled with scrupulous obedience - "holy" obedience, as the Constitutions call it. Obedience regulates prayer, work and recreation, defining time allowed for conversation and time for compulsory silence. Everything that happened in the convent day was strictly regulated by obedience; for every deviation from the regulations it was necessary to have separate permission. Helena, who was spontaneous and lively, on entering this new style of life, found herself constantly having to exercise self-control. She had to work out a new system of dealing with herself unlike that she had already achieved. But above all, she had to comprehend this new kind of obedience, which, because it forbade discussion, more than once led to misunderstandings, and even to undeserved humiliation, especially in those cases where personal animosities or the irritation of the person giving an order affected her. Helena, who was very sensitive and anxious to do well, and also used to personal independence, had great difficulties in submitting to the demands of holy obedience. Indeed she quickly realised it must be accepted with interior consent, but it was hard and painful to learn. However, as she was learning to fulfil the will of God, she put her whole self into it, trying to satisfy the demands of obedience.

But this was by no means all. The most thorny point lay elsewhere. The most difficult thing to bear was the limitation of time for prayer, which was dictated by the demands of her work, which were greater for the coadjutrix sister than for a member of the first choir. Helena was frequently reproved for spending too much time in prayer, for *only wanting to pray all the time.* After all, the main reason she had chosen the religious life was the conviction that everything in it was subordinated to the need for prayer. Logically speaking, for someone with such a strong predisposition to contemplative prayer and mysticism, the proper place would have been a contemplative order. Helena was born to be a contemplative and her soul was developing in that direction. Therefore she felt the limitations, in the sphere holiest and dearest to her, in a most painful manner. She was yet to learn that work is prayer, that it does not disturb even contemplation, from Jesus Himself. She had to undergo a long schooling from Jesus in order to possess and become familiar with this skill. Before this occurred, she fruitlessly attempted to fit herself within the too-narrow framework of her present possibilities.

It is therefore not at all strange that Helena should hesitate more and more. Had she made a mistake and was she not in the right place for her? The Congregation of Sisters of Our Lady of Mercy was an active community - was she to go to a contemplative Congregation? Her doubts increased, fed by her innate suspicion that that was the case. After being three weeks in the Congregation, a crisis occurred and Helena had decided to leave. But although the decision was taken, she kept putting off that final talk to her superior. The reason was simple: she had no confidence in herself. The situation was too complicated and she could not grasp the proper solution. After all, it was Jesus Himself Who had led her to this place! Where, then, lay the mistake? What was the will of God intending for her? She prayed fervently to be shown what to do next. She wanted to fulfil God's will, not her own. But among all these complicated problems she had lost her way.

She was persistent in prayer. She was like a child who keeps pestering until he achieves what he wants. Because God loves to be pestered so trustingly and continually, she did indeed receive the answer she wanted. Just as on a previous occasion in her life, it was Jesus Himself Who cast out her doubts. Helena gives an account of this in her Diary:

'I entered the cell full of anguish and discontent; I did not know what to do with myself. I threw myself headlong on the ground and began to pray fervently that I might come to know the will of God... After a while a brightness filled my cell, and on the curtain I saw the very sorrowful Face of Jesus. There were open wounds on His Face, and large tears were falling on my bed-spread. Not knowing what all this meant I asked Jesus, "Jesus, who has hurt You so?" And Jesus said to me, 'It

is you who will cause Me this pain if you leave this convent. It is to this place that I called you and nowhere else; and I have prepared many graces for you.' I begged pardon of Jesus and immediately changed my decision.

The next day was confession day. I related all that had taken place in my soul, and the confessor answered that, from this, God's will is clear that I am to remain in this congregation and that I'm not even to think of another religious order. From that moment on, I have always felt happy and content.'

(Diary, Notebook I, para. 19).

Jesus' answer, confirmed by her confessor, immediately ended Helena's spiritual crisis. The young woman calmed down, and experienced again that joy and equable disposition which was natural to her. Now she knew what she was to do, and she was decisive: if God wanted her to stay there, stay she would, putting every effort into understanding and submitting to the requirements of the religious life.

Up to this point, we have seen the shadows in Helena's new life. But we should not leave the picture in these sombre colours, for it might lead to the hasty and mistaken idea that only difficulties and painful experiences were her lot in the convent. We must throw some other light on the picture, to gain a fuller impression.

It is an old principle that one cannot know the truth about another human being from his words only. The picture presented will be fragmentary. It will be partial, even if the other speaks the exact truth, and thus in a sense it will be inaccurate. The account will show only that which the given individual was concentrating upon, that which he felt or experienced deeply. This reality for him must be seen in a more general context, illustrated by what others present also observed. Only then can we be sure that we see the real picture in the proper light.

Let us therefore pass to the problem which interests us from the other point of view: how did the community receive and judge Helena? There is no lack of material, so that, without pre-judging what happened, let us look first at the recollections of the convent superiors. We have the opinions of Helena's two direct superiors, the Mistress of the Postulants and the Sister in charge of the kitchen, where Helena was assigned to work. Both saw in her a soul closely connected with God and good material for becoming a nun.

The Mistress of Postulants in the convent on Żytnia Street, to which Helena had applied, was at that time Mother Jane Bartkiewicz. 'She quickly became aware of the young woman's qualities, and to more than one sister she said that Helena

> "was a person above the average, with a mystical disposition and a particular contact with God," and that "she must be a soul dear to God. She has her own special interior life, about which she does not say much".

The Sister in charge of the kitchen adds several particulars about the new candidate:

> "She completed her duties in the kitchen very well, for she was hard-working, capable and obedient...
> I noticed then that she was a modest girl who did not talk much, very much recollected and at one with God. She was always obedient and did what I told her. During the day she sometimes asked me, "Sister, I should like to pay a visit to the chapel for a moment." I did not always allow her to go, explaining that she was not yet a Religious and had no special duties. It was sufficient to visit the chapel morning and evening. Nevertheless she would ask for permis-

sion to pay just a little visit... I observed no obvious faults in her. The only thing she might be reproached for, and I met this reproach several times, was that she was always wanting to pray... I do not know whether she had any interior problems, for she did not mention anything... She was always smiling and accepted even a sharp reproof quietly and with a smile."

(Archives of S.F., Recollections).

It is also worth recalling that from the very beginning the then Superior of the convent on Żytnia Street in Warsaw, Mother Michael Moraczewska, had a positive and kindly attitude to Helena. Later, too, when from 1928 onwards Mother Michael was Superior General, her attitude to Helena remained the same. She always took special care of Sister Faustina, as she was by then, facilitating, as much as was possible in the Congregation, the fulfilment of the mission to spread the devotion to the Divine Mercy which Jesus was later to entrust to Sister Faustina.

For a final touch to this picture of the young postulant, we should see how her companions accepted her. Sister Joachim G., who spent the last months of the postulancy with her, followed by the novitiate in Cracow, said,

"I met Sister Faustina in the Postulancy in Cracow. She was cheerful and happy; she almost always had a smile on her lips. Her whole personality seemed to express that she had come gladly to serve the Lord Jesus. By her behaviour she encouraged me and other sisters towards such a joyful service of God.

She always had something to talk about, especially on matters concerned with God. She was always the most animated at recreation; she liked to speak in an emotional way; she was always conscious of the need to love one's neighbour; she never broke silence except

at recreation. The Mother Mistress recommended her as an example to me, especially as regards good humour and gaiety."

(Archives of S.F., Recollections).

Illuminated from all these angles, the picture of Helena certainly seems a cheerful one. The interior confusion she experienced on first seeing the reality of convent life - in an active rather than a contemplative order - was soon dissipated and does not appear to have been noticed by others. After a short period of doubt, the young woman realised that she was in the right place, and from this certainty a soothing peace descended on her, enabling her to overcome her difficulties and rise above the painful moments, little by little. Such moments must occur in daily life among a large group of people. In any case, the Lord was near, so near that not only might one run to Him at any moment of the day, but be forever confident of being within His reach. This was, for Helena, a new and very great joy. Close to the Christ of the Eucharist, she took her first steps trustfully on the path that was pleasing to God, though not always, in the beginning, easy for her.

8. Convent in which the Novitiate was situated, at 3 - 9 Wronia Street, Cracow

HELENA OBIIT, HIC NATA EST FAUSTINA

Three different Mistresses were responsible for the spiritual formation of Helena in the convent. For the first six months of her postulancy in Warsaw there was Mother Jane Bartkiewicz. When Helena was transferred to Cracow at the beginning of 1926, where she remained for the rest of her postulancy and throughout her novitiate, she came under the care of Sister Margaret Gimbutt. This Sister guided her through the first two months of the novitiate (and a few years later - in 1932 - over the five-month probation before Helena's perpetual vows). In June 1926 Sister Margaret was transferred to the same post in Warsaw, and her place in Cracow was taken by Sister Mary Joseph Brzoza, a much younger woman of 37 who had just arrived after training in France. Thus Sister Faustina had almost the whole period of her novitiate, which lasted two years, under the direction of Sister Mary Joseph, and it is principally to her that she owed her spiritual formation. But before we discuss in more detail the role of the last-named Sister let us pause with the two previous Directresses, for it was they who laid the foundations for that formation, and each of them had a specific part to play in it.

The first instruction on the requirements of the religious life was imparted to the newly-arrived candidate by Mother Jane Bartkiewicz. Under this Mistress of Postulants Helena became seized with doubts as to whether she was in the right convent for her. It is understandable, therefore, that we should ask to what degree, if any, her Directress contributed to this crisis.

Mother Jane was a senior nun aged 67, full of energy and with a well-developed sense of duty, but because for many years she had been Vicar General of her Congregation, deputizing for the Superior General in Poland, she was used to the absolute obedience of the Sisters, and it had made her something of a despot. Although she took a kindly care of the postulants, she was sometimes heavy-handed in bending the young candidates to fit the convent framework, which, in the beginning, in many cases, was not easy to accept. Her method of education might, in the case of the more sensitive postulant, weight the scales of mental perseverance down by inspiring anxiety and a lack of self-confidence.

Helena was just such a postulant. It is true that in general she found it easy to obey instructions, but hers was not a character that could be moulded by force. The spiritual strengths she had heretofore cultivated in her life in the world were above all adapted to resisting the world's negative influences. She now had to transform herself completely from one who resists to one who submits, which requires patience and time.

At the beginning of my religious life, suffering and adversities frightened and disheartened me, wrote Sister Faustina in her Diary (Notebook I, para. 56). This is an unusual expression for her, because she had a sturdy character capable of endurance. But in this case there were too many difficulties at once, which gave rise to a trauma, and, although this was overcome, it emerged years afterwards in the memory. Sister Faustina, even while urging her brother and sister to follow her into the religious life, could not refrain from remarking that the first period after entering is hard, and the adjustment to the requirements of the religious life needs patience and time. (Archives of S.F., Recollections of her brother Mieczysław).

And yet Mother Jane had a very favourable opinion of the young candidate. Mother Michael, then Superior of the Warsaw convent, said that a couple of months after Helena had arrived, Mother Jane described her as *"a soul in very close contact with the Lord Jesus"*. Was this perhaps why she wanted to test her?

However, it was not only the demands of her Mistress of Postulants which posed Helena a problem hard to accept. The Senior Sister of the kitchen, whom Helena was instructed to help, added quite other demands. The problem was one of prayer. Sister Sabina T. felt it was not necessary for Helena to visit the Blessed Sacrament or for frequent prayer during her duties, considering that when there was plenty of work it was not appropriate. She even explained that Helena, not yet being a nun, had no obligation to observe the required devotions strictly. It would be sufficient if she performed the most essential. This lack of priority for religious practices was impossible for a girl of Helena's type to accept, and it deeply offended her religious feelings. Thus, in these circumstances doing what Jesus had asked her, to stay in that convent, needed much effort, when she had taken the decision to leave. Her faith, the prime motivator of her behaviour, for the first time had to overcome what her reason was showing her. She had to accept, blindly and against her own inclinations, a style of life foreign to her because this was what Jesus wanted. She noted in her Diary,

"In the convent, at first it seems that the work and the life are hard, but later everything becomes pleasant and one is happy."

At the beginning of 1926, Helena went to Cracow to finish the postulancy and begin her novitiate. Here she found a quite different atmosphere and other attitudes. The Directress was Sister Margaret Gimbutt, an older woman but not at all like Mother Jane. Silent and humble, she formed people rather by her own example than by instructions. She herself was prayerful and placed prayer in its proper hierarchy among all the duties of the day. Under her wing, conflicts were dissipated and Helena quickly relaxed spiritually. "A happy child of God" was the description of Helena given by the senior novice, later Sister Crescentia (Sister K.), who had been asked to look after her. This phrase may best show Helena's then state of mind, both in the postulancy as well as subsequently in the first half of her novitiate.

She had a positive effect on those around her, because of her joy and enthusiasm, so that she was more than once put forward as a model, both for postulants, and, later, for novices. Her companions liked her and some admired her, and at recreation they gladly grouped themselves around her. She fascinated them, because in spite of her open gaiety and her ease in talking, verging on the talkative, she remained recollected. She could tell a story interestingly and "always knew how to speak about God and spiritual matters", as Sister Regina J. has said.

The recollections of her companions shed considerable light on the spiritual climate of those days. I give both those from the time of the postulancy as well as those from the first period of the novitiate. One of those most friendly with her, Sister Placida, says a great deal about the time when they were both undergoing their formation in the Congregation.

"When we were in the novitiate, Sister Faustina said that we should pray as the Apostles prayed: 'Lord, teach us to pray, multiply our faith'... She asked us often: "Sisters, do you pray for the Polish army? For miners working in difficult conditions? For sailors sailing the oceans?" I often wondered where she got these ideas from, because I felt that in praying for everyone, I was including in that intention the various groups of people. But she insisted that

*when praying it was necessary to particularize those
who needed our prayers more. Sister Faustina was
very anxious about the salvation of one's neighbour
and she spoke of it constantly... She often urged us to
pray for the intention that people should know God
better and love Him more... When we often received a
reproof or penance for some breaking of the rule, she
would encourage us by saying:" Dear Sisters, offer this
penance to atone to God for the sins with which
people insult Him". She added that sins are committed by religious also,.. One day she asked me during
recreation what were my duties that day. I said that
I had the heavy work of watering the young trees in
the garden, and that my hands were aching from it.
She encouraged me to do these duties as if they were
a penance, and to offer my labour for the sins of
mankind. Later, in the evening she asked me if I had
remembered what she had said to me in recreation."*

(Arch. S.F. Recoll.).

I have run somewhat ahead into the first period of
novitiate in these recollections only because they show
no new element and can as well serve to illustrate the
postulancy. There is still the same joyful spiritual
climate of living with those who had the same goals as
Helena herself.

It was in such a mood and with such companions
that Helena was preparing for her approaching taking
of the veil, the first, introductory vows to Jesus after
the end of the postulancy. The visible sign of all this
was the clothing in the habit and the taking of a new
name. This is a threshold in the religious life, the
moment when new religious are born.

Dressed in a white wedding gown, Helena went to
meet her Bridegroom at the altar. She returned as
Sister Faustina. To imitate the line of the Polish poet
Adam Mickiewicz: *Obiit Helena, hic nata est Faustina:*
Sister Faustina of the Blessed Sacrament.

Moved to the depths of her soul, Helena nearly fainted twice. The first time was when, with the other postulants, she was standing before the altar to accept the religious habit and to receive another name. The postulants knelt, but she slipped helplessly onto the priedieu. The sisters surrounded her at once and helped her to rise, and the clothing ceremony went ahead normally. She became faint once more, when being dressed in the habit in the parlour.

Sister Faustina noted the reason for her faintness in her Diary:

> *'The day I took the* (religious) *habit, God let me understand how much I was to suffer. I clearly saw to what I was committing myself. I experienced a moment of that suffering. But then God filled my soul again with great consolations.'*

(Diary, Notebook I, para. 22).

Helena had invited her parents to her Clothing. They did not come. Her elder sister explains this as follows: "She invited us to the Clothing, but because the letter was received so late, none of the family was at the ceremony."

Two years later, when Sister Faustina made her first vows, both her parents were present. Still against their daughter's decision, they hoped to persuade her to return home, but her happiness was so obvious and she was so radiant and in love with God, that despite their former attitude they looked at her as if they were bewitched. No. They had never met anything like this before. "As she is in love with Jesus, let us leave her there. This is the will of God," pronounced her father. Thus she had not only the consent of her parents, and their blessing, but their respect, and even their admiration for the path she had chosen for herself.

We know this from what Helena's cousin, Sophie Rulka, has to say:

"I remember that when Sister Faustina's parents went to Cracow on the occasion of her first vows, they visited us, and they came again on their way back from Cracow. Her mother said, on the second visit, that they were left alone with Sister Faustina for some time. They walked around the garden, but Sister Faustina said very little and was engaged in prayer. Knowing that her father was displeased with the path she had taken, and that he would have sons-in-law and grandchildren through his other daughters, she said to him: 'You see, Daddy, the One Whose bride I am is my husband and your son-in-law.' I remember that her father was very moved, and he and my father wept."

(Archives of S.F., Recoll.).

It was only then that her parents experienced regret for not having helped their daughter with her plans to become a nun. They felt proud of her. Though perhaps their hearts remained sorrowful that she had left them, they now of their own free will gave God, not indeed their first born, but the best of their children. In this way they gave God the sacrifice He had demanded of them.

NOVITIATE WITH JESUS

The novitiate, which directly succeeded the Clothing, began, for Sister Faustina, in a "honeymoon" atmosphere. The days passed happily and peacefully. The novitiate is a school where the programme has two aims: education in matters of the faith, and the formation of the character to provide a strong foundation for the work needed to obtain sanctity in the religious life and increasingly greater union with God.

Sister Faustina fervidly absorbed the lectures. In matters of faith, they revised the catechism, the Bible and the history of the Church. In learning the constitutions of her congregation she came to know the essence of conventual life and to understand its depth. At the same time, she was assisting in the kitchen. Her work did not clash with her studies: indeed, quite the opposite, for in it she learned little by little how to adapt prayer to the duties she undertook and to draw her work into a prayerful climate.

That same sister who described the atmosphere obtaining in the novitiate and whom I quoted in discussing the postulancy also had something to say on the topic of work:

"I recall that Sister Faustina as a novice was already working in the kitchen. She was very exact in her work. She took care that everything was clean, and paid attention to how to prepare dishes, so that they were tasty. She said that we should always cook

*as if Jesus Himself, or the bishop, were coming to a
meal.*

*"I also remember something that happened at this
time. On one occasion meat from an entire beef
carcase was delivered from the town. There was a
heat wave at the time and no suitable place to keep
the meat, and we did not want it to spoil. The Sister
Cook was ill; the Housekeeper Sister was busy with
other urgent work. Sister Josepha, who kept the
larder, did not want to know, having to finish some
work to a deadline. Sister Faustina was left alone to
cope with the carcase. I came to help. She told me,
"We will dish up lunch, and then we'll go to the
chapel and pray. I'll ask Jesus' advice, I'll tell Him
all about it, and He will give me the best advice on
what to do".*

*"After we had served lunch we did indeed go to the
chapel. After a moment's prayer Sister Faustina came
out as if overjoyed and filled with a new energy, and
she said, "I know what we'll do: the smaller pieces of
meat will be for minced meat burgers, and we will
sprinkle the large joints with vinegar and put them in
the cellar wrapped in cloth."*

*"We worked until late at night. I think the Novice
Mistress gave us someone else to help. I only remember that all the meat kept very well and nothing was
spoiled... When Sister Cook came back to work after
a few days, she praised Sister Faustina for having
done so well. Seeing the state in which the meat was
delivered, and recalling also the heat wave and lack
of appropriate methods of preserving it, for there was
only the cellar, without any ice, I think that for all
that meat to keep without going bad was almost a
miracle."*

(Archives of S.F. Recoll.).

The same sister has some interesting remarks about
the life of Sister Faustina in the community. She
recalls with respect her courage in matters concerning
God.

"In such instances she was capable of speaking up and reproving even sisters who were older or who held posts of responsibility. I remember a characteristic example...

"I once went to the kitchen for water. Three older sisters were chatting in the kitchen. Their subject was priests, our confessors. Their conversation was far from elevating. I was rather surprised that older sisters could talk in that way. I wanted to get out of the kitchen as fast as possible. Sister Faustina. who was working there, heard the conversation and said, "Excuse me, but Jesus does not like it, please finish your conversation, Sisters." I was full of admiration for a novice who had enough courage to oppose senior sisters. Afterwards at recreation, I asked her what had happened next, and if she had had any unpleasantness, but she said nothing happened, it wasn't worth speaking about because something might be said which would be against the principle of love of one's neighbour."

After seven weeks of novitiate, on 20th June 1926 there was a change, as I have already written, of Novice Mistress, but the newly arrived Sister Mary Joseph Brzoza directed the group entrusted to her in much the same way as Sister Margaret. She had, possibly, a more decided approach and went more deeply into spiritual needs. She was a true spiritual mother to them.

Of the three Novice Mistresses I have mentioned, Sister Mary Joseph had the strongest and most permanent effect on the spiritual formation of Sister Faustina. It was to her that credit must go for the strong, healthy foundation of monastic character and for the basic ordering of those elements essential for her own natural spirituality, to be finally completed by Jesus Himself. Sister Mary Joseph successfully diagnosed the specific needs of this chosen soul and was able to guide her with a steady, sure hand even through the dark night of the soul, that mysterious novitiate of Jesus Himself, which Sister Faustina experienced for a year and a half, commencing from the end of the first year of the novitiate. Sister Mary Joseph had a consummate intuitive knowledge of the human soul, and so was a sturdy and unfailing support even in the greatest conflicts and interior experiences of the young nun. Perhaps we might even boldly call her the first, in the full meaning of the term, spiritual director of Sister Faustina, a director whom Providence had sent to lead her through the testing time of mystical purification and maturing. We have every right to suppose that it was thanks to the wise direction of Sister Mary Joseph on the hand, and the trusting obedience of Sister Faustina on the other, that the latter's difficult time of God's highest trial lasted so briefly. In many, even in very great saints, it has lasted for years, during which they have struggled blindly with overwhelming spiritual experiences, trying alone to find a way out of what seemed to them to be a spiritual impasse.

Rev. Theodore Czaputa, aged 42, a penetrating and understanding confessor, supplemented in the confessional whatever Helena did not receive in the community. Her superiors cooperated well with the priest, dividing amongst themselves the responsibility for forming the novices entrusted to their care.

Over the whole house in Cracow the wise and generous-hearted Superior, Mother Raphael B., presided, one of the most distinguished individuals the Congregation then possessed.

It is therefore hard to imagine more fortunate conditions and a better chosen environment for the spiritual growth of the young generation in the community. Sister Faustina was surrounded by and in the care of its most valued members. She thus made great progress. As she had always had a marvellous memory and the interior readiness to submit, *"it was never necessary to repeat anything twice to her"*.

80

Thus passed the year 1926. The small daily trials unavoidable in such a large community and its life were no great problem. The "honeymoon", however, was drawing to a close. In the spring of 1927 Jesus led the soul of His young bride into the purifying fires of the dark night of the soul. Here it is necessary to understand, in the most general outline, what is meant by this expression, "dark night of the soul", or mystical night. I have taken information about this mystical darkness from the work of the Carmelite Edith Stein, "Wiedza Krzyza", or "The Knowledge of the Cross", in which she discusses the mystical experience of faith of St John of the Cross. A more extensive treatment can be found in Père A. Tanquerey's Outline of Ascetic and Mystical Theology (Zarys teologii ascetycznej i mistycznej), vol. 111, chapter II, art. II.

God makes Himself known to whom He wishes, outside the ordinary ways of prayer, in mystical experience. "Knowing God" consists of an awareness of Him and of the soul in union with Him. It is a "knowledge of acquaintance", indeed of intimacy, and differs from "knowledge about" God, which is possible for the mind which reasons about God from analogy with created things. An ascetic preparation for mystical experience, which heightens consciousness, can be undertaken, for example, under an experienced spiritual director in a contemplative religious community. Others, however, find that in passive states of mind, God also acts upon the soul as He pleases, making the soul aware of His indwelling in a flash of Divine condescension. A tendency to the disposition capable of this "infused contemplation", as it is sometimes called, had been observed by the wise senior nuns who knew Sister Faustina. God perfects the human faculties, while seeming to defeat their activity. Sister Faustina as a young novice was unprepared for the terrifying nature of this process.

Here we should add that the vocabulary in which mystics describe these unique, intense, arduous and ultimately ineffable experiences is, paradoxically, the vocabulary of others, describing the extremes of sensuous experience, for no other language seems adequate: cleansing "by fire", torment, loss, "death of the soul", love "flaming", "consuming", mystical "marriage", "union", and "intimacy".

To attain mystical experience, only the first step is man's: he is then led on by God. The time this preparation takes will vary - long enough for everything which hinders God from embracing the soul into His possession to be consumed and eliminated. God takes away the will of the human being, which, safely anchored in the spiritual life, has become courageous and sufficiently mature interiorly to be able to pass through the torment.

The soul has become able to deny the worth of mere earthly and familiar experience and attachments, as had the soul of Sister Faustina. All that is dearest to the soul in the enjoyment of the senses is surrendered, and a dark mystical night must be endured in which the soul lives without their help and comfort. This is called "the dark night of the senses", full of severe spiritual and physical disturbances. Temptations, violent emotions and even hatred of God are felt. The soul comes to "know" good and evil, and feels she stands before the divine judgment seat. Seeing her own nothingness in comparison with the Divine Reality, the soul is terrified and paralysed. However, the reward for this dark night is that the soul is cleansed and knows herself. The cleansing of the sensual and cognitive faculties allows them now to submit to the supremacy of the spiritual faculties. The soul then enters the "dark night of the soul", the experience most terrifying and difficult to endure, even for the bravest of God's lovers, without Divine aid. After cleansing comes enlightenment. The soul has sacrificed her prerogative of her own way of thinking and willing, and all the supports which make us self-sufficient, to take this next step beyond the light of reason. The whole process of enlightenment takes place deep in the subconscious, but consciously the despairing human being is convinced of having lost God and been condemned. Yet there begin to be glimpses, as the soul becomes more enlightened, which permit her to realise God's nearness, but these are still intermingled with recurrent dark clouds.

These mystical nights pass eventually, to be rewarded by the loving union of the soul with God. The soul regains strength, attains peace and is constantly recollected in God. God fills her so completely that He shares with her some of His own nature - the soul becomes transformed by the divine. Mystical nights last a very long time, prolonged the more the soul in the torment of purification and illumination resists or avoids the guiding hand of God. In Sister Faustina's case the process was astonishingly brief: altogether eighteen months, for the whole of the second year of the novitiate and six months after her first Vows, i.e. the years 1927 and 1928. This is what she wrote on the subject:

'Towards the end of the first year of my novitiate, darkness began to cast its shadow over my soul. I felt no consolation in prayer; I had to make a great effort to meditate; fear began to sweep over me. Going deeper into myself, I could find nothing but great misery. I could also see clearly the great holiness of God. I did not dare to raise my eyes to Him, but reduced myself to dust under His feet and begged for mercy. My soul was in this state for almost six months. Our beloved Mother Directress [Mary Joseph] encouraged me in these difficult moments. But this suffering became greater and greater.

'The second year of the novitiate was approaching. Whenever I recalled that I was to make my vows, my soul shuddered. I did not understand what I was reading; I could not meditate; it seemed to me that my prayer was displeasing to God.'

(Diary, Notebook I, para. 23).

'Every time I entered the chapel for some spiritual exercise, I experienced even worse torments and temptations. More than once, all through Holy Mass, I had to struggle against blasphemous thoughts which were forcing themselves to my lips.'

(Diary, Notebook I, para. 77).

'It seemed to me that by approaching the Holy Sacraments I was offending God even more... God was working very strangely in my soul. I did not understand anything at all of what my confessor was telling me. The simple truths of the faith became incomprehensible to me. My soul was in anguish, unable to find comfort anywhere.'

(Diary, Notebook I, para. 23).

'It sees what it does not want to see. It hears what it does not want to hear.'

(Diary, Notebook I, para. 97).

'One thing did surprise me: it often happened that, at the time when I was suffering greatly, these terrible torments would disappear suddenly just as I was approaching the confessional; but as soon as I had left the confessional, all these torments would again seize me with even greater ferocity.'

(Diary, Notebook I, para. 77).

"At a certain point, there came to me the very power-ful impression that I am rejected by God. This terrible thought pierced my soul right through; in the midst of the suffering my soul began to experience the agony of death. I wanted to die but could not... That dreadful thought of being rejected by God is the actual torture suffered by the damned. I fled to Jesus' Wounds and repeated the words of trust, but these words became for me an even greater torture. I went before the Blessed Sacrament, and I began to speak to Jesus: 'Jesus, You said that a mother would sooner forget her infant than God His creature, and that 'even if she would forget her infant, I, God, will never forget My creature.' O Jesus, do You hear how my soul is moaning? Deign to hear the painful whimpers of Your child. I trust in You, O God, because heaven and earth will pass, but Your word will last forever.' Still I found not a moment of relief."

(Diary, Notebook I, para. 23).

The frightened Sister Faustina, unable to help herself, went to her Directress of Novices and to her confessor.

Her Novice Mistress at once recognised the process which the soul of the novice was going through, calmed her and added,

"Know, dear Sister, that God has chosen you for great sanctity. This is a sign that God wants to have you very close to Himself in Heaven. Have great trust in the Lord Jesus."

(Diary, Notebook I, para. 23).

Her confessor took the same attitude. Above all, he confirmed that these were trials from God, and that

*'in your present condition, with all the torments of soul
you are experiencing you not only do not offend God, but
you even try to practise virtues.'*

(Diary, Notebook I, para. 68).

*'This is a sign,' he told me, 'that God loves you very
much and that He has great confidence in you, since He
is sending you such trials.'*

(Diary, Notebook I, para. 77).

He would not allow the penitent, on any account, full
of fear and doubt though she was, to miss Holy Communion, and he tried to unload her mental tensions by
carefully chosen penances.

But the meaning of the instructions she was hearing,
and even more so the penances, was not reaching
Sister Faustina. She was sure that she had been
unable to clarify the state of her soul to her confessor,
and that he therefore did not understand her. This is
well illustrated by the reminiscences of two of her companions, who shared the same dormitory.

Sister Simone N. says,

*"It was almost the day of confession, and after I
had been to confession I came back to change for my
duties in the kitchen. Shortly afterwards Sister
Faustina also came back from confession, knelt before
her bedside cupboard on which there stood a holy
picture, put her hands on her head and began to
weep loudly; her weeping became a shriek.*

*I was sorry for her and ran at once to the Novice
Mistress and told her what had happened. The
Mistress ran at once to our room, and I went straight
to the kitchen. After a little time, Sister Faustina also
came to the kitchen. You could see she had wept, but
she was quite calm. I did not ask her what difficulties she had, and she never told me of them."*

(Archives of S.F., Recoll.).

That this was not a single occasion can be seen from the recollection of a second companion in the novitiate, Sister P.;

"I recall that once when she came back from confession she was weeping silently. I was changing in the same dormitory, to go to work. At a certain moment I heard Sister Faustina fall to her knees weeping and saying, "Jesus, Jesus, no one understands me," and later, "Jesus, who will understand me?" When another sister entered, I said there was something the matter with Sister Faustina. That sister ran for the Novice Mistress. The Novice Mistress came and took Sister Faustina to her room. What they talked of I do not know, and during the next recreation I noticed that Sister Faustina again had some interior suffering."

(Archives of S.F., Recoll.).

Faustina herself noted her state in her Diary:

"The priest to whom I went to confession said to me, "I see very special graces in you, Sister, and I am not worried about you at all; why are you torturing yourself in this way?" But at that time I did not understand at all what he was saying and was extremely surprised when, by way of penance, I was ordered to say the Te Deum or the Magnificat (as thanksgiving for graces received) or to run fast round the garden in the evening, or else to laugh out loud ten times a day" (The latter was for the release of mental tension).

(Diary, Notebook I, para. 68).

Sister Faustina appeared deaf to the meaning of what was being said to her. Her suffering increased from day to day. The crisis came.

"One day, just as I had awakened, when I was putting myself in the presence of God, I was suddenly overwhelmed by despair. Complete darkness in the soul. I fought as best I could till noon. In the afternoon, truly deadly fears began to seize me; my physical strength began to leave me. I went quickly to my cell, fell on my knees before the Crucifix and began to cry out for mercy. But Jesus did not hear my cries. I felt my physical strength leave me completely. I fell to the ground... I wanted to go and see the Directress, but was too weak. I wanted to shout but I had no voice."

(Diary, Notebook I, para. 24).

"When my soul began to sink into this despair, I felt that the end was near. But I seized my little crucifix and clutched it tightly in my hand... and though I wanted to go to my Superiors, I no longer had the physical strength. I uttered my last words: "I trust in Your Mercy!" - and it seemed to me that I provoked God to an even greater anger. And now I was drowned in despair and all that was left me was a moan of unadulterated pain which, from time to time, tore itself from my soul... Every recollection of God opened up an unspeakable ocean of suffering, and yet despite this there is something within the soul which is drawn to Him, though it seems to her for this only - that she suffer more. The memory of the love with which God formerly surrounded it is still another kind of suffering. His gaze pierces it, and everything within the soul is burned by this gaze."

(Diary, Notebook I, para. 101).

Luckily, when words of persuasion have no effect, there is one unfailing remedy in the hands of a consummate spiritual directress - it is obedience. When Sister Faustina lay helplessly in spiritual agony, a second novice entered their cell. Frightened by the sight of her companion lying on the floor, she ran as fast as she could for the Novice Mistress who came at once, and - as Sister Faustina writes -

'in the name of holy obedience ordered me to get up from the ground. My strength returned immediately, and I got up, trembling. The Directress recognized immediately the state of my soul..'.

(Diary, Notebook I, para. 102).

'With kindly words she began to explain to me that this was a trial sent to me by God, saying, 'Have great confidence; God is always our Father, even when He sends us trials.' I returned to my duties as if I had come out from the tomb, my senses saturated with what my soul had experienced.'

(Diary, Notebook I, para. 24).

The relief did not last long. As evening approached, Sister Faustina's sufferings increased again. But in the night help came: the Mother of God visited her with the Infant Jesus on her arm. The Mother of God reinforced the spiritual strength of the tormented Sister, and gave her comfort and courage.

This heavenly aid enabled Sister Faustina to take a breath before the next wave of temptation, the most terrible of all she had so far undergone.

'It seemed as though hell had conspired against me. A terrible hatred began to break out in my soul, a hatred for all that is holy and divine.' (Diary, Notebook I, para. 25). *'The soul does its best to defend itself; it tries*

to stir up its confidence; but prayer is an even greater torment for it, as this prayer seems to arouse God to an even greater anger... The soul is drawn to God, but feels repulsed. All other sufferings and tortures in the world are as nothing compared with this sensation into which it has been plunged; namely, that of being rejected by God. No one can bring it any relief - says Sister Faustina impersonally - 'it finds itself completely alone; there is no one to defend it. It raises its eyes to heaven, but is convinced that this is not for her - for her all is lost. It falls deeper and deeper from darkness to darkness, and it seems that it has lost forever the God it used to love so dearly...

'If God wishes to keep the soul in such darkness, no one will be able to give it light. It experiences rejection by God in a vivid and terrifying manner... In the midst of this, the evil spirit adds to the soul's suffering, mocking it... "What have you gotten out of your mortifications", says Satan, "and out of your fidelity to the rule? What use are all these efforts? You have been rejected by God!' This word, 'rejected', becomes a fire which penetrates every nerve to the marrow of the bone. It pierces right through her entire being. The ordeal reaches its climax. The soul no longer looks for help anywhere. It shrinks into itself and loses sight of everything; it is as though it has accepted the torture of being abandoned. This is a moment for which I have no words. This is the agony of the soul.'

(Diary, Notebook I, para. 98).

Sister Faustina already knew that human help was insufficient. In her desperate prostration she turned to the Blessed Sacrament. Here there could be no doubt that God was present, though inaccessible to her. Lying prone in the shape of a cross or kneeling gazing at the Tabernacle, she admitted her despair, her powerlessness, and begged for mercy.

"Jesus, my Spouse, do You not see that my soul is dying because of its longing for You? How can You hide Yourself from a heart that loves You so sincerely?"
(Diary, Notebook I, para. 25).

But God was silent.

This hard interior struggle, lasting for months, exhausted her strength. She weakened physically and could perform her duties only with difficulty. Pale, with shadows under her bloodshot eyes, she evoked pity by her appearance and many sisters approached the Superior with the request that their obviously suffering companion be helped. Both the Superior and the Directress did all they could to relieve her lot. She was released from the more onerous duties at work, and all spiritual exercises were suspended, for she was to limit herself to short ejaculatory prayers. But how difficult it was perform this minimum!

So the year moved into spring, and with it came Lent. Sister Faustina joined her spiritual agony to that of Christ's Passion. And suddenly, on Good Friday, she received the longed-for grace: the sensation of the nearness of the beloved God inflamed her soul. It lasted only a short time; like a flash, but in that flash she understood how much Jesus had suffered for her. For her! A wave of love engulfed her heart. And when darkness shortly returned again, there remained the longing and thirst to love God, perhaps a painful comfort, but one which gave healing to her aching heart. She snuggled into this sensation, remembered and remained within it, forgetful of suffering. It was a lifeline to which she clung grimly, like a drowning man.

Not long after Easter, on 30th April 1928, Sister Faustina made her first vows - at the moment, temporary, for one year and to be renewed for five years, and to be followed by perpetual vows after this time.

Offering oneself to God in this state of spiritual prostration was an immense effort. But her thirst to love God helped her. To offer oneself meant to love. This she understood. She concentrated her will upon it. She would endure.

Sister Ludwina G., who was being clothed at the same time as Sister Faustina was making her vows, says,

> *"During the making of vows in the chapel she was very recollected, and later a great joy was visible in her face; it could be seen also during the celebrations which the wards arranged for the Sisters who were making their vows or being clothed that day."*

(Archives of S.F. Recoll.).

The novitiate was over. Now she was a nun. She had reached the goal to which the Lord had called her, four years previously in Łódź. The Directress, in sending her forth from her care to lead an independent life in the Congregation, well understood the dangers which might befall this elect soul, and tried to protect her against them. She instructed:

> *Sister, let simplicity and humility be the characteristic traits of your soul. Go through life like a little child, always trusting, always full of simplicity and humility, content with everything, happy in every circumstance. There, where others fear, you will pass calmly along, thanks to this simplicity and humility. Remember this, Sister, for your whole life: as waters flow from the*

mountains down into the valleys, so, too, do God's graces flow only into humble souls.'

(Diary, Notebook I, para. 55).

Her confessor in his advice placed the chief emphasis on practising love:

'Go through life doing good, so that I could write on its pages: 'She spent her life doing good.' May God bring this about in you... Act in such a way that all those who come in contact with you will go away joyful. Sow happiness about you because you have received much from God; give, then, generously to others... Keep well in mind the words I am telling you right now.'

(Diary, Notebook I, para. 55).

For herself, he added one sentence which in its brevity contained for her a basic maxim:

'Let God push your boat out into the deep waters, towards the unfathomable depths of the interior life.'

(Diary, Notebook I, para. 55).

For six months after professing her vows, darknesses still encompassed Sister Faustina's soul. Now they were not so impenetrable as before. The divine Light could be glimpsed more clearly through the clouds. There came a time when all the clouds dissipated and Sister Faustina found herself in the dazzling radiance of the presence of God. From then onwards, her soul could contemplate God, and contemplation is nothing other than - as St. John of the Cross says - the mysterious, peaceful, loving pouring-in of God into the soul, which, when not prevented, inflames that soul with the spirit of love. Sister Faustina opened herself completely to this Divine action within her.

FIRST YEARS AFTER PROFESSION

Sister Faustina's first vows coincided with changes among the superiors of the Congregation. In June 1928, Mother Leonarda Cielecka, who had up till then been the Superior General, the first in the post after the Polish branch had separated from the French mother house in 1922, ceased to be Mother General. Her place was taken by Mother Michael Moraczewska, she who had received Helena into the Congregation.

Mother Michael was to spend a long time as Superior General. The whole of the remaining eleven years of Sister Faustina's life in the Congregation was to be spent under her leadership. Mother Michael knew much about the interior life of Sister Faustina, and knew precise details of the apparitions of Christ to her. Because of the exceptional nature of the vocation of this spiritual daughter, she gave her special privileges: Sister Faustina might, in case of need, appeal direct to her for a decision, even circumventing her local superior. Always kindly and full of penetrating understanding, Mother Michael was able to assure Sister Faustina of uniform direction, whatever the local upsets might be. This was not, however, a purely one-sided arrangement: it often happened that Jesus, through the person of Sister Faustina as intermediary, affected the work of Mother Michael for the Congregation. She took these commands seriously. They always concerned difficult and complicated problems of the direction of the souls of the flock entrusted to her. All the interventions of Jesus concerned this aspect of her work.

In observing Mother Michael at a distance, it is difficult to resist the impression that in the work of the new devotion to the Divine Mercy she also had an important role to play, and that she was prepared for this by God. For it was to her, as Superior General, that was entrusted care for the gradually dawning comprehension, in Sister Faustina, of how she was to accomplish that which God was demanding of her. This required of Mother Michael a patient and calm awaiting of explanation, and subsequent help in bringing about this work. It is also thanks to her that Jesus' mission began to filter into the Congregation during the last years of Sister Faustina's life, and directly after her death.

Mother Michael must have been a spiritually mature soul, and with a rich interior life of her own. This appears in the calm and prudence with which she was able to meet the needs of the Congregation and at the same time those of the extraordinary mystic-contemplative personality of Sister Faustina with its apostolic mission.Such divergence could have split this group of God's handmaids, and that this did not happen was probably because Sister Faustina's spirituality was deeply rooted in the spirituality of the Congregation, and that in turn gave her the foundations on which God's grace built her new life. She was a flower which blossomed in the garden of the community, and which ornamented it in its own natural way, although the flower shot up to such a height that in time it overshadowed the entire Congregation. But the flower developed slowly, and it is only because of this that various particular sayings, hints, or even the behaviour of Sister Faustina give no impression of something unnatural or spiritually alien in her community. It is true that they said of her that she was "different", but by this they understood that she was entirely and completely absorbed in God. This is not common, even among nuns.

The devotion to the Divine Mercy as announced by Sister Faustina was so deeply intrinsic to the spirituality of her Congregation that it simply did not occur to anyone in her community that it might not fit their spiritual climate. This is why, although the truth was filtering through in the lifetime of Sister Faustina, when Mother Michael told the Sisters of Jesus' revelations after the death of Sister Faustina, it was a surprise for the majority. Here are the comments of companions who were close friends:

Sister F.P. said that *"in her lifetime Sister Faustina did not propose any special forms of devotion to the Divine Mercy. She merely encouraged this prayer frequently. When, for instance, any of the sisters did not perform her duties properly, Sister Faustina would ask for a prayer, saying, "Let us pray to the Divine Mercy for the intentions of that sister." Thus a devotion to the Divine Mercy could not scandalise anyone or surprise anyone."*

(Archives of S.F., Recollections).

Sister Justine G. confirms this opinion:

"As for the devotion to the Divine Mercy, Sister Faustina did not propagate any of its forms. She only spoke often in a general way of the Divine Mercy, and repeated the ejaculation: "Jesus, I trust in You." She also encouraged me to repeat often this prayer: " O Blood and Water, flowing from the Most Sacred Heart of Jesus, I trust in You.""

(Archives of S.F., Recollections).

Probably the most valuable for us of the many statements of the sisters on this topic is that of Sister Samuel W., that in the Congregation

"Sister Faustina was not the first to speak of the Divine Mercy, for that was the Foundress."

Indeed, devotion to the Mercy and Providence of God are a chief and most typical feature of the spirituality of this Congregation.

As Sister Faustina developed in the spirituality of this Congregation, it may be well to remind ourselves of its principal elements:

"Mercy is the essence of our congregation. If we remove mercy, we cease to be ourselves."

"Mercy forms the whole inner life of the Sisters of Our Lady of Mercy and prepares them interiorly and exteriorly for the joyful fulfilling of their high vocation. Mercy is the spirit of our work, the apostolic work of the Congregation."

"The degree of commitment to the love of God and the imitation of His desire to save sinners decides the degree of commitment to the spirit of the Congregation and also of the greatness of personal sanctity of each of the sisters... who, in accordance with the spirit of their vocation will offer for the intentions of the souls entrusted to them their prayers, mortifications and work, in other words everything, even efforts made for their personal sanctity, without which it would be impossible for them to work effectively for the improvement of others."

(Extracts from "Duchowość Zgromadzenia M.B. Miłosierdzia" 1967, i.e."The Spirituality of the Congregation of Sisters of Our Lady of Mercy").

The time at which Jesus revealed to Sister Faustina her great mission was one of dynamic growth for the Congregation. Established in Poland, it was now rapidly increasing. House after house was being established. Mother Michael opened four new ones: Józefinek at Grochow near Warsaw, and others at Rabka, in Lwow, and at Biała near Płock. They all required staff to run them, so sisters were transferred from place to place so frequently that at the time it was normal in the lives of the sisters of the Congregation.

A sensible use of the available people so that there should be harmony between the good of the Congregation and the need for workers was by no means easy to accomplish. There was increasing need to substitute for someone who was ill, or to fill the spiritual needs of particular sisters. Besides, many of them reacted badly to repeated changes and asked not to be moved.

Sister Faustina was among the few who made no opposition to any decisions of her superiors. Because for her their requests were the expression of the will of God, she obeyed them without grumbling and without regard for her personal feelings which she kept hidden so carefully that it never occurred to anyone that a change of place might cost her something interiorly. She was generally seen as one who readily adapted to new conditions. It even happened that she herself comforted more fearful sisters over this matter.

For example, Sister Damian Z. recalls that

"when she was afraid to go to Biała, to substitute for Sister Faustina who was returning from there, Sister Faustina comforted her, saying, "Don't be afraid, Sister. Jesus is there too. It is God's will."

(Arch. S.F., Recoll.).

But she was transferred so much more often than other sisters that it was noticed and it surprised her companions. When once Mother Mary Joseph Brzoza, who was then superior of the Warsaw house, was asked about this, she explained that

"there are usually two sorts of transfer. A nun may be transferred because of difficulties in getting along with others, either connected with her character or the unpleasant attitude of one of the sisters; or a transfer may be done in case of need and when one of the sisters can easily be moved. It was the second type of transfer that took place in Sister Faustina's case".

(Arch. S.F., Recoll.).

Itinerarium of Sister Faustina during her life in the Congregation

1925	in Warsaw	6 months	postulancy (kitchen work)
1926 from January	in Cracow	2 yrs 9m.	postulancy and novitiate (kitchen and garden work)
1927			
1928 till November			
1928 from November	in Warsaw	4 months	kitchen work
1929 till March			
1929 Feb.-June	in Vilnius	4 months	replacing kitchen worker
1929 from June	in Warsaw	8 months	in two Houses
1930 till spring			kitchen and garden work
1930 spring	in Kiekrz	2 months	replacing kitchen worker
1930 from June	in Plock	2 1/2 yrs	kitchen, bakery and shop work

Date	Place	Duration	Activity
1932 till November			
1932 from November	and in Biała in Warsaw	5 months	third probation, work in clothing store-room
1933 till April			
1933 from April till June	in Cracow 1	1/2 m.	final profession, garden work
1933 from June	in Vilnius	nearly 3 yrs	garden work
1934			
1935			
1936 till April			
1936 in May	in Walendów	few weeks	
	in Derdy	few weeks	
1936 from June	in Cracow	2 yrs 4m.	garden work. 2x hospital, portress at the gate from September 1937
1938			

Although Sister Faustina in general was thought of as an ideal nun, nevertheless there might be suspicions that these transfers were disciplinary and undertaken not only with the needs of the various religious houses in mind. Her apostolic activity sometimes created situations which were troublesome for her superiors. Her rather too rigid attitude to the faithful observance of the Rule and convent regulations, which annoyed certain sisters, was commented on. It then happened that bitter antagonism broke out. So that the statement that Sister Faustina was frequently transferred from place to place should not remain unsupported, I have included an itinerarium of her life in the Congregation in a separate table.

As the table shows, Sister Faustina in the 13 years of her life in the Congregation, was 4 times in one place for longer than a year. The first time was in the years 1926-1929 - i.e. for 2 years 9 months in the novitiate house in Cracow, which is understandable, for this was the period of her religious formation. The second, a two-and-a-half-year period, was at Płock in the years 1933-1932; the third was a period of almost three years in Vilnius in the years 1933-1936, and the fourth, beginning in Cracow in 1936, lasted until her death. This last period, which ended her earthly travels, resulted not from planning but from necessity. She was then too ill to fulfil normal religious duties. Physical weakness kept her tied to the Cracow house, which she left only for periodic stays in the hospital at Prądnik.

These four longer stays at particular houses add up to ten and a half years of her religious life. For the remaining two and a half years, she was 11 times moved from house to house.

Within these four longer stays, the chief part of Sister Faustina's religious life was contained. The first and last were, by God's will, destined for her own formation: the first, so that she might perform her life's apostolate on the earth, the last on her way to eternity; the two middle periods contained the revelations of Jesus concerning the devotion to the Divine Mercy.

The constant changes from house to house had an adverse effect which was clearly mirrored in the spiritual life of Sister Faustina. The most serious problem was the lack of uniform spiritual direction because of the changes of confessor, as there was a different one for each House. For those with active vocations this may not play too large a role, but it is a serious hindrance for those with contemplative vocations. Sister Faustina had constantly to explain afresh to each new confessor her own particular spiritual life, and this created difficulties for both sides, for it was not easy for the confessor rightly to recognise the state of the soul of his penitent. This required time, which was generally not available, as the next move was coming up. How very much Sister Faustina's life was made up of transfers can best be illustrated by the fact that the temporal vows, which were renewed annually for five years, in her case took place each time at a different House: the second renewal in 1929 was at Vilnius, the third in 1930 was at Kiekrz near Poznan, and the fourth and fifth in Płock.

Difficulties in the spiritual life were, for Sister Faustina, much more dramatic in character than in her companions, where their spiritual life was simpler. Perhaps it was these constant changes of place which speedily enabled her to recognise that without a permanent spiritual director, a priest who would guide her in strict obedience along God's chosen path for her, she would neither continue properly on the way to spiritual progress, nor fulfil God's will. This will of God was becoming more and more difficult to understand. Sister Faustina struggled to find the correct solutions to enable her to fulfil what Jesus demanded of her. In this situation - as always - she turned to God for aid. She asked for a permanent spiritual director, someone who would understand both herself and the voice of God in her soul. She never ceased in this prayer until God granted it to her. Before she received this grace, she lived through the most dramatic moments in her life. Interiorly, her soul was already purified and developed for close intimacy with Him after the experience of her dark nights of the soul. But yet another trial was awaiting her - a very difficult one - the mistrust of those people to whom she was directly subject: her confessors and superiors. Their mistrust was so serious as to sway her own certainty that she heard the voice of God in her soul. This is a long story, which will be the subject of the next chapter. It continued for more than two years, at the end of which Jesus heard her prayer: first He answered her directly, and then through the mouths of two successive priests. At last, in 1933, Sister Faustina found her proper spiritual director: he was Father Michael Sopoćko, the confessor of the sisters in Vilnius.

9. Convent in Płock, where the Servant of God received the vision of the Image of the Merciful Jesus

10. Lake Kierskie, over which Sister Faustina saw a vision of Jesus

THE VISION IN PŁOCK

Halfway through 1930, Sister Faustina found herself in Płock, assigned to work in the kitchen.

As Płock played a key role in her life - for it was here that she received from Jesus her chief mission in life - let us look more closely at the conditions of her life in the convent there. We are told of them by Sister Joachim G., then employed in the bakery.

"Kitchen work there required great resilience and patience. The kitchen formed a corridor through which everyone passed. The entire House and all its affairs had to pass through it." "And it was so narrow", added Sister P.K., "that one had to have absolutely angelic virtue not to be angry with those going through, who constantly jostled (Sister Faustina), and there was no other way. We were always being summoned to the gate by bells, and she was always smiling, calm, and not showing that it bothered her; only later, when another sister replaced her - after Sister Faustina had gone away - the complaints and lamentations began, that it couldn't go on like that... Then our eyes were opened to how much she could put up with, but she never showed her annoyance with so much as a word or a look."

(Archives of S.F., Recollections).

But the constant effort, unavoidable in such working conditions, proved too much for Sister Faustina. It was the proverbial last straw which broke the camel's back of her physical endurance. For the course of the preceding two years had left its mark on her indelibly. Always having to adapt to new conditions - six transfers - had weakened an already feeble body. Thus, after a few months in the kitchen at Płock, her state of health had worsened so considerably that the superior, Mother Rose Klobukowska, sent her to Biała, the daughter house of Płock, about six miles away, to rest and recover in more comfortable conditions, with easier work and in a smaller and quieter house.

The convent at Biała was indeed not large: there was a 70-hectare farm (about 175 acres) run by three sisters, including in that the help of the recently-arrived Sister Faustina. There was also a small group of wards, who came for occasional holidays or convalescence. Sister Faustina was really assigned to the kitchen, but she gradually came to deal with other kinds of work, because with such a small community it was often necessary to substitute for another sister, or even to change places with her. She did so willingly, as usual easy to get along with, quiet and cheerful, but "hiding herself", as Sister Zita J. noted uncharitably. This latest feature in her personality, noticed by her companion, was a new characteristic, indicating a coming inner transformation. This "secretiveness" about herself would increase as the years passed, because of the necessity of concealing her intimacy with Jesus. Towards the end of her life, Sister Faustina was to say very little.

In Biała, having less to do, Sister Faustina found time for the wards as well, who greatly appreciated her company. When the girls went home and recalled their impressions of Biała, they could not praise her enough. For example, the ward Ursula had no words for her admiration of Sister Faustina, who, after her work in the kitchen was done, would play with the girls there on holiday. She took part with them in their game of quoits. She would give them some variety and help them spend the time pleasantly. Ursula often said:

"Mother, Sister Faustina has lots of intelligence, and even more heart, because after all she works hard in the kitchen, so she could have just rested in the shade of a tree, but to give us pleasure, she would play with us."

(Arch.S.F., Recoll, S. Paulina K.).

Her stay in Biała was not be long. Stronger than she had been, at the beginning of 1931 she came back to Płock, this time to work in the bakery and the shop.

All our information about the experiences of Sister Faustina in the first part of her stay at the Płock house, before the departure for Biała, indicates that this was a time of spiritual relaxation, of a joyful, intimate familiarity with Jesus. Her companions unanimously emphasise the cheerful behaviour of their new work-mate. Weeping and other outward signs of suffering - such as occurred in Cracow during her mystical darkness - had vanished without trace.

Constant intimacy with God allows the elect souls to perceive God in the everyday affairs of daily life. The deeper the intimacy with Him, the greater the personal commitment, which leads in turn to closer cooperation with God. The lives of the saints provide us with sufficient examples. "You are not servants, but friends," said Jesus to His apostles and what He said has been proved true throughout the entire history of Christianity. Sister Faustina was no exception. She was one of the "friends" of God, according to Jesus' definition; she lived for God alone and her thoughts were busy only with Him.

Not much time had elapsed since she had been experiencing the mystical darkness in Cracow - barely eighteen months - enough for her to recover from her previous terrible spiritual experiences, and to regain her equilibrium and peace of mind, and to be strengthened again. Sister Faustina was burning with love which consumed her with overwhelming force. She sought some way to show the Lord her submission, using every opportunity. No effort seemed too great for her. She announced her readiness for anything.

"I love You, Jesus, with every drop of my blood, and I would gladly shed my blood for You to give You a proof of the sincerity of my love. O God, the more I know You the less I can comprehend You, but this 'non-comprehension' lets me realize how great You are! And it is this impossibility of comprehending You which inflames my heart anew for You, O Lord... In comparison with You, everything is nothing. Sufferings, adversities, humiliations, failures and suspicions that have come my way are splinters that keep alive the fire of my love for You, O Jesus. My desires are mad and unattainable. I wish to conceal from You that I suffer. I want never to be rewarded for my efforts and my good actions. You yourself, Jesus, are my only reward; You are enough, O Treasure of my heart!"

(Diary, Notebook I, para. 57).

These were no empty words, and God accepted the love sincerely offered to Him and her wish to cooperate with Him. Nor did He ask her to wait long for her heart's desire. Sister Faustina would receive an important mission to perform, prepared for her according to the eternal divine plan. She would be included in His plan for the redemption of the world.

Although it might seem that she was interiorly prepared and waiting for every command of the Lord, that which came was a total surprise for her. It was completely different from commands she had had before. Those were simple and unambiguous, and though often difficult to perform, they were at least easy to understand. Sometimes doing His will cost her a great deal, but she had had no doubts about how to fulfil His commands. The request she now heard did not resemble any of the others. On 22nd February 1931, when, after having finished all her daily tasks and taken part that evening in the community prayers in the chapel, she was alone in her cell... But let us pause and allow her to tell the story of the most important moment of her life:

"In the evening, when I was in my cell, I saw the Lord Jesus clothed in a white garment. One hand [was] raised in the gesture of blessing, the other was touching the garment at the breast. From beneath the garment, slightly drawn aside at the breast, there were emanating two large rays, one red, the other pale. In silence I kept my gaze fixed on the Lord. After a while, Jesus said to me, 'Paint an image according to the pattern you see, with the signature: Jesus, I trust in You. I desire that this image be venerated, first in your chapel, and [then] throughout the world. I promise that the soul that will venerate this image will not perish. I also promise victory over [its] enemies already here on earth, especially at the hour of death. I Myself will defend it as My own glory.'

(Diary, Notebook I, paras. 47,48).

In this Jesus was giving Sister Faustina two tasks to fulfil: 1. to paint His picture as she saw Him, 2. to undertake its propagation, commencing with the Congregation, whence she was to spread it over the whole of Christendom.

In this extraordinary revelation, the reader's attention is first concentrated on the Person of Jesus Christ Himself. It is so clearly the same Jesus of Nazareth that we know from the gospels. We recognize Him. Sister Faustina's account reminds us of those parts of the gospels in which is told how Christ, after His resurrection, sent His apostles and disciples out into the world to preach His teachings. There is such great similarity of approach that we are overwhelmed with the impression that both then and now the same Person is speaking. In both cases the commands are given in a short, laconic formulation of the aim itself. The methods by which this is to be accomplished are completely left out, as if they did not concern the Lord Who speaks. But the method of performing the task and the means to use are perhaps as important as the command. Yes, but they are entirely left to the initiative and forethought of the one who is to perform God's command, for Jesus, in giving the aim, at the same time indicated a sphere of independent action for any human being who is to bring into fruition God's business. God did not make any suggestions on how to carry out His plan. This is the sphere in which the free will of man is to act.

Jesus treated Sister Faustina as He did His apostles. For them, detailed indications on what and how to do things cease with the moment of His resurrection. From then on, they receive only short commands: **"Go and teach."** To Sister Faustina He spoke similarly: **"Paint the picture"**, and see **"that the picture is venerated"**.

Sister Faustina was astounded. She was faced with a problem which appeared insoluble: 1. she didn't know how to paint - how, then, could she reproduce the image which she had seen of the Lord? 2. She was a nun enclosed in a community and obliged to follow a strict inner rule and by her obedience - how, then, could she propagate veneration for this picture throughout the world?

But the command had been given, so thought had to be given to fulfilling it. For the moment, according to Sister Faustina's usual principle of action, all her attention was concentrated on the first stage of the work, the painting of the picture. She laid the problem before her confessor, expecting an explanation of the problem from him, together with further suggestions. The voice of the confessor is the voice of the Lord, thought Sister Faustina. He would certainly give her the right advice.

However, her confessor trivialised the affair. He represented the command of Jesus to his careworn penitent as being symbolic.

"That refers to your soul", he said, *'paint God's image in your soul.'*

Jesus protested at once:

"When I came out of the confessional, I again heard words such as these,' writes Sister Faustina, *'My image already is in your soul. I desire that there be a Feast of Mercy. I want this image, which you will paint with a brush, to be solemnly blessed on the first Sunday after Easter; that Sunday is to be the Feast of Mercy.'*

(Diary, Notebook.I, para. 48).

In this second revelation, confirming the first, there is an additional element. Jesus expresses another wish: one directed to Sister Faustina, another to priests.

'I desire that priests proclaim this great mercy of Mine towards souls of sinners. Let the sinner not be afraid to approach Me. The flames of mercy are burning Me - clamoring to be spent; I want to pour them out upon these souls.'

(Diary, Notebook I, para. 50).

In this revelation, Jesus expresses His wishes in full: He does not only require the reproduction of the vision in the form of a picture and its universal veneration, but also the establishment of the Feast of Divine Mercy, on the first Sunday after Easter. These two revelations together, the vision of Jesus in the cell and the words heard directly after confession, contain the whole substance of the divine wishes. And again: the method of giving the second revelation, like the first, is laconic, limited only to the aim. The entire theological motivation, the working out of the significance of the cultus required, and the Feast in the liturgy, have been left by Jesus to human beings. He confined Himself to showing His loving mercy, always awaiting sinners. The burning emotional fervour of this mission of love permeates every word the Lord said.

Sent away by her confessor, Sister Faustina went to her superior. This scene was described to Sister Felicia Z., after Sister Faustina's death, by Mother Klobukowska, and Sister Felicia Z. relates it thus:

> "At a certain time, she came to her (Mother Klobukowska) in her cell, and standing in the centre of the cell, Sister Faustina said to herself, sotto voce, so that Mother heard her, "Jesus told me to see Himself in my superiors", and then she turned to Mother Superior and said, "Jesus has told me to paint a picture of the Divine Mercy with the signature Jesus, I trust in You." Mother Rose did not take it very seriously and answered, "Then paint it, Sister." "
>
> (Arch. S.F., Recoll. Sister Felicia Z.).

Such an abbreviated account hardly shows the real course of the conversation. In Sister Faustina's Diary we find also a supplementary remark, that the Mother Superior, having learned of Jesus' wishes, said that if God really required that from her, He

should give some sign so that we could recognize Him more clearly.' (Diary, Notebook I, para. 51).

She did not offer any resistance to Sister Faustina's painting, and even supplied her with paints. But Jesus, when asked by the mortified Sister Faustina, did not wish to give an immediate sign, although He promised that He would give it to the superiors **"by means of the graces which I will grant through this image"**.

So both the confessor and the superior, awaiting further evidence of the genuine nature of the revelations, took up for the moment an expectant and rather doubting attitude. Sister Faustina, left more or less to herself, and for the first time in serious doubt of the voice of God in her soul, wanted **"to run away from these interior inspirations"**. But God again categorically protested and said **"that on the day of judgment He would demand of me a great number of souls."**

Sister Faustina was totally confused. She hesitated between two contrary emotions: once she tried to avoid being with Jesus, and again an overwhelming instinct in her soul propelled her towards Him. Despite the difficulties, she tried herself to solve the problem of the painting of the picture. Since she herself did not know how to paint, perhaps another Sister might do it at her request and under her direction. But who?

At this time a sister of the first choir, Bożena P., was given to her to help her in her work in the bakery and shop. It is worth hearing what she has to say about Sister Faustina at this time:

"The work was hard, and, it seemed, beyond her strength, but she knew how to organize it. In helping her I carried large baskets of loaves. While doing this once I haemorrhaged from the mouth. Sister Faustina was most concerned and wanted to tell the superior, but I asked her not to disturb the Mother Superior during the retreat. From that time on, she spared me: we put the loaves into other baskets, carrying half the weight. Sister Faustina behaved very lovingly and kindly to me, without grumbling that she had received such a feeble helper."

The work they did together, during which the sisters both said much on spiritual matters, brought them together and Sister Faustina decided to ask for her companion's advice.

"One time Sister Faustina asked me," says Sister Bożena, *"if I knew how to paint, because she needed a picture representing Jesus. "I would tell you what He is to look like". She added that she herself wanted to paint such a picture and had the brush and paint, which she could supply me with, because after all she could not paint the picture. I answered that I could not paint, I had never done so and could not undertake it. Not knowing exactly what she wanted, I wished to offer her one of the pictures I had, but Sister Faustina thanked me and said that she had turned to me about the matter because she knew I was discreet, and she asked me to say nothing to anyone. She also asked me if one of the sisters knew how to paint."*

(Archives of S.F., Recoll. Sister Bożena).

Following the suggestions of Sister Bożena, Sister Faustina continued to look for a nun who could paint the picture of Jesus as He commanded. But there was no outcome. She herself therefore began to sketch on the wall in charcoal, which is recalled by Sister Bożena T. and by Sister Simone N. It was therefore not surprising that news of the revelations reached some of the sisters. Rumour is always incomplete, with numerous gaps and many distortions of information; it is surrounded by mystery and sensation. The sensation rippled far beyond the convent walls. *"Children from the town stood in the street opposite the rooms of the nuns and saw rays coming from one of the windows. This was the window of Sister Faustina's cell".*

(Arch. S.F., Recollections of Sister Christine).

Sister Z.J. also recounts that

"one time during the stay in Biała, Sister Aloiza (the "Senior" in Biała) who was with us, asked me if I

had heard that Sister Faustina talked to someone at night. I answered that I had not heard this. We shared a bedroom; the beds were separated by curtains. Sister A. stated that there was no one else in the room and that Sister Faustina was talking to someone. I thought that perhaps she was talking to Jesus, because the sisters used to whisper among themselves that Sister Faustina had previously had some sort of revelation in Płock, that Jesus had appeared and talked to her. I am not able to say whether I personally believed in these revelations."

(Archives of S.F., Recollections.).

Around Sister Faustina there was woven a web of hints, vulgar curiosity, and sometimes mockery. Finally, suspicions of hysteria or even certain mental disturbances were voiced, and these multiplied the more rapidly as she herself, when asked by Sisters to confirm the rumours circulating and to give more details, did not react. Criticism came from various sides.

'... it seemed to my superior that these graces were unlikely,' notes Sister Faustina. *'She told me that it was impossible that God should commune with His creatures in such a way: "I fear for you, Sister; isn't this an illusion of some sort! You'd better go and seek the advice of a priest.'*

(Diary, Notebook I, para. 122).

'My only desire' - she writes further on - *'was that some priest would say this one word to me: "Be at peace, you are on the right road", or "Reject all this for it does not come from God." But I could not find such a priest who was sufficiently sure of himself to give me a definite opinion in the name of the Lord"*

(Diary, Notebook I, para. 127).

'The priest to whom I was going to confession at that time told me that one can often have illusions, and felt that he was somewhat afraid to hear my confession. This was a torture for me.'

(Diary, Notebook I, para. 74).

"... he said, 'You'd better go, Sister, and talk about these matters with your superiors.' And so I would go from the superiors to the confessor and from the confessor to the superiors, and I found no peace.'

(Diary, Notebook I, para. 122).

No matter to whom Sister Faustina now turned, spiteful remarks, whispers and knowing half-smiles went with her.

'I was regarded as one possessed by the evil spirit, and I was looked upon with pity, and the superior took certain precautionary actions in my respect. It reached my ears that the sisters also regarded me as such.. and to regard me as a hysteric and a fantasist, and the rumours began to grow louder. One of the sisters came to talk to me in private. She began by pitying me and said, 'I've heard them say that you are a fantasist, Sister, and that you've been having visions. My poor Sister, defend yourself in this matter.' She was a sincere soul, and she told me sincerely what she had heard. But I had to listen to such things every day. God only knows how tiring it was. Yet, I resolved to bear everything in silence and to give no explanations when I was questioned. Some were irritated by my silence, especially those who were more curious. Others, who reflected more deeply, said, 'Sister Faustina must be very close to God if she

has the strength to bear so much suffering.' It was if I were facing two groups of judges... There is no longer anything in me that had escaped the sisters' judgment.' (Diary, Notebook I, para. 125 et seq.) *'I could now see that everywhere I was being watched like a thief: in the chapel; while I was carrying out my duties; in my cell... There were times when I wondered whether I should undress to wash myself or not. Indeed, even that poor bed of mine was checked many times'.*

(Diary, Notebook, I, para. 128).

Used, until now, to living in an atmosphere of trust and the sense of inner freedom that this brings, Sister Faustina did not know how to steer a course between all these complicated trails of sensational rumours. Everything around her seemed hard to grasp, incomprehensible and unimaginable, nor could she find herself in the midst of it all. She had so far lost herself as not to believe in her own healthy common sense. She checked on herself through others. When Sister Simone N., a friend of hers, after making her final vows, on her way back to Biała stayed one night in Płock, Sister Faustina posed her an unexpected question: *"Sister Simone, we have not much time to talk, but tell me what you have heard about me."* Of course a request like that must have surprised her friend, who, knowing nothing of the reasons for what seemed strange behaviour for her, was scandalised and answered, *"Nothing"* and felt that Sister Faustina *"thought too much about herself, since she was interested in what was being said of her"* (Archives of S.F., Recollections).

A similar state of nervous tension continued throughout the entire time of Sister Faustina's stay in Płock. Depressed more and more by the opinion of those around her, which had begun to overwhelm her own judgment, Sister Faustina records:

"*...I began to grow a bit negligent. I did not pay attention to these interior inspirations and tried to distract myself. But despite the noise and the distraction, I could see what was going on in my soul. The word of God is clear, and nothing can stifle it. I began to avoid encounters with the Lord in my soul because I did not want to fall prey to illusions. However, in a sense, the Lord kept pursuing me with His gifts; and truly I experienced, alternately, torture and joy.*"

(Diary, Notebook I, para. 130).

"*One day, tired out with all these uncertainties, I asked Jesus, "Jesus, are You my God or some kind of phantom? Because my Superiors say that there are all sorts of illusions and phantoms. If You are my Lord, I beg You to bless me." Then Jesus made a big sign of the cross over me and I, too, signed myself. When I asked pardon of Jesus for this question, He replied that I had in no way displeased Him by this question and that my confidence pleased Him very much*"

(Diary, Notebook I, para. 54).

Sister Faustina at least did not cease to beg that the Lord would convince her of the genuineness of her revelations. She constantly renewed her pleas, seeking new ways or occasions to do so.

"*Seeing that I was getting very little help from people, I turned all the more to Jesus, the best of all teachers. At one time, when I was filled with doubts as to whether the voice I heard came from the Lord or not, I began to speak to Jesus interiorly without forming any words. Suddenly an inner force took hold of me and I said, "If You who commune with me and talk to me are truly my God, I beg You, O Lord, to make this ward go this very day to confession; this sign will give me reassurance.*" At that very moment, the girl asked to go to confession.

The Mother in charge of the class was surprised at this sudden change in her, but she undertook to call a priest immediately, and this person made her confession with great compunction. At the same time, I heard a voice within me say, "Do you believe Me now?" And once again a strange power pervaded my soul, strengthening and reassuring me to such a degree that I myself was surprised that I had allowed myself to doubt even for a moment.

But these doubts always come from without, a fact which inclined me to close myself up more and more within myself."

(Diary, Notebook I, para. 74).

Another eighteen months or more went by for Sister Faustina in similar perplexity and wavering between the extremes of disbelief and trust, and simultaneously in the constant search for ways to perform the Lord's command. Her stay in Płock was nearing an end, as the time for making her final vows approached. How would Sister Faustina now reply to Jesus' ultimate call to give herself to Him for ever?

PERPETUAL VOWS

Just a change of place brought mental relief. In Warsaw, where Sister Faustina had arrived, summoned to undertake her third probation, obligatory before taking perpetual vows, they welcomed her with tremendous kindness. She in turn reciprocated. She was happiest of all to see her first Directress of Novices, Mother Margaret Gimbutt, and to learn that she was to have that same post during Sister Faustina's probation.

This probation is the last stage in religious formation. It allows the nun to review her experience hitherto of life in the community and to think over once more her own vocation on the basis of what she has experienced, before she takes an irrevocable decision. For the community, the probation period decides the final acceptance of the candidate, who has been tested in community life, into the permanent membership of the Congregation. Probation is, then, a period of intense interior work, and is ended by a few day's retreat which, in cleansing the soul, prepares it for the approaching vows.

When Sister Faustina arrived in Warsaw, the annual eight-day retreat had just begun in nearby Walendow, about 12 1/2 miles away, where the Sisters ran an educational institution for girls. As Sister Faustina had not yet had a retreat, Sister Margaret directed her to go there at once.

Sister Faustina went with mixed feelings. She knew one thing: that in the interior confusion in which she had been living for the last two years she needed the special illumination of the Holy Spirit, to perform a proper examination of her life hitherto, and to be able to interpret the divine mission she had received and which she was yet to put into practice. She prayed fervently to receive this grace.

Jesus did not leave her without an answer.

"Jesus told me," writes Sister Faustina, *'that this retreat would be a little different from others. 'You shall strive to maintain a profound peace in respect to your communing with Me. I will remove all doubts in this regard. I know that you are at peace now as I speak to you, but the moment that I stop talking you will start looking for doubts. But I want you to know that I will affirm your soul to such a degree that even if you wanted to be troubled, it will not be in your power. And as a proof that it is I who am speaking to you, you will go to confession on the second day of the retreat to the priest who is preaching the retreat; you will go to him as soon as he has finished his conference and will present to him all your doubts concerning Me. I will answer you through his lips, and then your fears will end."*

(Diary, Notebook I, para. 169).

This was the promise of great grace and Sister Faustina breathed a sign of relief. Jesus' promise that the matter would be so soon clarified, the matter that lay like a stone in her heart and nightmarishly suffocated her whole religious life, the matter which had so far defied solution, freed within her a former confidence and gave her fresh courage. This was the first deep breath in her spiritual life through the suffocating atmosphere of the recent months. Mentally relaxed, she began the retreat in a mood of profound peace and prayerfulness.

The retreat was being given by Rev. Edmund Elter S.J., a professor of ethics and later of homiletics and rhetoric at the Gregorian (Papal) University in Rome. He was an enlightened priest with an extensive and profound education both in the humanities and theology, and even in law, who had just come from Rome to Poland.

Sister Faustina listened to his retreat conferences in great concentration, deaf to the invitations of some of the sisters to a chance of conversation. Nothing disturbed her communion with the Lord.

A day and a half went by. As the hour for confession drew nigh, her former sense of peace began to evaporate, and tension and restlessness began to grow. A few hours before the time, her doubts returned in full strength. Her memory obsessively recalled all the negative and even doubting replies of her superiors and confessors. The behaviour of some of the sisters, their hints, and the particularly sharp and brutal scolding given her recently in Warsaw, probably - for Sister Faustina does not name names - by Mother Jane Bartkiewicz, her former Mistress of Postulants, all now echoed through her aching head. Especially the most recent happening seemed to return as if lived through again:

> *'One of the Mothers, when she learned about my close relationship with the Lord Jesus, told me that I must be deluding myself. She told me that the Lord Jesus associates in this way only with the saints and not with sinful souls 'like you, Sister!'. After that, it was as if I mistrusted Jesus.'*

> (Diary, Notebook I, para. 29).

That incident was the last drop of bitterness in her chalice of sorrow and it had a considerable influence on her deepening and already great spiritual crisis. It confirmed that there was a clash between the spiritual experiences of Sister Faustina herself, and the adverse view of them held by outsiders. How difficult it was to live in that atmosphere of mistrust surrounding her! Always truthful, Faustina had never in her life up till now been in a similar situation. She did not know how to adopt the right attitude, either in her own inner life, or in respect of her superiors and her confessor. Now that she was to go to confession, her fear grew, because in addition the priest indicated to her by Jesus as her confessor was a stranger, and though he inspired trust he did not know her and it would be necessary to tell him everything from the beginning.

The time of her "appointment" approached. The priest gave a short talk and immediately afterwards sat down in the confessional. Sister Faustina watched him tensely. He was alone in the confessional and there was no one in front of the grating.

She arose on a unexpected impulse and scarcely knowing how it happened she found herself kneeling at the confessional. She told the confessor her business in a spontaneous reaction. Without reflection or choosing her words, she flung out, feverishly, everything that had collected within her during those difficult years, just as her memory had prompted her while she was waiting for confession. She poured out a chaotic mixture about the revelations in her mystic communion with Jesus, her own torment, her fear of others' opinion, her helplessness and her pain, during that confession.

The priest quickly realised he had an exceptional penitent. He stated,

Sister, you distrust the Lord Jesus because He treats you so kindly. Well, Sister, be completely at peace. Jesus

is your Master and your communing with Him is neither daydreaming nor hysteria nor illusion. Know that you are on the right path. Please try to be faithful to these graces; you are not free to shun them. You do not need at all, Sister, to tell your superiors about these interior graces, unless the Lord Jesus instructs you clearly to do so, and even then you should first consult with your confessor. But if the Lord Jesus demands something external in this case, after consulting your confessor, you should carry out what He asks of you, even if this costs you greatly. On the other hand, you must tell your confessor everything. There is absolutely no other course for you to take, Sister. Pray that you may find a spiritual director, or else you will waste these great gifts of God. I repeat once again, be at peace; you are following the right path. Take no heed of anything else, but always be faithful to the Lord Jesus, no matter what anyone says about you.'

(Diary, Notebook I, para. 174).

The priest replied with all the weight of his authority to all the problems successively put forward by Sister Faustina. He evaded no problem, he was not hesitant, nor did he leave anything unsaid. He gave his penitent clear directions as to how she was to conduct herself, both towards Jesus and towards her superiors or other sisters, and also how to talk to her confessor.

This confession was a turning-point in Sister Faustina's spiritual life. For the first time since the problem had arisen, her doubts were definitely quashed, and Sister Faustina found her Lord again. Now she knew what to do.

However, this did not get rid of the doubts forever. Fed by the mistrust of her superiors, doubts did not allow the wound to heal. Indeed, directly after the confession, Sister Faustina made a strong resolution:

'Faithfulness to inner inspirations, even though I would have no idea how much I would have to pay for it.'

(Diary, Notebook I, para. 176).

It turned out to be unenforceable, for she had not found a confessor who would agree to direct her. Neither the confessors in Warsaw, nor her superior had yet adopted a decisive standpoint on the matter of her spiritual life. Their doubts communicated themselves to her.

Nevertheless, although she still struggled with doubts, they had a somewhat different character. The opinion of Father Elter left its trace in her soul. The doubts never regained the strength they had formerly, when they were able to shake her spiritual life to its very foundations. This at least was not Płock, where the mistrust of Faustina herself was fairly widespread. At present she found support in the person of Mother Margaret, the Directress of her third probation, and then next in the Novice Mistress in Cracow, Sister Mary Joseph. Both of them treated Sister Faustina's inner life seriously and with confidence in her.

Of Mother Margaret, writes Sister Faustina,

'when I asked her about some particulars concerning progress in the spiritual life, this holy Mother answered everything with great clarity. She said to me, 'If you continue cooperating with God's grace in this way, Sister, you will be only one step away from close union with God... Your characteristic trait should be faithfulness to the

grace of the Lord. God does not lead all souls along such a path.'

(Diary, Notebook I, para. 204).

Sister Mary Joseph had a similar attitude:

'She clarified many things for me, and she set me at peace as regards my spiritual life, reassuring me that I was on the right path. I thanked the Lord Jesus for this great favor, for she is the first of the superiors who did not cause me any doubts in this regard.'

(Diary, Notebook I, para. 222).

Yet, despite everything, there were moments of doubt, and at these times, seeing that she was powerless, she tried to evade the demands of Jesus, which were beyond her strength. But Jesus again - as at Płock - warned her:

'Know that if you neglect the matter of the painting of the image and the whole work of mercy, you will have to answer for a multitude of souls on the day of judgment'.

(Diary, Notebook I, para. 154).

'After these words of Our Lord, a certain fear filled my soul, and alarm took hold of me. Try as I would, I could not calm myself,' she writes. *'I... fell on my face before the Blessed Sacrament and said to the Lord, 'I will do everything in my power, but I beg You to be always with me and to give me strength to do Your holy will; for You can do everything, while I can do nothing of myself.'*

(Diary, Notebook I, para. 154).

In this painful way, struggling with endlessly multiplying difficulties Sister Faustina learned gradually the elementary truth that not only everything that she received was through the grace of God, but that everything that she was to do could only be done by the help of His grace. She learned patience and perseverance, and gradually she began to achieve inner independence of people's opinion. In comparison with people, how compassionate and understanding is the Lord! Even her doubts resuming again, her hesitancy and unwillingness did not seem to annoy Him. On the contrary. To her amazement she noted:

"God is pleased, and rejoices when a soul distrusts Him for His own sake; because it loves Him, it is prudent and itself asks and searches for help to make certain that it is really God who is acting within it".

(Diary, Notebook I, para. 139).

How many times she went to Him. and, gazing towards the tabernacle, asked, *"Are You really Jesus?... Jesus, are You not an illusion?".* And Jesus reassured her patiently: **"My love deceives no one."**

Reminded by Jesus, Sister Faustina continued to ask Him for the spiritual director she needed for her task. During her retreat confession, the father had emphasized this, and even warned that without a director she could fall into error. When and where would she get one? She pestered Him again and again ceaselessly.

Jesus likes being asked persistently and does not remain deaf to prayer. So now, therefore, to strengthen Sister Faustina, He drew aside the curtain that hides the future, and in a short visionary glimpse He showed her the priest He intended for her spiritual director. The vision appeared twice: once at Warsaw during the third probation, and a second time in Cracow, where Sister Faustina had gone to make her final profession.

In the chapel between the altar and the confessional, there appeared to her the figure of the priest promised her as her confessor.

But this was not enough for Sister Faustina. Jesus had not specified when she would get her confessor. So she continued to pester Him in prayer. Her probation was ending and her perpetual vows were nearing. How could she espouse her Bridegroom? What would she bring to the espousal? More of these recurring doubts, that the One who speaks to her and communes so intimately with her is indeed Jesus? The interior pressure forcing Sister Faustina to make a definite decision did not so much arise from the pressure of her superiors' opinion as from the nearness of her taking perpetual vows. Here lay the chief reason for her importuning the Lord for an explanation of the doubts that had arisen in her as well as in those around her. She was begging for pity.

Jesus is His mercy showed her the pity she asked for. He again promised to answer her through the lips of the priest to whom she was to make her confession during the retreat to be made just before her vows.

The story of this confession is instructive, for it gives us much information on the kind of intimacy Sister Faustina had with Jesus. The detailed account of what happened left by her gives us a rare chance to see into her personal and quite intimate life.

Having learned by the experience of her confession to Father Elter, she now prayed both for the grace to reveal herself well to the confessor, and 110 for enlightenment for that confessor himself, so that having understood her he could give a decisive answer: yes or no. She writes:

'Throughout my probation, I prayed for light for the priest to whom I was to open up my soul to its depths. I asked God that He himself would help me and grant me the grace to be able to express even the most secret

thing that exist between me and Him and to be so disposed that, whatever the priest would decide I would accept as coming from Jesus himself. No matter what judgment he would pass on me, all I wanted was the truth and a decisive answer to certain questions... I looked forward to that moment which would decide the course of my actions for the rest of my life. I knew that everything would depend on this. It mattered little whether what he would say to me would be in accord with my inspirations or quite the contrary; this no longer mattered to me. I wanted to know the truth and follow it.'

(Diary, Notebook I, para. 131).

The priest to whom this time Jesus directed her was Rev. Joseph Andrasz S.J., a writer and editor, who had spent many years in publishing. He was at the time an extra-ordinary confessor to the Cracow house of the Sister of Our Lady of Mercy.

Jesus gave Sister Faustina detailed instructions as to how to make her confession to father Andrasz:

'My daughter, tell him everything and reveal your soul to him as you do before Me. Do not fear anything. It is to keep you in peace that I place this priest between your soul and Myself. The words he will speak to you are My words. Reveal to him your soul's greatest secrets. I will give him light to know your soul.'

(Diary, Notebook I, para. 232).

Sister Faustina herself was later amazed that she was able so easily to explain to this priest all the secret matters in her soul. This was not an ordinary occurrence for her. She could confess her sins easily, but when it was a matter of graces received, she had to struggle with herself to be able to speak of them. This time she had no problems. The words came fluently, and accurately depicted the state of her soul. Father Andrasz gave her the answer she expected.

"His answers brought a great peace into my soul. His words were, are, and always will be pillars of fire which enlightened and will go on enlightening my soul in its pursuit of the greatest sanctity... From the moment the priest assured me that what I had experienced was not an illusion, but the grace of God, I have tried to be faithful to God in everything!"

(Diary, Notebook I, paras. 233, 234).

These were the directions of Father Andrasz;

"You say to me that God demands great trust from souls; well then, you be the first to show this trust... accept all this with serenity."

(Diary, Notebook I, para. 55).

"You must not turn away from these interior inspirations, but always tell everything to your confessor. If you recognize that these interior inspirations refer to your own self; that is to say, they are for the good of your soul or for the good of other souls, I urge you to follow them; and you must not neglect them, but always do so in consultation with your confessor. If these inspirations are not in accord with the faith or the spirit of the Church, they must be rejected immediately as coming from the evil spirit. If these inspirations do not refer to souls, in general, nor specifically to their good, you should not

take them too seriously, and it would be better even to ignore them. But you should not make this decision by yourself, either one way or the other, as you can easily be led astray despite these great favours from God. Humility, humility, and ever humility, as we can do nothing of ourselves; all is purely and simply God's grace."

(Diary, Notebook I, para. 55).

Confession to Father Andrasz was not, for Sister Faustina, a single occurrence, strictly circumstantial, as it had been with Father Elter. As long as she remained in Cracow, she always had the chance to ask this confessor for counsel. As for almost a month after her final vows her fate was undecided - no decision had been taken about to which House she was to be sent - she went to confession to him a few more times. These confessions varied. She did not always go in a positive frame of mind. She admits that once she came to a downright negative decision. But Father Andrasz opposed her categorically. Sister Faustina writes:

"Once, exhausted because of these various difficulties which had befallen me because of what Jesus had said to me and what He had demanded of me for the painting of this image, I made up my mind to approach Father Andrasz before my perpetual vows and to ask him to dispense me from all these interior inspirations and from the duty of painting this image. After having heard my confession, Father Andrasz gave me this answer: "I will dispense you from nothing, Sister; it is not right for you to turn away from these interior inspirations, but you... must speak about them to your confessor..."

I was very upset by this. I thought that I would get myself free from everything, and it turned out quite the opposite - an explicit command to follow the requests of Jesus. And now, still another torment, as I had no permanent confessor... I asked Jesus to give these graces to someone else, because I did not know how to make use of them and was only wasting them.'

(Diary, Notebook I, para. 53).

Sister Faustina, who went to confession to Father Andrasz for the last time on the eve of her departure for Vilnius, i.e. on 24th May, and who had for the last month had the joy of having a spiritual director who was both infallible and decisive in his role, was now overwhelmed with fear for the unknown future awaiting her in a town that was new to her. Too well she knew the savour of being mistrusted. She therefore complained to Jesus:

"Jesus, You gave me this Father who understands my inspirations, and now You are taking him away from me again. What am I going to do in this Vilnius? I don't know anyone there, and even the dialect of the people there is foreign to me." And the Lord said to me, 'Do not fear; I will not leave you to yourself.' ...Suddenly I remembered the vision in which I had seen that priest between the confessional and the altar... And the words I had heard came back vividly: 'He will help you to fulfil My will here on earth.'

(Diary, Notebook I, para. 258).

And at her last confession to him, Father Andrasz *stressed that I must be faithful to God's grace and said, "No harm will come to you if, in the future, you con-*

tinue to keep this same simplicity and obedience. Have confidence in God; you are on the right path and in good hands, in good hands, in God's hands.'

(Op. cit. para. 257).

Following step by step after Sister Faustina and reading her writings with care, we have the opportunity to observe at close quarters her simply heroic attempts to stand before the altar as a worthy spouse of the Lord. As she understood matters, above all it was necessary to clarify and arrange two matters: communion with Jesus, and work for Him, both that undertaken by herself, and that which He requested of her. She tried to do this resolutely ignoring the unpleasantness and humiliation this afforded her, since she believed that in this way she was fulfilling the will of God. Her whole attention was concentrated upon these two problems.

Meanwhile, Jesus - as we shall see in a moment - wanted something more. He wished that she, as His spouse, would place her whole self at the disposal of His love for sinners, and that, like Himself, she would make a sacrifice of herself to God to atone for their sins. He wished that not only should she faithfully follow His instructions, but also that she should supplement His sacrifice both passively and actively: passively, through bearing humiliations without complaint - all those unjust judgments on her, spiteful deeds and tormenting; actively, through her permanent readiness to give charitable aid and service to her neighbour without counting the cost she would have to pay, even to emptying herself completely. Here we enter the greatest mystery of the intimacy of the soul with God when the Son of God wishes to bring the soul closer to Himself by including its fate with His own. Jesus did not make this request suddenly. He did not shock His spouse. He wished that she decide herself, fully conscious of what she was doing. He had therefore for years prepared and made her used to the idea of joining Him in sacrifice. He began at the threshold of her religious life, from the moment of her taking the habit. In Sister Faustina's Diary we find a short note from that period:

"The day I took the [religious] habit, God let me understand how much I was to suffer. I clearly saw to what I was committing myself."

(Diary, Notebook I, para. 22).

This was a short revelation, almost a flash, but so strong that it brought about a faint, which was remembered by her companions and engraved itself on the memory of Sister Faustina.

For a second time the knowledge that God called her to the role of a victim returned during the making of her first vows. Again, the Diary gives only a few words on the subject:

"First vows. An ardent desire to empty myself for God by an active love, but a love that would be imperceptible, even to the sisters closest to me."

(Diary, Notebook I, para. 27).

Both of these religious impulses were given to direct the will of Sister Faustina towards limitless sacrifice when offering herself to the Lord. Throughout the whole of this time the religious life itself was preparing this readiness in her. Jesus returned to His request directly before her final vows, this time clearly stressing the wish of His Heart and requiring from her a decisive answer.

"During the third probation, the Lord gave me to understand that I should offer myself to Him so that He could do with me as He pleased. I was to remain

standing before Him as a victim offering. At first, I was quite frightened as I felt myself to be so utterly miserable and knew very well that this was the case. I answered the Lord once again, '**I am misery itself; how can I be a hostage for others?**' '**You do not understand this today. Tomorrow, during your adoration. I will make it known to you.**'...

When I came to the adoration, I felt within my soul that I had entered the temple of the living God, whose majesty is great and incomprehensible... Although I saw nothing externally, God's presence pervaded me. At that very moment my intellect was strangely illumined. A vision passed before my eyes of my soul; it was like the vision Jesus had in the Garden of Olives. First, the physical sufferings and all the circumstances that would increase them; [then] the full scope of the spiritual sufferings and those that no one would know about. Everything entered into the vision: false suspicions, loss of good name... My name is to be: 'sacrifice'. When the vision ended, a cold sweat bathed my forehead. Jesus made it known to me that, even if I did not give my consent to this, I could still be saved; and He would not lessen His graces, but would still continue to have the same intimate relationship with me, so that... God's generosity would not lessen thereby. And the Lord gave me to know that the whole mystery depended on me, on my free consent to the sacrifice given with full use of my faculties. In this free and conscious act lies the whole power and value before His Majesty... At that moment, I realized I was entering into communion with the incomprehensible Majesty. I felt that God was waiting *for my word, for my consent. Then my spirit immersed itself in the Lord, and I said, "Do with me as You please, I subject myself to Your will... I will be faithful to Your commands with the help of Your grace..." Suddenly, when I had consented to the sacrifice with all my heart and all my will, God's presence pervaded me. My soul was... inundated with such happiness that I cannot put in writing even the smallest part of it... I was extraordinarily fused with God. I saw that God was well pleased with me and, reciprocally, my spirit drowned itself in Him. Aware of this union with God. I felt I was especially loved and, in turn, I loved with all my soul... At that moment I felt transconsecrated. My earthly body was the same, but my soul was different; God was now living in it with the totality of His delight... A great mystery took place... between the Lord and myself".*

(Diary, Notebook I, paras. 135-7).

A new intimacy therefore took place between Sister Faustina and God. God, having accepted her consent to join with Him sacrifice for sinners, from now on leads her ever deeper into the essence of this relationship, and develops in her the ability to consecrate herself without reservation. We know that although the community in which Sister Faustina lived did not observe traces of selfishness in her, overcoming her own ego did not always come easily to her. Many parts of her Diary show this. She was helpful, kind and generous, but how many times she complained to Jesus of ingratitude or the thoughtless or selfish use that others made of her, or of her own lack of strength! Jesus never left her bitter complaints without a reply. He explained the very essence of sacrifice, He commended to her a perseverance and a total lack of self. Barely a

few days after the revelation which took place imme-
diately before her vows, Jesus again appeared to Sister
Faustina when she knelt in the chapel saying the "Holy
Hour".

*"As soon as I entered the chapel, God's presence
enveloped me. I was distinctly aware that the Lord was
near me. After a moment I saw the Lord, all covered
with wounds; and He said to me, 'Look at whom you
have espoused'. I understood the meaning of these words
and answered the Lord, "Jesus, I love You more when I
see You wounded and crushed with suffering like this
than if I saw You in majesty'. Jesus asked, "Why?" I
replied, "Great majesty terrifies me, little nothing that I
am, and Your wounds draw me to Your Heart and tell
me of Your great love for me..." I fixed my gaze upon
His sacred wounds and felt happy to suffer with Him.
I suffered, and yet I did not suffer, because I felt happy
to know the depth of His love..."*

(Diary, Notebook I, para. 252).

Sister Faustina, led by her Divine Master, now
became used to living always in the shadow of His
suffering. Her understanding of this greatest mystery
of God's Mercy grew ever deeper. She now understood
that the essence of her intimacy with the Lord would
depend on taking part in His Passion, and that it was
precisely this which would be the core of her vocation.
One day Jesus appeared before her

*"stripped of His clothes, His body completely covered
with wounds, His eyes flooded with tears and blood, His
face disfigured and covered with spittle. The Lord then
said to me, 'The bride must resemble her Betrothed.' I*

understood these words to their very depth. There is no room for doubt here. My likeness to Jesus must be through suffering and humility.'

(Diary, Notebook I, para. 268).

Jesus varied His teaching: sometimes there were visions, at others there were words of instruction. Here are two of them:

'I desire that you know more profoundly the love that burns in My Heart for souls, and you will understand this when you meditate upon My Passion. Call upon My mercy on behalf of sinners; I desire their salvation.'

(Diary, Notebook I, para. 186).

'I desire that your heart be formed after the model of My merciful Heart. You must be completely imbued with My mercy.'

(Diary, Notebook I, para. 167).

There was no need to repeat such appeals to Sister Faustina. She responded with fervent love and complete readiness to do His Sacred Will. His love challenged her to increase her own efforts, for with all her soul she wanted to be like Him.

'I want to resemble You, O Jesus - You crucified, tortured and humiliated. Jesus, imprint upon my heart and soul Your own humility. I love You, Jesus, to the point of madness. You who were crushed with suffering as described by the prophet [cf. Isaiah 53: 2-9], as if he could not see the human form in You because of Your great suffering... O eternal and infinite God, what has love done to You?'

(Diary, Notebook I, para. 267).

Following Jesus' instructions, Sister Faustina made meditation on His Passion her daily duty. In the Congregation, saying the Stations of the Cross is recommended, but not compulsory. Many witnesses state that this was her favourite prayer and frequently performed.

On 1st May 1933 Sister Faustina made her perpetual vows. Jesus Himself had been her Teacher, and Father Andrasz had so confirmed her interior life as genuine that she could now lean without hesitation on the strong base of her relationship with God. The "annunciation" was past. So too was the period of her spiritual "engagement". Her trials, searchings and painful spiritual maturing were also behind her. She had developed to her fullness, so that, in absorbing God with her whole person, she could now perform the task entrusted to her for life and pass on God to souls, and thus draw Him to herself in order to give to others.

Sister Faustina could hardly grasp the thought of the happiness that was to come. It surpassed all her expectations. She was flooded with joy in her soul. She had received "full measure and flowing over." An enormous gratitude to God arose within her for this immeasurable gift of His love.

'When I think of my perpetual vows and Who it is that wants me to be joined with Him, for hours I become absorbed in the thought of Him. How can this be; You are God and I - I am Your creature. You, the Immortal King and I, a beggar and misery itself! But now all is clear to me; Your grace and Your love, O Lord, will fill the gulf between You, Jesus, and me.'

(Diary, Notebook I, para. 199).

Sister Faustina made her perpetual vows before Bishop Stanislaus Rospond. When he put the wedding ring on her finger, the bishop solemnly intoned the sacramental formula:

'I betroth you to Jesus Christ, the Son of the Father Most High may He keep you unblemished. Take this ring as a sign of the eternal covenant you are making with Christ, the Spouse of Virgins. May it be for you the ring of faith and the sign of the Holy Spirit, that you may be called the bride of Christ and, if you serve Him faithfully, be crowned [as such] *for all eternity'.*

(Diary, Notebook I, para. 248).

Sister Faustina herself, kneeling during the nuptial Mass in humble prayer, gave herself to God as she had promised:

'Today I place my heart on the paten where Your Heart has been placed, O Jesus, and today I offer myself together with You to God, Your Father and mine, as a sacrifice of love and praise. Father of Mercy, look upon the sacrifice of my heart, but through the wound in the Heart of Jesus.'

(Diary, Notebook I, para. 239).

Sister Faustina did not shut herself up in her joy even in this moment of the greatest emotional tension. She knew that on such a solemn day Jesus could refuse her nothing, so she took to Him all her requests, which she had arranged in three separate groups so as to forget nothing and no one. She remembered the people close to her, those to whom she owed gratitude, those to whom she had a personal obligation and to whom God had bound her in obligation. She remembered the Congregation, her country, and the universal Church. At the end, she included a personal request, torn from the bottom of her soul, though very simple and brief:

'For myself, I ask, Lord, transform me completely into Yourself: maintain in me a holy zeal for Your glory, give

*me the grace and spiritual strength to do Your holy will
in all things."*

(Diary, Notebook I, para. 240).

Sister Faustina was aware how difficult it would be
to fulfil her vocation. She knew that she must learn
long and perseveringly, before she could obtain the
appropriate virtues to be able to carry it out. She had
already learned humility, and understood that she
herself could do nothing. She therefore asked Jesus:

*"O Jesus, hidden in the Blessed Sacrament, You see
that in pronouncing my perpetual vows I am leaving the
novitiate today Jesus, You know how weak and little I
am, and so, from today on, I am entering Your novitiate
in a special way. I continue to be a novice, but Your
novice, Jesus, and You will be my Master to the last
day. Daily I will attend lectures at Your feet. I will not
do the least thing by myself, without consulting You as
my Master. Jesus, how happy I am that You yourself
have drawn me and taken me into Your novitiate; that
is to say, into the tabernacle. In making my perpetual
vows, I have by no means become a perfect nun. No, no!
I am still a weak little novice of Jesus, and I must
strive to acquire perfection as I did in the first days of
the novitiate, and I will make every effort to keep the
same disposition of soul which I had on that first day
the convent gate opened to admit me... ...I leave You
complete freedom in directing my soul. Guide me along
the paths You wish. I won't question them. I will
follow You trustingly."*

(Diary, Notebook I, para. 227-228).

According to Sister Faustina herself, *'A great mystery has been accomplished between God and me.'* (Diary, Notebook I, para. 138) on the day of her perpetual vows. She does not wish to say much about it. It is a matter between her and God. It is too personal. and perhaps too difficult to put into words, to explain it. She only says:

'My heart is a permanent dwelling place for Jesus. No one but Jesus has access to it. It is from Jesus that I derive strength to fight difficulties and oppositions. I want to be transformed into Jesus in order to be able to give myself completely to souls. Without Jesus I would not get near to souls, because I know what I am of myself. I absorb God into myself in order to give Him to souls. I desire to struggle, toil and empty myself for our work of saving immortal souls. It does not matter if these efforts should shorten my life; it is no longer mine, but belongs to the Community. I want to be useful to the whole Church by being faithful to my Community.'

(Diary, Notebook I, para. 193-194).

So the vows were made, the solemn day ended and life returned to its daily normality. Sister Faustina, united with God for eternity, went back to her usual duties. She saw them differently,and new horizons opened before her:

'Now a gray, ordinary day has begun. The solemn hours of the perpetual vows have passed, but God's great grace has remained in my soul. I feel I am all God's; I feel I am His child, I feel I am wholly God's property. I experience this in a way that can be physically sensed. I am completely at peace about everything, because I

know it is the Spouse's business to look after me...

My Jesus, I will now strive to give honor and glory to Your Name, doing battle till the day on which You yourself will say, enough! Every soul You have entrusted to me, Jesus, I will try to aid with prayer and sacrifice, so that Your grace can work in them... O you days of work and of monotony, you are not monotonous to me at all, for each moment brings me new graces and opportunity to do good.'

(Diary, Notebook I, para. 245).

Life took on new colours for Sister Faustina. For the first time we hear from her lips that daily life, in which she so painfully felt a lack of time for prayer, had now become full of a divine meaning and grace. Henceforward, she would have no difficulty in permeating her work with prayer. Work, and with it her whole life, would become prayer. Sister Faustina had now had that culminating moment of union with God. She had taken on herself an enormous commitment for the Lord. How would her future life turn out?

THE YEARS IN VILNIUS
- THE PORT IS IN SIGHT

For a month after her perpetual vows, Sister Faustina waited in Cracow to be re-assigned to work. As, by helping in the garden, she was generally working alone, she used the time to make a retreat in the style of St Ignatius, which gave her the opportunity to reflect on the meaning of her vows, and once again to consider how she was to act in her life as Jesus' spouse so as to fulfil worthily those duties in particular which had been laid on her before her vows.

She was assigned to Vilnius. Depressed, she thought how far from Cracow that was. Probably no departure from the Cracow house cost her as much as the present one. She would have to leave the priest who, having understood her special vocation, had already begun to put her inner life in order: he explained her uncertainties and the complications in which she herself was confused, and he was directing her on the right path of conduct.

Hardly had she begun to feel secure under the direction of Father Andrasz, S.J., when God, in the name of religious obedience, snatched her away from him for the spiritual unknown.

In this atmosphere of returning fears, Sister Faustina thought the fact that she had received permission to visit Jasna Gora in Częstochowa, to see the miraculous shrine of Our Lady of Częstochowa, was a special act of Divine Providence. She sat there for many hours, and travelled on now much more at peace, for she had confided her future life to Our Lady, whom from the time of her final vows she considered as her Mother in a fuller manner; for was she not now the spouse of Her Son?

Sister Faustina knew Vilnius. She had been there four years before, as a replacement for help in the kitchen. In comparison with the Cracow convent, it now seemed to her to be small: there were 18 Sisters and some wards. Among the sisters, what a joy it was to find three who were known to her from earlier years in the convent: Sister Felicia Z., Sister Justine G., and Sister Fabiana P. Also, the Superior was the same as in 1929, Mother Irene Krzyżanowska, kindly and understanding, and Sister Faustina had great confidence in her.

Her main fear was not over the necessity of adapting herself once more to the requirements of a new surrounding and the style of life there, nor awe of new religious superiors, the more so as she now knew that she was not obliged to tell them everything about matters concerning her soul. Father Andrasz had explained what needed to be said to superiors and what was for the confessor alone. Her present problem was confined, in reality, to the question of the choice of a suitable confessor. Where would she be able to find one?

Jesus Himself solved the problem. Just as He had promised in Cracow before her departure, He did not leave her alone. Further, He arranged a surprise for her: Sister Faustina did not need to seek a confessor. At the first Saturday confession she made, she recognized the priest in the confessional as the one who had been shown to her twice before by Jesus, the chaplain whom He had designated to be her spiritual director, and who was also to help her in the accomplishment of the task the Lord had set her.

This was Father Michael Sopoćko, the new chaplain to the Sisters in Vilnius, who had been assigned to them a bare six months before.

We should spend a little time to get acquainted with Father Sopoćko, for it was he of all the confessors of Sister Faustina who accepted the request of Jesus as a personal charge, and he was to do so with such seriousness that, when he had become engaged in it, he devoted all his energy, education and pastoral opportunities, and even his money, to this end. Everything he had, or could use, was consecrated to the mission given by the Lord through the medium of Sister Faustina, and he was neither discouraged by the difficulties which seemed to pile up before him, nor by the uncharitable treatment or contempt which was frequently to be his fate. He persistently and thoroughly prepared the theological basis of the new devotion, at the same time introducing it gradually through pastoral practice.

He was a highly educated man with extensive pastoral experience. Born in the area of Vilnius, he came into the world on 1st November 1888 in the hamlet of Nowosady in the Oszminski district. He completed his studies at the Seminary in Vilnius and was ordained in 1914.

His vocation drew him not only to pastoral work but also towards teaching and scholarship. As he was energetic and with a great deal of initiative, he undertook various kinds of work as the need arose from whatever he encountered, and, in everything he did, he achieved above average results.

The First World War took him from his pastoral duties during his first years as a priest, and he found himself in Warsaw. At once he applied to study theology at the University of Warsaw, but as the military situation grew more threatening, he broke off his studies and joined the Polish army as a military chaplain. He took part in action on the south-eastern front. Unfortunately, typhus fever confined him to a hospital for some time, On his recovery, he returned to Warsaw, and there, combining duties as an army chaplain with the university studies that the war had forced him to discontinue, he graduated in 1923, supplementing theology with study at the State Higher Institute of Education, which he finished a year later.

The Bishop of Vilnius called Father Sopoćko back to Vilnius after he had finished his doctoral studies, and there he began to work energetically as an army chaplain and in teaching the local civilian population. He commence the latter by lecturing on educational matters for the Higher Teachers' Course in Vilnius, and on the methodology of religion at vacation courses for teachers, which took place all over the Vilnius archdiocese. In addition, in 1927, Archbishop Jałbrzykowski appointed him spiritual director of the Vilnius Archdiocesan Seminary, and one year later the Polish Ministry of Religious Affairs and Public Education appointed him to the Chair of Pastoral Theology at Vilnius' Stefan Batory University. The latter appointment was sufficient to give Father Sopoćko the impetus to complete his studies, as a result of which he defended a thesis at the University of Warsaw in pastoral theology, and returned to the Stefan Batory University as a Docent (i.e. as holder of a research degree above the level of a doctorate. -Translator's note).

Despite his dynamic energy, Father Sopoćko could not manage all these many and varied tasks. He would have to resign from some part of his work. In 1932 the army bishop released him from his duties as military chaplain, and Archbishop Romuald Jałbrzykowski released him from his post of spiritual director of the Seminary. Now he could concentrate on his studies and teaching work. In addition, he was confessor to the local men's and women's religious congregations; from January 1933 he had become the usual confessor of the Sisters of Our Lady of Mercy.

It was this priest, with his extensive knowledge of moral and pastoral theology, so capable and practical in carrying out his pastoral duties, that God had prepared for Sister Faustina as her spiritual director.

Recognition of Father Sopoćko as the priest promised her by Jesus astonished Sister Faustina at a time when she was not prepared, though the question of a confessor was then always in her thoughts. But her whole attention at the time was concentrated on the person of Father Andrasz. She reflected that he had too great an influence upon her life to be just a chance confessor, even as just such an eminent and holy priest as Father Elter had been during the time of her third probation. Perhaps he was the chaplain promised her? He understood her so easily and so well!

A letter of hers written to Father Andrasz just after her arrival in Vilnius has been preserved, and from its contents it appears that Sister Faustina was weighing up that possibility. The wish that it should be so, suggested to her appropriate arguments which clearly illuminate her sensible reasoning. Although events quickly showed that she was wrong, she preserved towards Father Andrasz the same confidence and openness she was to adopt to Father Sopoćko, and when she was later in Cracow she went to confession to him, with the knowledge and full approval of the latter. We even have the impression that Father Sopoćko sometimes checked his own judgments by the reactions of Father Andrasz.

But let us return to that decisive confession. Sister Faustina was waiting her turn in the chapel to make her weekly confession. She was amazed to see Father Sopoćko. She knew there could be no mistake: the priest sitting in the confessional was the same she remembered well from her two visions, one in Warsaw, one in Cracow. This must mean that she would err no more, blindly feeling her way. She could sigh with relief. From now on, her life would be strictly regulated by the decision of the priest before her. He would solve every problem, while she would obediently follow his directives. Jesus had kept His promise - she had obtained what she asked for. In the chaotic whirl of thoughts and feelings, one seemed paramount: a vivid feeling of gratitude, enveloping her as she fell at the Lord's feet in thanksgiving.

But when it came to making her confession, it became more complicated. The fear she had for so long hidden in the depths of her soul kept her silent. She was not able to trust herself to this chaplain at their first meeting. For the next few confessions she was unable to overcome her inner resistance, although Jesus at once put an end to her doubts by assuring her once more that this was the promised confessor. Sister Faustina's inner state is best mirrored in her own words:

'I heard these words in my soul: 'This is My faithful servant; he will help you to fulfill My will here on earth.' Yet, I did not open myself to him as the Lord wished. And for some time I struggled against grace. During each confession, God's grace penetrated me in a very special way, yet I did not reveal my soul before him. and I had the intention of not going to confession to that priest. After this decision, a terrible anxiety entered my soul, God reproached me severely.' (Diary, Notebook I, para. 263). *"...'I made him known to you even before your superiors had sent you here. As you will act towards your confessor, so I will act towards you. If you conceal something from him even though it be the least of My graces, I too will hide Myself from you, and you will remain alone'...* (Diary, Notebook I, para. 269)." *'I myself am your director; I was, I am,. and I will be. And since you asked for visible help, I chose and gave you a director even before you had asked, for My work required this. Know that the faults you commit against him wound My Heart. Be especially on your*

guard against self- willfulness; even the smallest thing should bear the seal of obedience.' "

(Diary, Notebook I, para. 362).

Sister Faustina's resistance to submitting herself to the will of Jesus, as it is here so clearly revealed, is surprising. It indicates that though in theory she recognized absolute obedience and tried to observe it strictly, in practice she had difficulty submitting her own wishes and judgments to the Lord's will. To no one does it come easy to lay oneself bare interiorly, even to reveal the most godly wishes and inclinations. This problem was to recur for Sister Faustina more than once in her life. She had yet to suffer much within herself, to overcome and to work upon herself, before she could totally submit to the will of God without reservations. In this case, she had to give up the direction of a priest whom she already knew, to whom she had become attached as the person sent by God's will, and to accept this new strange priest with whom - who knew?-she might once more have to struggle through some difficult moments.

After almost a month of struggle with herself, at last Sister Faustina uncovered the whole secret of her soul to Father Sopoćko.

"When I did lay bare my soul completely to this priest, Jesus poured an ocean of graces into it. Now I understand what it means to be faithful to a particular grace. That one grace draws down a whole series of others.'

(Diary, Notebook I, para. 263).

But to understand something does not mean that one is ready to adopt it in one's life. Time is needed for the "new" reality of the spirit to make itself at home in the soul and to find its proper field of action. Submitting blindly to the will of the confessor introduced a basic

153

change in the spiritual life of Sister Faustina up to this time. She writes of it with her customary frankness:

'For many years [Jesus] himself educated me, until the moment when He gave me a spiritual director. Previously, He himself had made clear to me what I did not understand; but now, He tells me to ask my confessor about everything and often says, I will answer you through his mouth. Be at peace. It has never happened to me that I have received an answer which was contrary to what the Lord wanted of me, when I presented it to the spiritual director [Father Sopoćko]. It some times happens that Jesus first asks certain things of me, about which no one knows anything, and then when I kneel at the confessional, my confessor gives me the same order - however, this is infrequent.'

(Diary, Notebook I, para. 145).

The process of adaptation was experienced quickly and without upset by Sister Faustina, although - as we shall see - Fr. Michael Sopoćko submitted her to humiliating observation. Constantly strengthened by Jesus, once having entrusted herself to her confessor, she was able to uncover her soul to him without difficulty and she followed his direction in everything. She was, after all, well drilled in "holy" religious obedience - Jesus Himself had taught it to her - and now she possessed a new kind, higher, the "holy" obedience to her spiritual director.

Let us leave Sister Faustina at the threshold of having her inner life put into order. Let us allow her to recover from her first impressions, to become used to the certainty of having found a safe haven. We shall turn our attention to the other partner in that unusual Divine "adventure", Father Sopoćko. It does not often happen that God "interferes" so much in someone's life as He did in this case. Sister Faustina assured him that Jesus expected his co-operation in the execution of the mission entrusted to her. Because her mind was then full of the question of the painting of the image, she at once turned to him for help in the matter.

What a pity that we know so little of the story of how, in the soul of this priest, there grew to maturity the response to God's appeal. Everything happened between God and him alone. A certain sidelight is thrown on the matter by the short recollection of the then Sister Infirmarian, Sister Borgia T. She said,

"The arrival of Sister Faustina from Płock to us in Vilnius almost deprived the convent of its confessor... More or less at this time we had a change of confessor..., and the new one was Father Sopoćko. Not long after, one day at tea Father Sopoćko seemed shocked or not himself, and he informed the Superior - Mother Irene - in my presence, that he thought he would probably not be able to continue to be confessor to the Sisters, and that we should look about for another confessor, though he said that his decision was not final..., but that he would probably have to resign his office as his health was not good, and he advised applying to the Archbishop in good time for a successor to him"

(Arch. of S.F., Recollections).

"We were amazed at this. During the conversation I felt that other factors were at work about which he could say nothing, but which I could conjecture. He was simply reluctant to mix himself up in something uncertain by any imprudence. This conjecture was confirmed for me because after his recommendation to have Sister Faustina examined by psychiatrists, when the diagnosis indicated nothing untoward, her spiritual director was obviously reassured and from that time onwards there was no more talk of a change of

confessor... *Father Sopoćko remained our confessor,"* Sister Borgia concludes her statement

(Arch. S.F., Recollections).

The then superior of the convent in Vilnius, Mother Irene Krzyzanowska, also made a statement on this matter, but she confined herself to a dry relation of the facts, a discreet silence covering everything which might throw light on the psychological reactions of Father Sopoćko.

However, Father Sopoćko himself gives a fuller picture of his actions at the time, intended to check up on Sister Faustina as a person before he committed himself to a personal intervention in the divine dilemma she laid before him. He tested her prudently and thoroughly, but so discreetly that, apart from those persons to whom he turned directly in this matter, no one else knew anything of it. Here are his own words:

"Sister Faustina of course could not herself paint, and complained to Jesus. He apparently then showed her a priest sitting in the confessional and told her that this priest would help her. When she next came to Vilnius, she realised that I was the chaplain whom Jesus had showed her... I was not at all pleased, I did not want to think about it at all and I tested Sister Faustina and did not even want to hear her confession. But wanting to get to the bottom of the problem, I recommended that Sister Faustina be examined by a psychiatrist. Dr Maciejewska examined her and gave a positive opinion that Sister Faustina was in perfect mental health. I also asked the Superior of the convent in Vilnius, Mother Irene, for her opinion of Sister Faustina in the community. Mother Irene's view was also favourable, she had nothing adverse to say of Sister Faustina, and the Superior General, Mother Michael, in sending Sister Faustina to Vilnius, also gave a very good report of her."

(Archives of Sister Faustina, Recollections).

Reassured over his fears that Sister Faustina might be of unsound mind, and having learned the worth of the character of his unusual penitent, Father Sopoćko did not long delay, and after a period of about five months' observation of her, he proceeded to act. It was not in his nature to postpone unsolved problems, the more so as there was the probability that it was the will of God to tackle them.

Sister Faustina underwent this whole period of humiliating testing in these months without protest. In her Diary we find no words of accusation, which is the more noticeable as she often had the habit of grumbling to Jesus about various people. Father Sopoćko is indeed the subject of her thoughts and "conversations" with Jesus, but the tone of what she writes about him is always full of respect and affection, which is expressed in various forms of fervent prayer for him. She writes:

> *"Father Sopoćko must be well loved by God. I say this because I myself have experienced how much God defends him at certain moments. When I see this, I rejoice greatly that God has such chosen ones."*

(Diary, Notebook I, para. 63).

To augment this picture, we should add that Father Sopoćko did not leave Sister Faustina without guidance even during the period when he was testing her. He drew her attention to the dangers which threatened, as well as to the necessity of developing the right attitude within herself. One of the first pieces of advice he gave her was as follows:

> *"Without humility, we cannot be pleasing to God. Practise the third degree of humility; that is, not only must one refrain from explaining and defending oneself when reproached with something, but one should rejoice at the humiliation.*

If the things you are telling me really come from God, prepare your soul for great suffering. You will encounter disapproval and persecution. They will look upon you as a hysteric and an eccentric, but the Lord will lavish His graces upon you. True works of God always meet opposition and are marked by suffering. If God wants to accomplish something, sooner or later He will do so in spite of the difficulties. Your part, in the meantime, is to arm yourself with great patience.

(Diary, Notebook I, para. 270).

Sister Faustina remembered well the advice of her confessor. It was the yardstick for the constant stream of new efforts she was making to adopt his counsel appropriately to her life.

Oh, how great a grace it is to have a spiritual director! One makes more rapid progress in virtue, sees the will of God more clearly, fulfills it more faithfully, and follows a road that is sure and free from dangers. The director knows how to avoid the rocks against which the soul could be shattered. The Lord gave me this grace rather late, to be sure, but I rejoice in it greatly, seeing how God inclines His will to my Director's wishes

(Diary, Notebook I, para. 331).

This very positive and submissive attitude of Sister Faustina towards Father Sopoćko is also confirmed by Mother Borgia, who from March 1935 as Superior had a close insight into the spiritual lives of the Sisters in Vilnius:

"Sister Faustina particularly revered Father Sopoćko, thinking that God had given him specially to her as her confessor, though he was at times very exacting."

THE FIRST REQUEST OF JESUS IS FULFILLED

The request of Sister Faustina to accept the spiritual direction of her life occurred at a very busy time in the life of Father Sopoćko. He was then combining the work of lecturing at the university and at the seminary with the final preparations for his degree of Docent (the post-doctoral research degree) which was to be conferred halfway through May 1934. His time was fully occupied and he could not give as much to Sister Faustina as she needed. But he found a method which took up less time than the prolonged weekly confessions, and which gave him the additional chance to think over quietly the matters she raised.

"So that Sister Faustina's confessions should not become too long," writes Father Sopoćko, *"I asked her at confession to accuse herself of her sins only, and if she had anything else to say, to write it and give it to me to read. At first she wrote only the briefest little pages... later she wrote of her experiences in the form of a journal... At first she sometimes mentioned the names of people or the Christian names of sisters, which might give rise to unpleasantness, so I requested her to avoid the particular designation of individuals, which, of course, she did."*

Thus the Diary came to be written, and Sister Faustina continued to write it to the end of her life, although it was not quite three years later that Sister

Faustina left Vilnius for Cracow and never returned to it. From then onwards she was able to keep in contact with Father Sopoćko only by letter. She saw him again only a few times during his short visits to Cracow.

The Diary caused Sister Faustina a great deal of trouble. It was the cause of misunderstandings, and even painful scenes. Her companions, not knowing the situation, argued, with the logic of the practical, that she was wasting her time, of which she had none too much, on scribblings. As she was unable to reveal why she wrote, Sister Faustina began to conceal her writing, and did so with such success that those around her ceased to notice. Mother Borgia, her superior, recalls this unusually awkward situation:

"From the time that Father Sopoćko became our confessor, Sister Faustina was writing her diary, at his request. Of course, Mother General also knew of this. Sometimes other sisters complained that Sister Faustina, despite her hard work, had still time to write a diary. It is possible that she wrote it at the cost of her sleep, but", writes Sister Borgia, *"I never said anything about that as the superior of the house, for I had confidence in her good sense."*

Unfortunately, barely had Sister Faustina learned to put her mystical experiences in the form of a continuous diary, and become reasonably skilled at this, when something happened which caused her to destroy everything she had written over almost her entire first year's stay in Vilnius. This is described by Father Sopoćko:

"In 1934 I went to Palestine and was not in Vilnius for some months... When I came back, Sister Faustina told me that she had burned the diary she had written so far. She said that on a certain occasion a young man appeared to her and said that the writing was no use and could only be a source of anxieties,

*and he ordered her to throw the diary into the fire,
which she did. I told her that she had not done well,
that this had been a temptation from the devil, and
I requested her to try to re-create what she could
remember from that diary, and to continue to write a
diary".*

Obedient to the command of her confessor, Sister
Faustina went back to her writing. She began her diary
again on 28th July 1934.

"I am to write down", she says at the beginning, *"the
encounters of my soul with You, O God, at the moments
of Your special visitations. I am to write about You, O
Incomprehensible in mercy towards my poor soul... I have
received this order through him who is for me Your
representative here on earth, who interprets Your holy
Will to me. Jesus, You see how difficult is for me to
write, how unable I am to put down clearly what, I
experience in my soul. O God, can a pen write down
that for which many a time there are no words? But
You give me the order to write, O God; that is enough
for me."*

But the writing she now undertook was much more
complicated and a far more difficult task than it was
before. It was necessary to harmonize the description of
what was currently happening with what had gone
before. Not having divided her Diary into two halves,
Sister Faustina mixed up the two accounts. And
because she wrote episodically, forced to break off, she
often returned to the same theme yet again, to finish
or to supplement it. This has had an effect upon the
clarity of the text, for passages from the former part
are entered without preamble into current matters, and
the boundary between them is so imprecise that it is

sometimes hard to know to what period a given text refers. Sister Faustina had no special time set apart for writing. She wrote when she had a spare moment from work. Also, she never corrected her text once it was written, which was probably not only because she had no time, but also because she did not realise that a text requires corrections, putting in order, or improvements. How could she have had even an elementary knowledge of the writer's craft and its requirements? To her credit, she showed an understanding of the difficulties arising when seeking the appropriate expression to show her thoughts. The difficulty of interpreting her text was further increased by Father Sopoćko's command, accepted by her, not to indicate clearly the person of whom she is writing nor the place where the action happened. It is sometimes impossible therefore to determine of whom she may be writing.

Sadly, the part of her Diary which was destroyed also contained the story of how the image of Jesus of the Divine Mercy came about, which was written as it happened, for it was at that time that it was painted. Before Sister Faustina returned to writing her diary, the picture was ready. In the new version of her Diary she does not often revert to that theme. Luckily, we have the supplementary account of the then superior, Mother Irene, and of Father Sopoćko.

Having lost all fear that his penitent was not in full mental health, and been reassured of her moral qualities, Father Sopoćko went into action. Mother Irene relates,

> "after having received the doctor's verdict, with my knowledge Father Sopoćko looked for an artist who would paint the image of the Merciful Jesus in the manner in which He appeared to Sister Faustina in Płock. Prof. Eugeniusz Kazimierowski undertook to paint the picture. In order not to alert the sisters to the interior experiences of Sister Faustina, every Saturday morning I went with her to Holy Mass at

*the Ostra Brama Gate, and after Mass we would go
to the painter, to whom Sister Faustina would give
exact details as to how he was to paint the picture of
the Merciful Jesus. The painter tried assiduously to
adapt himself to all Sister Faustina's requirements."*

To what Mother Irene wrote, Father Sopoćko adds
information from his point of view:

*"I was not at that time convinced of the genuine
nature of the revelations, and I was simply curious to
see what would come of it. Kazimierowski was not a
great painter, but he lived in my neighbourhood, I
knew him and therefore I turned to him. From
January 1934 Sister Faustina came once or twice a
week with Sister Borgia to me and to this painter,
and Kazimierowski painted the image of the Merciful
Jesus according to her directions."*

In the statements of Mother Irene and Father
Sopoćko there is a certain contradiction and it is better
to correct it at once. Namely, Mother Irene says that it
was she who went to the painter with Sister Faustina,
while Father Sopoćko says that it was Sister Borgia.
The matter is explained thus: at first the superior
alone went with Sister Faustina, but later she sent
Sister Borgia more and more frequently in her place.

In June 1934 Kazimierowski finished the painting
and gave it to Father Sopoćko. The picture shows Jesus
in a long white robe with wide sleeves and with a cord
belt - He is moving towards us stepping quickly. He is
already so near that He knows we must have seen
Him, so He has raised His right hand in the gesture of
blessing - as if He intended to make the Sign of the
Cross - and His left hand, lifting aside a fold of the
robe at His breast, shows two rays coming from His
invisible Heart: one ray is transparent and one is red.
Their stream of light falls slantingly before Him
towards the earth.

In this image it is not we who approach the Lord, but He who makes the first step, coming towards us with a gesture of blessing and merciful forgiveness. The central point in this picture is formed by both the rays. A double action is taking place: we are drawn into the orbit of the action of Divine Mercy by the gesture of blessing, and simultaneously made conscious of this by the indication to us of the source from which Mercy flows to us, which is hidden in the breast of the Lord as if within a costly shrine. Thus contact between us who look, and Jesus, is made above all by His movement and gesture. Jesus directs our whole attention to the contents of His Heart. Even His slightly downcast eyes take us in the same direction.

Father Sopoćko was not delighted with the picture when he saw it. It was obvious that Kazimierowski had not portrayed the marvellous vision of Sister Faustina sufficiently convincingly. But he had faithfully followed the directions she had given him. There must have been many detailed instructions, for if we calculate on only one visit a week - and we know that there were more, though not regular - Sister Faustina must have been in the artist's studio more than a score of times. She had thus had the chance to check exactly, as work progressed, that there were no deviations from her vision and to supplement instructions detail by detail. Hence this picture, although not an artistic masterpiece, is the basis for the devotion, for it is an irreplaceable witness as to how Jesus appeared to Sister Faustina as King of Mercy. It augments, in a visual form, what we can find in the Diary on this subject.

Sister Faustina was even less pleased than Father Sopoćko. Disappointed, and depressed because the artist had not re-created the dazzling charm of what she had passed on to him, she complained to Jesus:

"Once, when I was visiting the artist who was painting the image and saw that it was not as beautiful

as Jesus is, I felt very sad about it, but I hid this deep in my heart. When we had left the artist's house, Mother Superior stayed in town to attend to some matters while I returned home alone. I went immediately to the chapel and wept a good deal. I said to the Lord, "Who will paint You as beautiful as You are?" Then I heard these words: *'Not in the beauty of the color, nor of the brush lies the greatness of this image, but in My grace.'*

(Diary, Notebook I, para. 313).

Father Sopoćko looked at the picture with a critical eye. For him as a priest it was most important to understand the iconographical significance of the image of Jesus, and the symbols of the picture were not altogether clear to him. He therefore asked Sister Faustina for a further explication.

"I admit that the picture did not please me greatly from the artistic standpoint," writes Father Sopoćko. *"I then asked Sister Faustina what the red and light rays meant. She did not give me an answer at the time. I then told her that if this came from the vision, Jesus should be asked to explain, and she should ask Him in prayer what they meant."*

(Archives of S.F., Recollections).

She answered,

"Very well, I will ask the Lord."
During prayer I heard these words within me: 'The two rays denote Blood and Water. The pale ray stands for the Water which makes souls righteous. The red ray stands for the Blood which is the life of souls. These two rays issued forth from the very depths of My tender

mercy when My agonized Heart was opened by a lance on the Cross. These rays shield souls from the wrath of My Father. Happy is the one who will dwell in their shelter, for the just hand of God shall not lay hold of him."

(Diary, Notebook I, para. 299).

In this revelation, Jesus repeats His request that the first Sunday after Easter is to be the Feast of Mercy. This is the first request in the matter which is made directly to Father Sopoćko. Sister Faustina is here only the medium through which Jesus transmits. Here are the further words of Jesus:

'I desire that the first Sunday after Easter be the Feast of Mercy. Ask of My faithful servant that, on this day, he tell the whole world of My great mercy; that whoever approaches the Fount of Life on this day will be granted complete remission of sins and punishment. Mankind will not have peace until it turns with trust to My mercy. Oh, how much I am hurt by a soul's distrust! Such a soul professes that I am Holy and Just, but does not believe that I am Mercy and does not trust in My Goodness. Even the devils glorify My Justice but do not believe in My Goodness. My Heart rejoices in this title of Mercy. Proclaim that mercy is the greatest attribute of God. All the works of My hands are crowned with mercy.'

(Diary, Notebook I, para. 299-301).

The explanation of Jesus concerning the role and significance of His Mercy was the answer given to Father Sopoćko for his doubts and hesitations. Jesus tried to turn the attention of His priest to the importance of the mission entrusted to him. For it was not Sister Faustina who had to carry out further attempts to put into practice God's intentions - now it was the turn of the confessor. It is within a priest's competence to decide whether a picture may be hung in a church, and it was his will which here made the decision. This is why Jesus, constantly prompting Sister Faustina, now changes her task, as regards the practical side. She is to transmit His desires to Father Sopoćko: **"Ask of My faithful servant... Tell him..."** etc.

That Father Sopoćko indeed was in need of helpful suggestions is shown by his own words:

> *"There are truths of the faith which we are supposed to know and which we frequently refer to, but we do not understand them very well, nor do we live by them. It was so with me, concerning the Divine Mercy. I had thought of this truth so many times in meditations, especially during retreats, I had spoken of it so often in sermons and repeated it in the liturgical prayers, but I had not gone to the core of its substance and its significance for the spiritual life; in particular, I had not understood, and for the moment I could not even agree, that the Divine Mercy is the highest attribute of God, the Creator, Redeemer and Sanctifier. It was only when I encountered a simple holy soul who was in close communion with God, who, as I believe, with divine inspiration told me of it, that she impelled me to read, research and reflect on this subject."*

It is clear that Father Sopoćko was confused not only by his continuing checks as to whether what Sister Faustina told him was true, and whether these were really revelations from Jesus, but by the question of Divine Mercy, which had not been thought through by him; these difficulties had to be overcome, his doubts removed, before he could commit himself. The words of Jesus, repeated to him by Sister Faustina, went to the very heart of the problem which was tormenting him, and brought illumination. But he was not interiorly ready to receive the words of the Lord with an open heart. He had still to seek, research and go through his own investigative reflections before his soul had matured towards understanding this Divine mystery in all its theological depth and, at the same time, the wide pastoral horizons opened up in the matter entrusted to him to undertake. He needed more time.

At the moment he was occupied by the picture. He wished to have everything connected with it completely explained. This he could obtain only from Sister Faustina. Her Diary records:

> *"Once, my confessor asked me where the inscription should be placed, because there was not enough space in the picture for everything. I answered, "I will pray and give you an answer next week." When I left the confessional and was passing before the Blessed Sacrament, I received an inner understanding about the inscription. Jesus reminded me of what He had told me the first time; namely, that these three words must be clearly in evidence "Jesus, I trust in You."* [Jezu, Ufam Tobie]... **"I am offering people a vessel with which they are to keep coming for graces to the fountain of mercy. That vessel is this image with the signature: "Jesus, I trust in You."**

(Diary, Notebook I, para. 327).

Father Sopoćko, still undecided and unconvinced, put forward to Sister Faustina another suggestion for the signature under the image: Christ, King of Mercy. So once more she asked Jesus to express His desire.

> *"I asked Jesus whether the inscription could be: "Christ King of Mercy". He answered, **"I am King of Mercy"**, but He did not say "Christ".*

(Diary, Notebook I, para. 88).

Father Sopoćko was obviously delaying; he had so far not overcome his interior objections. He writes:

"This image's content was somewhat new, so that I could not hang it in a church without the permission of the archbishop, which I was embarrassed to ask for, and especially to have to relate its origins. I therefore placed it in a dark corridor beside the church of St. Michael in the convent of the Bernardine Sisters, of which I had at the time been appointed rector... Sister Faustina asked that at all costs the picture should be placed in a church, but I was in no hurry."

The image was only put permanently into a church three years later, i.e., in 1937, which does not mean that for all that time it remained in that dark cloister. Gradually, the matter of the devotion to the Divine Mercy progressed. One thing had been definitely accomplished: the vision of Sister Faustina had taken on a tangible form - it was preserved. The picture was ready in its final form and had been approved by Jesus. Now it was the turn of the interior preparation appropriate to those who were to devote themselves to this works: Sister Faustina and Father Sopoćko. Jesus did not delay: He began the next stage in the realization of His desire: the preparation of both as apostles of Divine Mercy.

11. Jesus, I trust in You! Image of the Merciful Jesus
painted by Kazimierowski, 1934

APOSTLE OF DIVINE MERCY

The religious life of Sister Faustina had, from the very beginning, been focused around devotion to the Divine Mercy. She was doubtless predestined to this by the type of community to which she belonged. But it must not be forgotten that to this community's life-style there was added her own great personal devotion to the Eucharist, and thus to that very Sacrament which expresses in itself the Divine Mercy acting for us now. So, both personally and in her Congregation, she lived in a spiritual climate which was always aware of the Divine Mercy. It is not surprising that she should cleave to it with all her soul, and when Jesus gave her the mission, after four and a half years of life in the convent, of reminding the world of His Mercy, she should have been - humanly speaking - sufficiently well prepared spiritually to undertake this work, and the question of Divine Mercy sufficiently thought through by her and adapted to the needs of the life and the work she was doing.

But God obviously thought otherwise. It is possible that within her there were still some lacunae in her thought, and possibly an as yet incomplete personal commitment in this sphere. It is, however, probable that commitment was insufficient for the aim for which God had destined her, She was to be an apostle of Divine Mercy. Proclaiming it in word and deed, she was to become a living witness of it in cooperating in the closest intimacy with Christ in His work of the redemption of souls. He thus desired to have her even closer to Him that she had hitherto been, so close that she could not only freely survey the whole "breadth and depth" of His Mercy, but, by immersing herself in Him, scoop up a full measure for other souls.

Jesus prepared her for this work at length and slowly, and His teaching ran concurrently with the painting of the image, augmenting and explaining more fully the substance in the vision of His face seen by her in the revelation at Płock. The core of His teaching was the question of the salvation of human souls. In newer and yet fresher lights He showed Sister Faustina the action of His Mercy, and at the same time He asked with greater and greater insistence that she should commit herself yet more fully.

How closely His request conformed to the intention of serving Him which Sister Faustina had earlier announced! God was actually adapting Himself to her will! He had simply accepted the gift offered to Him so often of loving readiness, and in turn was now making her aware of what He wanted from her. And because He had her agreement, He began the teaching which would prepare her for this work

In order to see the way in which Jesus prepared Sister Faustina for this mission, we must go back to the time when, after her mystical nights were over, she attained union with God. The consciousness of the presence of God and life in Him had at the time possessed her with greater and greater clarity, and her loving and adoring thoughts had centred on the Holy Trinity, attempting clumsily to penetrate Its mysterious life. When she was once adoring, she writes:

'I absolutely wanted to know and fathom who God is... In an instant my spirit was caught up into what seemed to be the next world. I saw an inaccessible light, and in this light what appeared like three sources of

light which I could not understand. And out of that light came words in the form of lightning which encircled heaven and earth. Not understanding anything, I was very sad. Suddenly, from this sea of inaccessible light came our dearly beloved Saviour, unutterably beautiful with His shining Wounds. And from this light came a voice which said, 'Who God is in His Essence, no one will fathom, neither the mind of Angels nor of man.'

(Diary, Notebook I, para. 30).

And just then, while Sister Faustina was absorbed in the form of Jesus emerging from this threefold light, He taught her to get to know God **"by contemplating His attributes."**

Not long afterwards, this first instruction was supplemented by another illumination. The divine voice within her soul told her that the attribute she was given to meditate upon in particular was His Mercy, which

"has passed into souls through the divine-human Heart of Jesus as a ray from the sun passes through crystal." I felt in my heart and understood that every approach to God is brought about by Jesus, in Him and through Him", wrote Sister Faustina in her Diary, Notebook II, para. 528.

This brief note contains more than at first meets the eye. Sister Faustina, who is so communicative when expressing love and submission to God, becomes laconic and summarises when writing of interior enlightenment, to such a degree that she sometimes encapsulates the whole matter in one sentence. It is therefore necessary to follow her thought closely, so as not to miss some piece of information which may be important to us.

173

The attitude of Sister Faustina to Jesus now took on a new colouring. Although in principle it was the same as before, it had become deeper and richer. As she felt it, her consciousness that God is approached in Christ was clearly emphasized. She understood that through Him she attained not only God, but also came to know and contemplate His Mercy.

Jesus confirmed Sister Faustina in this deeper understanding of His Person and mission, and, without allowing her to roam freely in the Divine regions, He Himself gave her the subject on which she was to concentrate.

'Today Jesus said to me, 'I desire that you know more profoundly the love that burns in My Heart for souls, and you will understand this when you meditate upon My Passion' "she writes in the Diary, Notebook I, para. 186.

When Sister Faustina began the meditation she was given, Jesus helped her with visions of the stages of His Passion: once she saw Him in the Crown of Thorns, another time scourged, spat upon and covered in blood. The frequency and intensity of these visions allows us to suppose that He wished to engrave on her soul for ever precisely this image of Himself.

Again it is necessary to stress how very much His present teaching harmonizes with her devotion to Him up to this point. It was just such a tormented Jesus she found it easiest to love, it was for such a Divine Bridegroom that she wished to be a spouse, and for her He was most approachable in this form. It is therefore not surprising that she quickly understood the Lord's supplementary teaching and responded with even more fervent love, imbued with a feeling of gratitude and the wish to comfort Him in His suffering.

'O my Jesus, my only hope, thank You for the book which You have opened before my soul's eyes', prayed Sister Faustina. *'That book is Your Passion which You underwent for love of me. It is from this book that I ham learned how to love God and souls.'*

(Diary, Notebook I, para. 304).

'Hidden Jesus, Eternal Love, our Source of Life, Divine Madman, in that You forget Yourself and see only us... O Love, O depth of Your abasement, O mystery of happiness, why do so few people know You? Why is Your love not returned? O Divine Love, why do You hide Your beauty? O Infinite One beyond all understanding, the more I know You the less I comprehend You;but because I cannot comprehend You, I better comprehend Your greatness'.

(Diary, Notebook I, para. 278).

'O Jesus, Divine Prisoner of Love, when I consider Your love and how You emptied Yourself for me... I lock up my poor heart in this tabernacle, that it may adore You without cease night and day. I know of no obstacle in this adoration, and even though I be physically distant, my heart is always with You. Nothing can put a stop to my love for You. No obstacles exist for me. O my Jesus, I will console You for all the ingratitude, the blasphemies, the coldness, the hatred of the wicked, the sacrileges. O Jesus, I want to burn as a pure offering and to be consumed before the throne of Your hiddenness.'

(Diary, Notebook I, para. 80).

The last fragment of this prayer shows that, together with her growing love, Sister Faustina's spiritual outlook is being widened. Totally absorbed in the contemplation of Christ the Lord, she, however, sees not only His Divine Person, but as she examines more closely His act of redemption, she begins to observe particular human souls, to whom He has brought salvation. The interior problems of persons in her surroundings, hidden from others, became crystal clear to her. So life itself gave her ample material to contemplate : examples of holiness in some, resistance in others, who were sinful and cold. This new psychical ability in Sister Faustina was perceptible by others during her stay in Vilnius. Up to this point, we have no mentions of this, either in her Diary, or in the recollections of her companions. But now her community noticed this extraordinary gift of Sister Faustina. Both the Sister and the wards agree in stating that she read their souls, like an open book, and that it "was impossible to hide anything from her."

This newly-uncovered world of human souls was a serious problem for Sister Faustina and she needed time to come to terms with it. It became the groundwork for many meditations. Something had changed in her interior life, and the change was great. It had now ceased to be her and Jesus, alone together. Into this world other souls had now entered, and Sister Faustina had to find an appropriate place for herself among them.

"My Jesus, when I look at this life of souls, I see that many of them serve You with some mistrust. At certain times, especially when there is an opportunity to show their love for God, I see them running away from the battlefield. And once Jesus said to me, 'Do you, my child, also want to act like that?' I answered the Lord, 'Oh, no, my Jesus, I will not retreat from the battlefield, even if mortal sweat breaks out on my brow I will not

let the sword fall from my hand until I rest at the feet of the Holy Trinity!" Whatever I do, I do not rely on my own strength, but on God's grace. With God's grace a soul can overcome the greatest difficulties."

(Diary, Notebook I, para. 287).

As she saw and understood more, Sister Faustina also prayed more. Her prayer extended in time, coming into every moment of the day, whether at prayer or recreation, and imbued her conversation and her silence; it was ever-present and unceasingly wove itself into all of her life. Whatever she noticed during the day, she brought to the Lord. From her heart came more and more fervent cries for mercy for particular souls. Jesus not only looked kindly on her entreaties, but aided her by explaining when and under what conditions He gave His graces:

'On one occasion, Jesus gave me to know that when I pray for intentions which people are wont to trust to me, He is always ready to grant His graces, but souls do not always want to accept them: 'My Heart overflows with great mercy for souls, and especially for poor sinners. If only they could understand that I am the best of Fathers to them and that it is for them that the Blood and Water flowed from My Heart as from a fount overflowing with mercy. For them I dwell in the tabernacle as King of Mercy. I desire to bestow My graces upon souls, but they do not want to accept them. You, at least, come to Me as often as possible and take these graces they do not want to accept. In this way you will console My Heart. Oh, how indifferent are souls to so much goodness, to so many proofs of love! My Heart drinks only of the ingratitude and forgetfulness of souls

*living in the world. They have time for everything, but
they have no time to come to Me for graces.*

(Diary, Notebook I, para. 367).

Living in a community, Sister Faustina must have
met with sinful souls. There were more then a few
among the wards, where there were cases of stubborn
resistance to God, inaccessible to any persuasion or
arguments. Also, not all the sisters were automatically
holy. They, too, had to undergo various inner crises,
through apathy during which selfish impulses were
given free rein, and at such times there came to the
surface everyday little sins, those which in time
surround the soul with a hard coating that becomes
difficult to pierce under the influence of the now
victorious inclination to justify one's own compromises
and to rationalize them. In such cases, Sister Faustina
with her always fervent and constant love for God and
her unceasing striving to fulfill His Most Holy Will was
a live pang of conscience for the guilty, and thereby she
was also particularly irritating. She often had to bear
a cross, if she wished to remain as she was.

And now Jesus desired that she should saturate all
her daily life, and its burdens, with the spirit of His
mercy. As if this was not enough, the very basis of His
teaching of her at present required that she should
transform it into an unceasing sacrifice of herself,
making atonement for the sins of those around her,
and include in it the humiliations she was receiving.

*'Once during an adoration, the Lord demanded that I
give myself up to Him as an offering, by bearing a
certain suffering in atonement, not only for the sins of
the world in general, but specifically for transgressions
committed in this house. Immediately I said, "Very good;
I am ready." But Jesus gave me to see what I was going*

to suffer, and in one moment the whole passion unfolded itself before my eyes. Firstly, my intentions will not be recognized; there will be all kinds of suspicion and distrust as well as various kinds of humiliations and adversities. I will not mention everything here. All these things stood before my soul's eye like a dark storm from which lightning was ready to strike at any moment, waiting only for my consent. For a moment, my nature was frightened. Then suddenly the dinner bell rang. I left the chapel, trembling and undecided. But the sacrifice was ever present before me, for I had neither decided to accept it, nor had I refused the Lord. I wanted to place myself completely in His will. If the Lord Jesus himself were to impose it on me, I was ready. But Jesus gave me to know that I myself was to give my free consent and accept it with full consciousness, or else it would be meaningless. Its whole power was contained in my free act before God. But at the same time, Jesus gave me to understand that the decision was completely within my power, I could do it or not do it. And so I then answered immediately, "Jesus, I accept everything that You wish to send me; I trust in Your goodness." At that moment, I felt that by this act I glorified God greatly. But I armed myself with patience. As soon as I left the chapel, I had an encounter with reality. I do not want to describe the details, but there was as much of it as I was able to bear. I would not have been able to bear even one drop more."

(Diary, Notebook I, para. 190).

Once undertaken, the sacrifice multiplied with Sister Faustina like the bread in the hands of the Lord. She took more and more initiatives. Her well-developed observation allowed her to recognize the state of the souls of others. A whole world of the interior of another's life opened before her. She could distinguish its ups and downs, the struggle with self, and, yet more threatening to the soul, the resignation, as also the many sufferings, often acute, that accompany resignation. But it was not in her nature to observe another's suffering while she remained passive. Her heart, so full of sympathy, especially for the wards, for whom the Congregation bore responsibility, reacted quickly and compelled her to offer help. The first help at hand was to ask God to transfer to her a part of the pain that some ward was going through. Her reasoning was simple: when the other person's burden was easier, it would be also easier for her to overcome self.

Both Jesus and her confessors allowed Sister Faustina to undertake this kind of action (Diary, Notebook I, para. 192). She did this at various times right up to the end of her life. In her spiritual activity she took on herself above all the sufferings of souls weighed down with sins, but this does not mean that she was indifferent to the needs of God's workers. She supported more than one of her companions in this way while they were in great difficulty, not forgetting even the needs of her superiors, among others Father Sopoćko above all. An entry in her Diary at the beginning of 1936 gives the description of an interesting event which illustrates very well this sphere of Sister Faustina's "activity"; and shows that it had become one of the important elements in her apostolate.

The event concerns Father Sopoćko. Sister Faustina always prayed a lot for him. She knew his cares and difficulties, for Jesus had lifted the veil and shown her both his present difficulties and events connected with the activities and life of this priest which were yet to happen. Sister Faustina was amazed that there was so much suffering to come. She therefore asked Jesus to explain:

"Once when I saw how much my confessor was to suffer because of this work which God was going to carry out through him, fear seized me for the moment, and I said to the Lord, "Jesus, this is Your affair, so why are You acting this way towards him? It seems to me that You are making difficulties for him while at the same time ordering him to act."

(Diary, Notebook I, para. 86).

God did not leave her without an answer in a matter so important to her. But before we give the answer, let us tell the story of the event itself. Father Sopoćko had asked Sister Faustina to pray for him. She relates:

"I promised to pray, and asked for a mortification. When I received permission for a certain mortification, I felt a great desire to give up all the graces that God's goodness would intend for me that day in favor of that priest, and I asked the Lord Jesus to deign to bestow on me all the sufferings and afflictions, both exterior and spiritual, that the priest would have had to suffer that day. God partially answered my request and, at once, all sorts of difficulties and adversities sprang up out of nowhere, so much so that one of the sisters remarked out loud that the Lord Jesus must have a hand in this because everyone was trying Sister Faustina... what some sisters put forward, others denied, while I offered all this in silence on behalf of the priest.

But that was not all; I began to experience inner sufferings. First, I was seized by depression and aversion towards the sisters, then a kind of uncertainty began to trouble me. I could not recollect myself during prayer, and various things would take hold of my mind. When,

181

tired out, I entered the chapel, a strange pain seized my soul, and I began to weep softly. Then I heard in my soul a voice, saying, *"My daughter, why are you weeping? After all, you yourself offered to undertake these sufferings. Know that what you have taken upon yourself for that soul is only a small portion. He is suffering much more."*

(Diary, Notebook II, para. 596).

This explanation was insufficient for Sister Faustina. She repeated the question she had posed before:

"Why are You treating him like that? The Lord answered me that it was for the triple crown meant for him: that of virginity, the priesthood and martyrdom."

(Diary, Notebook II, para. 596).

Calmed and reassured by Jesus, Sister Faustina said the Te Deum as thanksgiving for this particular grace, that He had given her to understand how "God treats those He intends to have close to Himself. Thus, all sufferings are nothing in comparison with what awaits us in heaven." This is how she concludes, happy in the assurance of Jesus, indirectly also for her own difficulties

We can find the account of the same event in the recollections of Father Sopoćko:

"The great difficulties foretold by Sister Faustina in connection with my sojourn at St. Michael's Church began, and grew worse, and finally culminated in January 1936. I had spoken to almost no one about these problems, until on the day of the crisis I asked Sister Faustina to pray for me. To my great surprise, all these difficulties disappeared that same day, as if a soap bubble had burst, and Sister Faustina said

*that she had accepted my sufferings for herself, and that very day had had more than ever before in her life. When, next, in the chapel she asked Jesus for some relief, she heard these words: **"You yourself offered to undertake these sufferings for him, and now you are reluctant? I have given you only a small portion of his sufferings."** And here, with complete accuracy, she told me the reason for my difficulties. Her accuracy was the more amazing as she could not have known the details by any means. There were several other instances,"* stated Father Sopoćko

In giving this account of an event in 1936, we have leaped ahead in this story of Sister Faustina. However, it was necessary, in order to give a more complete picture. Besides, it illustrates very well how the intimacy through prayer of Sister Faustina and her confessor was developing. But let us return to 1934.

When she was striving to relieve the sufferings of sinners, Sister Faustina understood that this was rather an indirect and incomplete aid, and that at the same time it must be supplemented by prayer. At every free moment she asked Jesus for mercy for them:

"Every soul You have entrusted to me, Jesus, I will try to aid with prayer and sacrifice, so that Your grace can work within them. O great lover of souls, My Jesus, I thank You for this immense confidence with which You have deigned to place souls in our care."

(Diary, Notebook I, para. 245).

"O Jesus, eternal Truth, our Life, I call upon You and I beg Your mercy for poor sinners. O sweetest Heart of my Lord, full of pity and unfathomable mercy, I plead with You for poor sinners. O Most Sacred Heart, Fount of Mercy from which gush forth rays of inconceivable

graces upon the entire human race, I beg of You light for poor sinners. O Jesus, be mindful of Your own bitter Passion and do not permit the loss of souls redeemed at so dear a price of Your most precious Blood.'

(Diary, Notebook I, para. 72).

Jesus looked in tenderness at Sister Faustina praying so fervently. After all, He Himself had encouraged her to take part in the work of saving souls. How self-sacrificingly she had responded to His call! Bent low over this soul consecrated to Him without reserve, He mingled with His words of teaching some expressions of His Divine love. At every opportunity He reassured her again of how close He held her to His Heart, and how He Himself rested in her heart. This unceasing intensive communion with the Lord taught Sister Faustina what love is and what is sacrifice for souls. He confirmed her in prayerful fervour, repeating:

'Call upon My Mercy on behalf of sinners; I desire their salvation.'

So that her prayers would be efficacious, He dictated a suitable text for intercession:

'O Blood and Water, which gushed from the Heart of Jesus as a fount of Mercy for us, I trust in You.'
'When you say this prayer, with a contrite heart and with faith on behalf of some sinner, I will give him the grace of conversion.'

(Diary, Notebook I, para. 186-187).

It is not easy to study in the school of Jesus. God gives incomparably much Himself, but He demands the maximum effort from His spouse. Her entire programme of the Lord's instruction at the time revolved around the problem of suffering. Jesus not only desired

Sister Faustina to accept suffering, but herself to seek it out as the best material to be fashioned into a precious substance for God. He ordered her to reflect on and digest this subject as deeply as possible, for it is the basic manifestation of the Divine proposition.

But standing before God as a sacrifice of atonement for the sins of others, and in addition attempting to ease the burden of sinners by taking on oneself a part of their moral and mental suffering, if only to protect them from despair or discouragement, leads in consequence to a situation in which suffering is an inescapable companion. Without regard for which of the two motives it is undertaken, it leaves hardly a moment free. It is always necessary to be in a state of physical and mental readiness, not to protect oneself against any form of suffering that may be given, and always accepting it of one's own free will to transform it within the self into an offering of atonement to God. The hardship of such a role is, however, rewarded by joy, for Jesus does not hide His pleasure and is not slow to praise and encourage His spouse.

'Jesus made known to me how very pleasing to Him were prayers of atonement. He said to me, 'The prayer of a humble and loving soul disarms the anger of My Father and drew down an ocean of blessings.'

(Diary, Notebook I, para. 320).

It was astounding how many constant small vexations multiplied themselves along the path of the daily life of Sister Faustina. Vilnius was, for her, certainly, the promised land, for here the task given her by Jesus was made capable of realization. Nevertheless, probably in no other convent in which she had been, with the exception of Płock, did she have such very difficult and hard to bear conditions at work, increased at times by the spite of a couple of nuns who disliked her. So Vilnius was at one and the same time for her both heaven and purgatory; there was the joyful, fruitful and creative intimacy with Jesus, and suffering, used in a fertile soil, the soul of Sister Faustina, as a penance for the souls of sinners.

With her delicate and sensitive nature, and her well-developed sense of dignity, she by no means found it easy to bear, without defending herself, the unjust and mistaken remarks, accusations, humiliations and gibes she suffered. It required constant self-control from her. But Jesus demanded that this self-control be not merely external - for this was not the heart of the matter - but also internal. He desired that she should attain such interior equilibrium that anger or a wish for retaliation should slip away from her, leaving no trace, and that she should remain constantly at peace, kindly, always understanding and forgiving. Sister Faustina realized that she might not be able to undertake such a huge task. In spite of all her charitable qualities, it surpassed her ability. However, she longed with all her heart to be able to do so. She therefore sought help from the Lord:

'O My Lord, I can see very well that from the time when my soul first received the capacity to know You, my life has been a continual struggle which has become increasingly intense. Every morning during meditation, I prepare myself for the whole day's struggle. Holy Communion assures me that I will win the victory; and so it is. I fear the day when I do not receive Holy Communion. This Bread of the Strong gives me all the strength I need to carry on my mission and the courage to do whatever the Lord asks of me. The courage and strength that are within me are not of me, but of Him who lives in me - it is the Eucharist.

O my Jesus, the misunderstandings are so great; some-times, were it not for the Eucharist, I would not have the courage to go any further along the way You have marked out for me.

Humiliation is my daily food. I understand that the bride must herself share in everything that is the groom's; and so His cloak of mockery must cover me, too. At those times when I suffer much, I try to remain silent, as I do not trust my tongue which, at such moments, is inclined to talk for itself, while its duty is to help me praise God for all the blessings and gifts which He has given me.'

(Diary, Notebook I, paras. 91,92).

'Do not be surprised that you are sometimes unjustly accused. I myself first drank this cup of undeserved suffering for love of you', were Jesus' words to Sister Faustina noted in her Diary, Notebook I, para. 289.

Jesus took the edge off her suffering by making her contemplate Himself. Turning her attention away from her own suffering, He led her without difficulty towards forgetting herself for the souls of others. He had an infallible way to encourage Sister Faustina. When He held out His hand to aid her, it was always a hand stretched down from the Cross. And the comparison of her own love with the Divine Love as shown by Jesus always had the same effect: it called up from the soul of Sister Faustina inexhaustible spiritual strengths and became the leaven giving rise to her heroic efforts to fulfill His desires. Sister Faustina never could have enough of contemplating God's love. It was the guide which led her to develop her own. It is also a love which reveals itself in the acceptance of suffering. Thus it is not surprising that Sister Faustina came to love suffering as an infallible way of pleasing God, that she carefully garnered every one of its appearances and transformed it in her own way into a gift of the prayer which she was constantly offering Him with that same fervent love.

> *'From the moment I came to love suffering, it ceased to be a suffering for me. Suffering is the daily food of my soul.'*

(Diary, Notebook I, para. 276).

The interior transformation which changed the whole mentality of Sister Faustina - the passage from a defensive position to one of enthusiastic acceptance - happened within her as if of itself, simply through her constant intimate communion with Jesus. This does not at all mean that Sister Faustina ceased to be sensitive to suffering. But, heedless of the cost, she took it up in both hands, as much as she could bear.

> *'O you small, everyday sacrifices, you are to me like wild flowers which I strew over the feet of my beloved Jesus. I sometimes compare these trifles to the heroic virtues, and that is because their enduring nature demands heroism.'*

(Diary, Notebook I, para. 208).

This latter confession indicates the struggle she had with herself to attain generosity of spirit in the measure which the Lord demanded of her. But was this the most important aspect? She herself writes:

> *'God made known to me what true love consists in and gave light to me about how, in practice, to give proof of it to Him... And the Lord said to me, 'My child, you please Me most by suffering. In your physical as well as your mental suffering. My daughter, do not seek sympathy from creatures. I want the fragrance of*

your suffering to be pure and unadulterated. I want you to detach yourself, not only from creatures, but also from yourself... The more you will come to love suffering, My daughter, the purer your love for me will be."

(Diary, Notebook I, para. 279).

Oh, Sister Faustina understood very well what kind of love God was asking from her! From her practical experience she knew how to give it substance.

'True love is measured by the thermometer of suffering. Jesus, I thank You for the little daily crosses, for opposition to my endeavors, for the hardships of communal life, for the misinterpretation of my intentions, for humiliations at the hands of others, for the harsh way in which we are treated, for false suspicions, for poor health and loss of strength, for self-denial, for dying to myself, for lack of recognition in everything, for the upsetting of all my plans.

Thank you, Jesus, for interior sufferings, for dryness of spirit, for terrors, fears and incertitudes, for the darkness and the deep interior night, for temptations and various ordeals, for torments too difficult to describe, especially for those which no one will understand, for the hour of death with its fierce struggle and all its bitterness.

I thank You, Jesus, You who first drank the cup of bitterness before You gave it to me, in a much milder form. I put my lips to this cup of Your holy will. Let all be done according to Your good pleasure; let that which Your wisdom ordained before the ages be done to me. I want to drink the cup to its last drop... In bitterness is my joy, in hopelessness is my trust'.

(Diary, Notebook I, para. 343).

Holy Thursday - the chief feast of the Blessed Sacrament - was to be an important date in the spiritual formation of Sister Faustina, in the sphere of her participation in the salvation of souls. It seems that her love, tested by so many trials, was at last sufficiently purified and strongly established. Jesus, Who had so far limited His demands to asking her to make a sacrifice of herself for the sins of persons more or less well known to her, now made this demand in a greatly extended version. It was the same demand, but it embraced sinners in general, and in particular those who were most threatened, for, doubting in salvation, they had fallen into despair or apathy. Here are Jesus' words:

'1934, Holy Thursday. Jesus said to me. 'I desire that you make an offering of yourself for sinners and especially for those souls who have lost hope in God's mercy.'

Sister Faustina did not hesitate for a second. The desire of Jesus was her command, which she was ready to meet with all speed. She only needed enough time to ask for the permission of her confessor. When she had received this, she made the act demanded by the Lord.

'Act of oblation: Before heaven and earth, before all the choirs of Angels, before the Most Holy Virgin Mary, before all the Powers of Heaven, I declare to the One Triune God that today, in union with Jesus Christ, Redeemer of souls, I make a voluntary offering of myself for the conversion of sinners, especially for those souls who have lost hope in God's mercy. This offering consists in my accepting, with total subjection to God's will, all the sufferings, fears and terrors with which sinners are filled. In return, I give them all the consolations which

my soul receives from my communion with God. In a word, I offer everything for them: Holy Masses, Holy Communions, penances, mortifications, prayers. I do not fear the blows, blows of divine justice, because I am united with Jesus. O my God, in this way I want to make amends to You for the souls that do not trust in Your goodness. I hope against all hope in the ocean of Your mercy. My Lord and my God, my portion - my portion forever, I do not base this act of oblation on my own strength but on the strength that flows from the merits of Jesus Christ. I will daily repeat this act of self-oblation by pronouncing the following prayer which You yourself have taught me, Jesus: 'O Blood and Water which gushed forth from the Heart of Jesus as a Fount of Mercy for us, I trust in You!'

S.M. Faustina of the Blessed Sacrament
Holy Thursday, during Holy Mass, March 29, 1934."
(Diary, Notebook I, para. 309).

The consequences of her act of oblation swiftly appeared, so that Sister Faustina was certain that it had been accepted by Jesus. She writes in her Diary, Notebook I, para. 311:

'I soon learned that it was pleasing to God, because I immediately began to experience its effects. In a moment my soul became like a stone - dried up, filled with torment and disquiet. All sorts of blasphemies and curses kept pressing on my ears. Distrust and despair invaded my heart. This is the condition of the poor people, which I have taken upon myself. At first, I was very much frightened by these horrible things, but during the first [opportune] confession, I was set at peace.'

The act of oblation on Holy Thursday may be called the final diploma thesis, written by Sister Faustina in the school of Christ, concerning that of His teaching which she had studied up to this point. Nonetheless, in spite of everything, it is not evidence of "completion of studies". To be an apostle of Divine Mercy, Sister Faustina had yet to learn to voice the teaching of the Divine Mercy, or she would not be a complete apostle. Full apostleship means witnessing to a given truth both in words and deeds. Jesus had begun His teaching by showing her how to witness to mercy in deed. Only when Sister Faustina had absorbed that type of apostolate did He direct her attention to action by word. The main concentration of this new phase of His teaching fell in the year 1935. It coincided with the first public exposition of the now ready image of Jesus the Merciful in the Ostra Brama or Dawn Gate, of Vilnius during the solemn celebrations of the Jubilee of the Redemption of the World at Eastertide - which we shall have more to say about in the next chapter. Father Michael Sopoćko at that time took up the theme of the Divine Mercy in his sermons. The effect of the image was therefore augmented by the instruction then publicly given, and Sister Faustina was greatly affected by this solemnity. Now she had the opportunity to be convinced by the evidence of her own eyes of the significance of the spoken word in the apostolate entrusted to her by Jesus.

At the same time, Jesus called her more and more insistently to take up the task she had been given. He therefore explains and encourages:

'I grant you as many graces as you can hold. As often as you want to make Me happy, speak to the world about My great and unfathomable mercy.'

(Diary, Notebook I, para. 164).

'With souls that have recourse to My mercy and with those that glorify and proclaim My great mercy to others, I will deal according to My infinite mercy at the hour of their death.'

(Diary, Notebook I, para. 378).

Jesus confides the desire of His Heart to His spouse in a moving way. In His requests at that time, more than once there is a note of pitiful accusation, which perhaps most strongly of all hastened Sister Faustina towards action:

'My Heart is sorrowful,' Jesus said, *'because even chosen ones do not understand the greatness of My mercy. Their relationship [with Me] is, in certain ways, imbued with mistrust. Oh, how much that wounds My Heart! Remember My Passion, and if you do not believe My words, at least believe My wounds.'*

(Diary, Notebook I, para. 379).

The constant emphasis that Jesus places on His Mercy ever awaiting us and the insistence that we are to implore it, gave Sister Faustina the first intimations of the greatness of the task God had given to her.

'I feel that God will let me draw aside the veils [of heaven] *so that the earth will not doubt His goodness... I feel within myself a power greater than human. I feel courage and strength thanks to the grace that dwells in me.'*

(Diary, Notebook I, para. 386).

Sister Faustina readily accepted the commands of the Lord. Her soul was filled with one thought only, a concept which occupied her brain, heart and will. She radiated confidence in, and adoration for, the Divine Mercy. She lost no opportunity to speak of this divine attribute. Her private conversations and her part in group discussions were full of this theme. Whoever was in contact with her at this time says that everything led back to this one subject. In spite of this, Sister Faustina's conduct did not surprise anyone, nor did she especially draw the attention of the community. It was generally thought that she simply particularly loved and had adapted in her own way one of the principal aspects of the spirituality of the Congregation. Sometimes this was thought to be exaltation, but most often it was said that "Sister Faustina is in love with Jesus", and she was held up as an example to other sisters.

At the end of 1935 Jesus fully revealed His intentions about her:

'My daughter, look into the abyss of My mercy and give praise and glory to this mercy of Mine. Do it in this way: Gather all sinners from the entire world and immerse them in the abyss of My mercy. I want to give Myself to souls; I yearn for souls, My daughter. On the day of My feast, the Feast of Mercy, you will go through the whole world and bring fainting souls to the spring of My mercy. I shall heal and strengthen them.'

(Diary, Notebook I, para. 206).

'I have inclined My heart to your requests. Your assignment and duty here on earth is to beg for mercy for the whole world. No soul will be justified until it turns with confidence to My mercy...'

(Diary, Notebook II, para. 571).

So Sister Faustina was fully informed as to what God wanted of her. Her vocation was clearly defined by Him: she had received a mission, the greatness of which might have terrified her if not for the certainty that Jesus Himself was acting through her, and that He would therefore assuredly support and strengthen her too-feeble capacity for the work. Indeed, Jesus left no room for doubt on that score:

'The graces I grant you are not for you alone, but for a great number of other souls as well... And your heart is My constant dwelling place, despite the misery that you are. I unite Myself with you, take away your misery and give you My mercy. I perform works of mercy in every soul. The greater the sinner, the greater the right he has to My mercy. My mercy is confirmed in every work of My hands. He who trusts in My mercy will not perish, for all his affairs are Mine, and his enemies will be shattered at the base of My footstool.'

(Diary, Notebook II, para. 723).

'My daughter, if I demand through you that people revere My mercy, you should be the first to distinguish yourself by this confidence in My mercy. I demand from you deeds of mercy, which are to arise out of love for Me. You are to show mercy to your neighbours always and everywhere. You must not shrink from this or try to excuse or absolve yourself from it.

'I am giving you three ways of exercising mercy toward your neighbour: the first - by deed, the second - by word, the third - by prayer. In these three degrees is contained the fullness of mercy, and it is an unquestionable proof of love for me. By this means a soul glorifies and pays reverence to My mercy.'

(Diary, Notebook II, para. 742).

Knowing that she had such a spiritual backing, Sister Faustina could, with complete confidence, undertake the requests of the Lord, and could devote herself without reservations to the work which, according to human judgment, was beyond her capability. Of course, she had attacks of anxiety, but it was not the apostolate as such which was their main cause. Somewhere in the bottom of her soul there grew a limitless adoration and ecstatic joy, which found expression in the Diary in verse, with greater frequency. These verses gave her the opportunity to express the emotions crowding her heart. She, too, sang a Magnificat.

'The mercy of the Lord is praised by the holy souls in heaven who have themselves experienced that infinite mercy. What these souls do in heaven, I already will begin to do here on earth. I will praise God for His infinite goodness, and I will strive to bring other souls to know and glorify the inexpressible and incomprehensible mercy of God.'

(Diary, Notebook II, para. 753).

Such a great mission is, obviously, a serious temptation to the vanity which lies in each of us. It is therefore unavoidable that we ask how Sister Faustina coped with the problem.

Jesus had given her a task which might easily have turned her head, but at the same time He had promised her aid. The picture of His instruction would not be complete if we did not mention how He preserved a spirit of humility in her.

He acted in a similar way to that which He had used throughout all His teaching of her up to this point. He made comparisons with Himself. He began not long after Sister Faustina's act of oblation for sinners on Holy Thursday 1934. At the time, He directed her attention to the Incarnation. At first He asked her to contemplate It, and shortly He appeared to her in the form of a little Child. These visions were frequently repeated, usually during Mass. Almost to the end of her life, Jesus did not cease to remind her of Himself under this form.

Sister Faustina was surprised and could not understand either the purpose or the meaning of this type of vision. According to her reasoning, she had been familiarized with all the mysteries of the Lord's Passion, so that Jesus even allowed her to partake of His sufferings, and this should surely indicate that He found her sufficiently "adult" to comprehend the full greatness and depth of the Redemption. There had already been the full intimacy of a spouse with the Bridegroom. Why, then, did Jesus - that same Divine Spouse - suddenly begin to appear in the shape of an Infant? Why? she asked herself, full of mixed feelings. What could have caused the Lord to do this?

She was used to come to Him with all her doubts and problems, and she did so again.

"Once, when I saw Jesus in the form of a small child, I asked, "Jesus, why do you now take on the form of a child when You commune with me? In spite of this, I still see in You the infinite God, my Lord and Creator." Jesus replied that until I learned simplicity and humility, He would commune with me as a little child."

(Diary, Notebook I, para. 335).

A similar explanation was repeated by Jesus to Sister Faustina more than once, while visions of this type were sufficiently frequent for that thought to remain ever vivid before her mind.

"When I started the Holy Hour," she writes of another occasion, *"I wanted to immerse myself in the agony of Jesus in the Garden of Olives. Then I heard a voice in my soul: "Meditate on the mystery of the*

Incarnation.' And suddenly the Infant Jesus appeared before me, radiant with beauty. He told me how much God is pleased with simplicity in a soul. *'Although My greatness is beyond understanding, I commune only with those who are little. I demand of you a childlike spirit.'*

(Diary, Notebook I, para. 332).

Sister Faustina, of course, did not cease to meditate upon the Passion. This kind of prayer was her daily food, without which she could not live. Although Jesus Himself had commanded her to do so, and basically approved of her custom, he supplemented it, showing her that if He had not humbled Himself to assume the body of a child, in order to become human, there would have been no work of Redemption.

"Holy Hour. During this hour, I tried to meditate on the Lord's Passion. But my soul was filled with joy, and suddenly I saw the Child Jesus. But His majesty penetrated me to such an extent that I said, "Jesus, You are so little, and yet I know that You are my Creator and my Lord." And Jesus answered me, 'I am, and I keep company with you as a child to teach you humility and simplicity.'

(Diary, Notebook I, para. 184).

Humility, and at the same time a great sense of dignity; great tasks, and the little means leading to their completion; simplicity in communion together with the consciousness of her own worth, and above all love, which is the bond of perfection - these are the charac'-eristics which Jesus developed in Sister Faustina, especially beginning with her time in Vilnius.

THE PLACING OF THE PICTURE
IN THE OSTRA BRAMA GATE, VILNIUS

In the convent in Vilnius, various difficulties and troubles, not all connected with the mission entrusted to her by Jesus, awaited Sister Faustina. The first cares were associated with her change of work. Sister Faustina was an excellent cook. She had reached a large measure of perfection in this sphere, and so she expected to work in the kitchen. However, unexpectedly she was assigned to running the garden.

She had little idea of gardening, and the extensive grounds around the convent in Vilnius, with their different vegetable, fruit and flower plots, appeared to her to indicate a task beyond her capability and strength. To aid her, seven wards were put in her charge, too few for the work entailed, considering her lack of experience. Her working conditions were therefore hard, much more so than those of her predecessor, who, although she was a qualified gardener and physically far stronger then Sister Faustina, had received much more capable help: fourteen carefully-picked wards.

How was she to manage? Sister Faustina asked herself this question, frightened by this new assignment of duty, though, as always, without protest she obediently agreed to the wishes of her Superior.

The Mother Superior had her own reasons for preferring Sister Faustina to work in the gardens and not the kitchen. Outside in the gardens, she was more separated from other sisters than she would have been at any other kind of work. Her Superior wanted Sister Faustina to have as much freedom of movement as possible without drawing attention to herself. While gardening, her weekly visits to the painter were far easier to conceal. Besides this, the work-plan for gardening gave greater freedom by far to dispose of her time in additional prayer or mortifications, for which she sometimes asked her Superior's permission.

Although timorous about it, Sister Faustina did manage her new assignment. Above all else at first, she looked for an expert adviser. He was a Brother in the nearby Redemptorist monastery. Wherever she could, she gathered the information she needed. All this helped so much that in a short time not only was she doing all the essential garden work, but she had even started hot-beds so as to be able to provide fresh flowers for the altar in winter. Te results of her efforts were impressive. Jesus blessed her attempts: the fruit and vegetables gave good healthy crops, and the flowers were especially beautiful, though it is true that she gave them great attention. What a joy it was to decorate the Lord's altar with them!

Neither her cares nor her hard daily work could deflect Sister Faustina from the main task Jesus had set her. She had already crossed the threshold which might divide these two spheres of work. While fulfilling her daily duties, she was simultaneously able to be constant in her thought of the Divine Mercy and its action, and, taking new confidence from it, she developed her thinking in the direction her Divine Master had given it.

Sister Faustina was already at the first stage of fulfilling her mission: she had found a spiritual director, and the image was painted. But her former doubts had not completely died down and they continued to course within her, with this difference, that they now were principally concerned with the Feast of Divine Mercy and the measures necessary to establish it. There can be no doubt that the mistrust felt by Father

Sopoćko had a certain effect on his penitent. Also Father Sopoćko still had reservations as to the revelations of which Sister Faustina had informed him. He was then unable to find theological confirmation that the Divine Mercy is the greatest of the attributes of God, which is what she affirmed. He only solved this problem in 1936, after Sister Faustina had left Vilnius. As he writes,

"I began to search in the writings of the Fathers of the Church for a confirmation that this is the greatest of the attributes of God, as Sister Faustina had stated, for I found nothing on this subject in the works of more modern theologians. I was very pleased to find similar statements in St. Fulgentius, St. Ildephonse, and more still in St. Thomas and St. Augustine, who, in commenting on the Psalms, had much to say on Divine Mercy, calling it the greatest of God's attributes. From then onwards, I had no serious doubts of the supernatural revelations of Sister Faustina."

(Archives of S.F., Recollections).

However, this was not until 1936. For the time being, Father Sopoćko held the whole matter in suspension, himself neither for nor against. It is true that he was impressed with Sister Faustina herself, both as a truthful speaker and for her personal reliability. Father Sopoćko also persistently sought a key to decipher the proper meaning of the information and commands given to him through her. He asked again and verified, coming back over and over to the same theme. She always answered him, but not at once, only after having checked with Jesus. Her answers then were always genuine.

But the tension caused by this protracted mistrust and checking on the part of her spiritual director exhausted Sister Faustina's mental strength and her inner powers of recuperation. In addition, from early spring in 1934, Father Sopoćko was away for quite a time. First he went to the Holy Land for a few weeks, then he was in Warsaw defending a post-doctoral thesis before taking the degree of "Docent". During his absence, Sister Faustina's doubts in the truth of all that she had experienced grew more severe. Satan made a frontal attack, for the first time appearing to her, as she relates, in the form of a young man. Satan attained his aim in that he persuaded her to burn her diary, for she feared that it might be the cause of unnecessary misunderstandings and troubles.

When he returned to Vilnius, Father Sopoćko was able to to convince her that she had fallen victim to the lying words of the evil spirit, and her confessor categorically ordered her to re-write her diary and to continue to write it, but a trace of all these experiences remained in her soul. Perhaps it was only a shadow of her former fears, but nevertheless it did continue to torment and depress her. It was not so easy to extinguish all her troublesome doubts, when they constantly recurred in those around her. Despite her own efforts, she seemed incapable of comprehending the full significance of her revelations. Each successive question posed by her spiritual director again left her helpless and confused. Once more she had to ask Jesus for an explanation. As usual, she entrusted Him with this trouble too:

"November 5, 1934. One morning, when it was my duty to open the gate to let out our people who deliver baked goods, I entered the little chapel to visit Jesus for a minute and to renew the intentions of the day. Today, Jesus, I offer You all my sufferings, mortifications and prayers for the intention of the Holy Father, so that he may approve the Feast of Mercy. But, Jesus, I have one more word to say to You: I am very surprised that You

bid me to talk about this Feast of Mercy, for they tell me that there is already such a feast and so why should I talk about it? And Jesus said to me, 'And who knows anything about this feast? No one! Even those who should be proclaiming My mercy and teaching people about it often do not know about it themselves. That is why I want the image to be solemnly blessed on the first Sunday after Easter, and I want it to be venerated publicly so that every soul may know about it."

Jesus encouraged Sister Faustina to pray for the Holy Father's intentions, even prescribing the way she should do so:

'Make a novena for the Holy Father's intention. It should consist of thirty-three acts; that is, repetition that many times of the short prayer - which I have taught you - to the Divine Mercy.'

(Diary, Notebook I, para. 341).

On another date, Sister Faustina records a different uncertainty:

'January 10, 1935. Thursday. In the evening during benediction, such thoughts as these began to distress me: Is not perhaps all this that I am saying about God's great mercy just a lie or an illusion...? And I wanted to think about this for a while, when I heard a strong and clear inner voice saying, 'Everything that you say about My goodness is true; language has no adequate expression to extol My goodness.' These words were so filled with power and so clear that I would give my life in declaring that they came from God. I can tell this by the

profound peace that accompanied them at that time and that still remains with me. This peace gives me such great strength and power that all difficulties, adversities, sufferings, and death itself are as nothing. This light gave me a glimpse of the truth that all my efforts to bring souls to know the mercy of the Lord are very pleasing to God. And from this springs such great joy in my soul that I do not know whether it could be any greater in heaven."

(Diary, Notebook I, para. 359).

The very dates, of the two accounts by Sister Faustina that we have here quoted of her "conversations" with Jesus, speak for themselves. A period of seven months separates them, and there is a marked change of tone. The last "conversation" shows that indeed her doubts have not yet vanished, but that she already accepts the explanations of Jesus with a completely open soul, and that they totally satisfy her.

But it was not only doubts which tormented her.

Equally painful was a feeling of her own incapability and powerlessness. She had expressed this many times to Jesus when the problem of the painting of the image arose, and she confessed this feeling to Him again about the difficulties of establishing the Feast of Divine Mercy and the spreading of the devotion. She felt helpless in the face of the duty imposed on her. There seemed no way out. There was not even a clue as to how to approach it.

Jesus did not leave her without support when she experienced this overwhelming sense of impotence:

"Once the Lord said to me, "Act like a beggar who does not back away when he gets more alms [than he asked for], *but offers thanks the more fervently. You too should not back away and say that you are not worthy*

of receiving greater graces when I give them to you. I know you are unworthy, but rejoice all the more and take as many treasures from My Heart as you can carry, for then you will please Me more. And I will tell you one more thing: Take these graces not only for yourself, but also for others; that is, encourage the souls with whom you come in contact to trust in My infinite mercy. Oh, how I love those souls who have complete confidence in Me. I will do everything for them.'

(Diary, Notebook I, para. 294).

Having been so fortified by Jesus, Sister Faustina could now completely trust the words of the Lord, and thanks to this she could give herself up to His behests in a radiant preparedness. She confessed to Jesus:

'It is my greatest desire that souls should recognize You as their eternal happiness, that they should come to believe in Your goodness and glorify Your infinite mercy.'

(Diary, Notebook I, para. 305).

'I desire to struggle, toil and empty myself for our work of saving immortal souls. It does not matter if these efforts should shorten my life; it is no longer mine, but belongs to the Community. I want to be useful to the whole Church by being faithful to my Community.'

(Diary, Notebook I, para. 194).

'My heart is a permanent dwelling place for Jesus. No one but Jesus has access to it. It is from Jesus that I derive strength to fight difficulties and oppositions. I want to be transformed into Jesus in order to be able to

give myself completely to souls. Without Jesus I would not get near to souls because I know what I am of myself. I absorb God into myself in order to give Him to souls.'

(Diary, Notebook I, para. 193).

Jesus did not allow Sister Faustina to stay peacefully content with what had already been attained. He roused her more and more forcefully towards further activity in the two directions which had been previously shown her: the apostolate of Divine Mercy, and causing the painting by Kazimierowski, the visual sign of His Divine Mercy, to be placed in a church and to receive public devotion.

In a short time, opportunity for this arose. In 1935, the entire world of Christendom was celebrating the Great Jubilee - 1900th anniversary of the Redemption of the World. The chief solemnities fell at Eastertide. In Vilnius, a triduum organized at the Ostra Brama Gate collected crowds of the faithful. The end of the triduum fell on Low Sunday, the first Sunday after Easter, that day that Jesus had wished to be consecrated to His Mercy.

Reminded again by Jesus, Sister Faustina approached Father Sopoćko, asking him to expose the image of the Divine Mercy at the Ostra Brama* chapel over the

---

* Translator's note: Ostra Brama - the "Dawn Gate" or "Sharp Gate", a former gateway through the fortified walls of old Vilnius. It is known that by the end of the sixteenth century there was veneration here for a painting on wood, covered later by an enamel jewelled revetement, of the Blessed Virgin at the moment of the Annunciation; the image was formerly suspended in a wooden chapel over the fortifications. It resides now in a chapel, rebuilt in 1839, over a street in Vilnius, exposed to great public veneration, and miracuvlous powers are attributed to it, in Poland and Lithuania in particular.

roadway. At first, this seemed impossible to Father Sopoćko but events happened exactly as foretold by Sister Faustina: namely, the parish priest of the Ostra Brama district, Canon Stanislaus Zawadski, asked the Reverend Professor Sopoćko to give a sermon during the celebrations. The latter took the opportunity to agree, with the condition that the parish priest expose the painting by Kazimierowski in the window of the galleried chapel over the roadway at the Ostra Brama. The priest made no objection, and the picture, garlanded by Sister Faustina, was placed next to the famous picture of Our Lady of Ostra Brama. There, according to Father Sopoćko "it looked imposing, and drew everybody's attention, more than did the image of Our Lady". There was nothing odd about that: people were used to seeing the picture of Our Lady, but the picture of Jesus was unknown to any, and interested them by the unfamiliar representation, which was the more intriguing because its meaning was not entirely clear to everyone. People wondered what the picture represented, and most concluded that it was a new version of the Sacred Heart.

Sister Faustina recorded a detailed account of the celebrations in her Diary:

"*I desire that this image be displayed in public on the first Sunday after Easter. That Sunday is the Feast of Mercy.*' (Jesus had repeated this many times to her.) *'Strangely, all things came about just as the Lord had requested. It was on the first Sunday after Easter [April, 1935] that the image was publicly honored by crowds of people for the first time. For three days it was exposed and received public veneration. Since it was placed at the very top of a window at Ostra Brama [Shrine of Our Lady above the "Eastern Gate" to the city of Vilnius], it could be seen from a great distance.*

At Ostra Brama, during these three days, the closing of the Jubilee of the Redemption of the World was being celebrated, marking the nineteen hundred years that have passed since the Passion of our Savior."

(Diary, Notebook I, para. 88/9).

"On the eve of the exposition of the image, I went with our Mother Superior to visit our confessor [Father Sopoćko]. When the conversation touched upon the image, the confessor asked for one of the sisters to help make some wreaths. Mother Superior replied, "Sister Faustina will help." I was delighted at this and when we returned home, I immediately set about preparing some greens, and with the help of one of our wards brought them over. Another person, who works at the church, also helped. Everything was ready by seven o'clock that evening, and the image was already hanging in its place. However, some ladies saw me standing around there... and on the next day they asked the sisters what this beautiful image was and what was its significance. Surely these sisters would know, [they thought] as one of them had helped adorn it the day before. The sisters were very surprised as they knew nothing about it; they all wanted to see it and immediately they began to suspect me. They said, "Sister Faustina must certainly know all about it."

When they began asking me, I was silent, since I could not tell the truth. My silence increased their curiosity, and I was even more on my guard not to tell a lie and not to tell the truth since I had no permission [to do so]. Then they started to show their displeasure and reproached me openly saying, "How is it that *outsiders know about this and we, nothing?" Various judgments were being made about me. I suffered much for three days, but... I was happy to suffer for God and for the souls that have been granted His mercy during these days.*

(Diary, Notebook I, para. 421).

The scene described above throws much light on the kind of hardship that Sister Faustina usually suffered at the hands of her companions. There was too much secrecy around her person: it was not possible always to hide everything. Whatever did come to light was fragmentary, unclear and incomplete. This must have caused many sisters to have the impression either that special rules applied to Sister Faustina, or that they themselves were thought unworthy of confidence, since even matters concerned with religious life were being kept secret from them. This supposition is not baseless. There were some very difficult situations. It is a fact that whilst in Vilnius, the very place where Jesus' desires came to pass, and where much activity in connection with this occurred, Sister Faustina caused a number of her companions to feel irritated to a much greater extent than anywhere else she remained. This irritation was most obvious during the period she was increasingly active in connection with the exposition of the image.

But here we should pause and look back once more to the time when the picture was painted. We know that it was ready in June 1934, and given to Father Sopoćko. But we do not know when Father Sopoćko put it in the cloister at the convent of the Bernardine Sisters. This probably happened only by the autumn, for Father Sopoćko was still checking the iconographical significance of certain elements in the picture which were insufficiently clear to him.

The statement of the superior of the Vilnius convent

has been preserved from which it appears that the picture was there in the late autumn. The Mother Superior says:

"In November 1934, I became superior of our house in Vilnius. One day, Sister Faustina came to me with the request that I accompany her to the cloisters of St. Michael's Church to see the image of the Merciful Jesus painted by Kazimierowski. I gladly agreed and we went there. My first impression of the picture I saw was not favourable. It seemed to me that artistically it was fairly mediocre. The face of Christ was like a Byzantine painting, the whole body was out of proportion and too short, the feet clumsily placed, etc...."

(Archives of S.F., Recollections).

Sister Borgia's judgment was severe, too severe and partial. We should therefore explain why this happened, and try to soften this arbitrary critique.

The picture was certainly hung badly, not only because of the lack of suitable light, but because there was a lack of space deep enough in the cloister. When the Mother Superior looked at it, she was unable to stand at a proper distance: the picture hung too near and too low, and thus was seen at a disadvantage. The same picture, when later placed in the Ostra Brama (Dawn or Easter Gate) and then seen from a distance and looking upwards, made a far better impression, which Father Sopoćko mentions, and its symbolical content was sufficiently vivid to draw the attention of all who saw it

But however poorly lit and hung, the picture, in that cloister, was at least accessible to others, even if only the Bernardine sisters. It can therefore be accepted that, even in this restricted sphere, we can count its effect on human souls as beginning. But this minimal solution could not satisfy Jesus, who never ceased to remind Sister Faustina that the image should be placed in a church. But before it became better known, it remained for almost six months in the cloister without change of position.

The exposition of the image to the public gaze in the Ostra Brama was a threshold in the development of the devotion to the Divine Mercy, and, when we read the relevant parts of her diary, we note how carefully Jesus prepared Sister Faustina for this event. It was not enough for Him to educate her as His apostle. He wished her not only to understand the concept of how His Mercy operates, but to see it with her own eyes. Observing how His forgiving love penetrated the human soul, she would still better respond to this mystery.

Thus, within a few months of the finishing of the painting, a cycle of visions began, in which the figure of Jesus from the painting took on life and appeared to Sister Faustina as she was working. It is significant that these visions began before the picture was placed in the Ostra Brama. The diary records five in this period. However, they do not cease with the exposition there, but, more rarely, they still appear, and Sister Faustina continued to experience them after she had left Vilnius for Cracow.

The first vision in this cycle happened at the end of October 1934, and probably coincided with the date of the placing of the picture with the Bernardine nuns. Under the date, 26 X 1934, Sister Faustina records:

'On Friday at ten minutes to six, when I and some of our wards were coming in from the garden to supper, I saw the Lord Jesus above our chapel, looking just as He did the first time I saw Him and just as He is painted in the image. The two rays which emanated from the Heart of Jesus covered our chapel and the infirmary, and spread out over the whole world. This lasted about four minutes and then disappeared.'

(Diary, Notebook I, para. 87).

This was an important vision. It was different from all others she had experienced, not only in kind, but in the circumstances in which it took place. It was not only a visible synthesis of the devotion to the Divine Mercy, but it also contained prophetic elements as regards the development of the devotion. Also, for the first time Sister Faustina had a vision during her daily work, when she was with the wards. It is true that the girls did not see the same phenomenon, but they were aware that something strange had happened: one of them even saw the rays, and although she did not understand their meaning, she was absolutely certain that this was no ordinary reflection of the light. Overwhelmed by what she had seen, she continued to ask Sister Faustina insistently for an explanation, which, of course, she did not receive.

More or less at the same time - although we cannot tell exactly when: a little later or a little earlier - there was another vision connected with the image, but quite different. This commenced a whole series, stretching over a period of years. It is a particularly interesting vision, because it indicates the connection between the devotion to the Divine Mercy and the Eucharist. For the first time, Jesus drew the attention of Sister Faustina to the idea that the image revealed by Him is nothing other than a visual representation of His Mercy concealed in the Blessed Sacrament. This vision took place in the convent chapel in the autumn of 1934.

'During Holy Mass, when the Lord Jesus was exposed in the Blessed Sacrament, before Holy Communion I saw two rays coming out from the Blessed Host, just as they are painted in the image, one of them red and the other pale. And they were reflected on each of the sisters and wards, but not on all in the same way. On some of them

the rays were barely visible. It was the last day of the children's retreat.'

(Diary, Notebook I, para. 336).

These two visions, the one in the garden in the presence of the wards, and the other in the chapel during the exposition of the Blessed Sacrament, together give a complete picture of the action of Divine Mercy. These visions, showing Jesus granting His Mercy - whether in the form shown in the image, or under the concealment of the Blessed Sacrament (with a preponderance of the latter) - appeared with several variations and in differing circumstances. There would be two more within that same winter of 1934-1935. The theme of both visions was the Eucharist.

The first took place on 29th December 1934. Sister Faustina writes:

'One evening as I entered my cell, I saw the Lord Jesus exposed in the monstrance under the open sky, as it seemed. At the feet of Jesus I saw my confessor, and behind him a great number of the highest ranking ecclesiastics, clothed in vestments the like of which I had never seen except in this vision; and behind them, groups of religious from various orders; and further still I saw enormous crowds of people, which extended far beyond my vision. I saw the two rays coming out from the Host, as in the image, closely united but not intermingled; and they passed through the hands of my confessor, and then through the hands of the clergy and from their hands to the people, and then they returned to the Host... and at that moment I saw myself once again in the cell which I had just entered.'

(Diary, Notebook I, para. 344).

Exactly a month later, on 29th January 1935, the next vision appeared:

'That same day, when I was in church waiting for confession, I saw the same rays issuing from the monstrance and spreading throughout the church. This lasted all through the service. After the Benediction, [the rays shone out] to both sides and returned again to the monstrance. Their appearance was bright and transparent like crystal. I asked Jesus that He deign to light the fire of His love in all souls that were cold. Beneath these rays a heart will grow warm even if it were like a block of ice; even if it were as hard as a rock, it will crumble into dust.'

(Diary, Notebook I, para. 370).

After an interval of a couple of months, Sister Faustina records one more vision, the last before the exposition of the image in the Ostra Brama Gate. This vision took place at the end of Lent, and thus almost immediately before the Jubilee celebrations. It was closely connected with the liturgy of Good Friday and concentrated upon the person of Christ:

'On Good Friday, at three o'clock in the afternoon, when I entered the chapel, I heard these words: 'I desire that the image be publicly honored.' Then I saw the Lord Jesus dying on the Cross amidst great suffering, and out of the Heart of Jesus came the same two rays as are in the image.'

(Diary, Notebook I, para. 414).

The greatest concentration of visions occurred in the time the image was displayed in the Ostra Brama Gate. For the whole period of the Triduum, day by day, the visions came one after the other. They form, on an enormous scale, a demonstration of the universality of the action of the Divine Mercy. With what mounting emotion Sister Faustina must have contemplated the infinite reach of His Mercy, where it gathers in human souls, where it penetrates deeply into God's people and soars beyond space, fettered only by human will.

In these visions, Satan also figured. In this kind of depiction of the colossal struggle between human sins and the Redemption, the evil spirit, ever bound up with our destiny, has his part to play. This was nothing new to Sister Faustina. She had come to know his fury and his destructive works.

She knew well that she was no passive observer but an active participant in the struggle she saw going on before her eyes. This could be seen particularly in the behaviour of the evil spirits to her.

'When the image was displayed, I saw a sudden movement of the hand of Jesus, as He made a large sign of the cross. In the evening of the same day, when I had gone to bed, I saw the image going over the town, and the town was covered with what appeared to be a mesh and nets. As Jesus passed, He cut through all the nets and finally made a large sign of the cross and disappeared. I saw myself surrounded by a multitude of malicious figures burning with hatred for me. Various threats came from their lips, but none of them touched me. After a moment, this apparition vanished, but for a long time I could not get to sleep.'

(Diary, Notebook I, para. 416).

The exact time of this vision was not noted down by Sister Faustina, but it was probably on the Thursday before the evening when the image, garlanded by her, was placed in the Ostra Brama shrine.

In the diary we have a detailed account of the course of the solemnities and the accompanying visions on two days of the Triduum: Friday and Sunday, i.e. the first and the last. Of Friday, Sister Faustina writes as follows:

April 26. On Friday, when I was at Ostra Brama to attend the ceremony during which the image was displayed, I heard a sermon given by my confessor [Father Sopoćko]. This sermon about Divine Mercy was the first of the things that Jesus had asked for so very long ago. When he began to speak about the great mercy of the Lord, the image came alive and the rays pierced the hearts of the people gathered there, but not all to the same degree. Some received more, some less. Great joy filled my soul to see the grace of God. Then I heard the words,

You are a witness of My mercy. You shall stand before My throne forever as a living witness to My mercy.

When the sermon was over, I did not wait for the end of the service, as I was in a hurry to get back home. When I had taken a few steps, a great multitude of demons blocked my way. They threatened me with terrible tortures, and voices could be heard: "She has snatched away everything we have worked for over so many years!" When I asked them, "Where have you come from in such great numbers?" the wicked forms answered "Out of human hearts; stop tormenting us!"

Seeing their great hatred for me, I immediately asked my Guardian Angel for help, and at once the bright and radiant figure of my Guardian Angel appeared and said to me, "Do not fear..."

(Diary, Notebook I, paras. 417-418).

It is characteristic of her that in these Jubilee celebrations Sister Faustina is only interested in what concerns the devotion to the Divine Mercy. She retails everything connected with it very graphically, and show the logic of it and the connections to each other that succeeding events possessed. This is what she wrote concerning Sunday:

Sunday, [April] 28, 1935. Low Sunday, that is, the Feast of The Divine Mercy, the conclusion of the Jubilee of Redemption. When we went to take part in the celebrations, my heart leapt with joy that the two solemnities were so closely united. I asked God for mercy on the souls of sinners. Towards the end of the service, when the priest took the Blessed Sacrament to bless the people, I saw the Lord Jesus as He is represented in the image. The Lord gave His blessing, and the rays extended over the whole world. Suddenly, I saw an impenetrable brightness in the form of a crystal dwelling place, woven together from waves of a brilliance unapproachable to both creatures and spirits. Three doors led to this resplendence. At that moment, Jesus, as He is represented in the image, entered this resplendence through the second door to the Unity within. It is a triple Unity, which is incomprehensible - which is infinity. I heard a voice, 'This Feast emerged from the very depths of My mercy, and it is confirmed in the vast depths of My tender mercies. Every soul believing and trusting in My mercy will obtain it.'

(Diary, Notebook I, para. 420)

The Jubilee celebrations were a great mystical experience for Sister Faustina, centring upon the symbols of the image and the devotion to the Divine

Mercy. This is why, after the celebrations were over, she had the feeling that she now well understood the close connection between the Redemption and the Divine Mercy.

'I see now that the work of Redemption is bound up with the work of mercy requested by the Lord.'

(Diary, Notebook I, para. 89).

The great feast had passed, and the rhythm of everyday life was reestablished. But Sister Faustina was not the same as she had been before. She had emerged as an apostle, fully conscious of the greatness of the mission entrusted to her, burning with the desire to save souls. Everything she had been given to experience was only the perfecting of the tool Jesus had chosen to do His work. Each of her painful and difficult experiences had ended in victory for her mission. Now she lived with only one thought, which imbued everything she did.

What of the further history of the painting? Father Sopoćko tells us:

"After the service, the painting was put back in its former place of concealment and remained there for another two years. It was only on 1st April 1937 that I asked His Grace the Metropolitan Archbishop of Vilnius for permission to hang the image in the Church of St. Michael, where I was still the rector. His Grace said that he did not wish to decide on this by himself, and he asked a commission to look at the picture.

Being occupied with work at the Seminary and the University, I was not present when the commission looked at the painting, nor do I know who served on the commission. On 3rd April 1937, His Grace the Metropolitan Archbishop informed me that he now had exact information about the painting, and that he would allow it to be consecrated and placed in the church, on condition that it was not to be hung over the altar, and that no one should be told of its origin.

On that day the painting was blessed and hung beside the main altar on the side where the lessons are read, and from there it was taken several times to the parish of St. Francis, the formerly Bernardine church, on the occasion of Corpus Christi processions to specially arranged altars. On 28th December 1940, the Bernardine Sisters took it to another place, and the picture was slightly damaged; in 1942, when the Sisters were arrested by the German authorities during the war the picture was returned to its former place by the main altar, where it remains, greatly venerated by the faithful and decorated with many votive offerings."

(Archives of S.F., Recollections of Rev.
M. Sopoćko, dated 27th January, 1948).

What happened to the picture after 1948 is not known exactly. Father Sopoćko only mentions briefly that in 1965 the picture was "in the little church at Nova Ruda near Grodno [in Lithuania]." There was then no contact for a number of years, until recently when it was learned that the picture was still in the same place.[*]

Sister Faustina's destiny then separated her from that of the painting. At the time the painting was placed in the church, she had already been transferred to Cracow, and she never saw the painting again. Father Sopoćko, having then lost all doubts as to the supernatural origins of the revelations passed on to him by Sister Faustina, now of his own initiative tried to ensure that the image was publicly venerated.

---

[*] More recently still, it has been restored and transferred to another church in Vilnius - Translator.

The devotion to the Divine Mercy continued, and even preceded the hanging of the image in the church, as Sister Borgia recalls:

> "Concerning the devotion to the Divine Mercy, at the beginning Sister Faustina did not figure particularly in this... With time, after the picture had been painted by Professor Kazimierowski in Vilnius, the devotion began to spread. It cannot be said that the devotion caused surprise or, of course, any kind of scandal. Some of the nuns were devoted to it; others, who were very critical of Sister Faustina, thought that perhaps the Superior General and Father Sopoćko were too credulous of Sister Faustina's ideas. Lay people, when they saw the painting of the Merciful Christ, tended to think it a variation on the image of the Sacred Heart, with the strange difference that the Heart was not visible, but only the rays. Nevertheless, this very interest helped the spread of the cult of the Divine Mercy."

(Archives of S.F., Recoll.).

The devotion spread quietly and discreetly. Deprived of any element of sensationalism, it spoke to human souls because of their inner need, and not because of superficial attraction, as is so often the case with private revelations. The speed of its becoming widespread is therefore the more surprising. When the Second World War came, with the tragedy of the Polish nation's sufferings, devotion to the Divine Mercy was already established among the people of Vilnius, and it spread to other towns [in Poland itself] as masses of refugees left. This was barely in the second year after Sister Faustina's death.

SISTER FAUSTINA'S
MOST DIFFICULT TRIAL

The year 1935 was an emotional one. It began with April, crowned with the celebrations of the Great Jubilee of the Redemption of the World. The experiences Sister Faustina had then made her understand fully her mission in life. The Lord had most beautifully included her in His plans for salvation: she was not only to strive that the visible expression of the Divine Mercy in the form of the image revealed to her should be made available to the public and publicly venerated, and that Divine Mercy be honoured in the establishing of Its solemn feast on the first Sunday after Easter; she was also to remind those who had grievously sinned and lost hope of their salvation that Divine Mercy always awaits the sinner who has repented.

It was this latter duty which now increasingly absorbed Sister Faustina. The spirit of the apostolate consumed all her being like a flame, changing her into a fire of that single longing. With her whole soul she absorbed the great mystery of the Divine Mercy. She adored the patient and trusting, ever ready to forgive, love of her Lord. She too entrusted herself to it, and simultaneously strove - like some careful housewife - to bring to the Lord all obstinate and rebellious souls, often so unhappy and abandoned to despair, which like a dark wall cut them off from the arms of God awaiting them.

Up until now, the role of Sister Faustina had mainly been to inspire Father Sopoćko, who was to be the executive of God's will. At least, that is what she had herself believed. But his task - as it turned out - was confined to the ordering and carrying out of all that concerned the official and liturgical side of the devotion. However, she had received her own role to be performed independently: to bring in great numbers of sacrificial souls, who would give themselves up to the new apostolate. She was to think of a new congregation completely devoted to reparation to the divine justice for the sins of the world and to prayer beseeching mercy for sinners. This happened not long after the end of the Jubilee celebrations. It is sadly impossible to establish the exact date of this new divine inspiration. Sister Faustina, who until now had noted down the desires of Jesus with scrupulous detail, gave the latest with great reserve, skirting the problem while full of misgivings. The first record of this, with no date, comes from May 1935:

"When I became aware of God's great plans for me, I was frightened at their greatness and felt myself quite incapable of fulfilling them, and I began to avoid interior conversations with Him, filling up the time with vocal prayer. I did this out of humility, but I soon recognized it was not true humility, but rather a great temptation from the devil. When, on one occasion, instead of interior prayer, I took up a book of spiritual reading, I heard these words spoken distinctly and forcefully within my soul, 'You will prepare the world for My final coming.' These words moved me deeply, and although I pretended not to hear them, I understood them very well and had no doubt about them. Once, being tired out from this battle of love with God, and making constant excuses on the grounds that I was unable to carry out this task, I wanted to leave the chapel, but some force held me back

*and I found myself powerless. Then I heard these words,
"You intend to leave the chapel, but you shall not get
away from Me, for I am everywhere. You cannot do
anything of yourself, but with me you can do all
things."*

(Diary, Notebook I, para. 429).

This text is unclear, for Sister Faustina does not
define what the "great" plans of God for herself were.
She confines herself to giving her own reaction in
answer to God's call. The reader has difficulty in
resisting the impression that she is trying to hide by
silence, to wipe out of her consciousness the request of
the Lord she had heard. Nor did she only in her Diary
avoid speaking of what had happened. When she next
went to confession to Father Sopoćko, she also kept
silent about it, only revealing to him the state of her
soul:

*"When, in the course of the week, I went to see my
confessor [Father Sopoćko], and revealed the condition
of my soul to him, especially the fact that I was
avoiding interior conversations with God, I was told that
I must not shrink from interior conversations with God,
but should listen intently to the words He speaks to me."*

(Diary, Notebook I, para. 430).

So we still have no information as to what gave
Sister Faustina such a deep shock to her psyche. It is
not until an entry for 9th June that we find in the
Diary a mention which can throw light on this request
of Jesus. But here too the fact that she is not telling
everything is obvious:

*"As I was walking through the garden in the evening,
I heard these words: "By your entreaties, you and your*

223

companions shall obtain mercy for yourselves and the world.' I understood that I would not remain in the Congregation in which I am at the present time. I saw clearly that God's will regarding me was otherwise. But I kept making excuses before God, telling Him that I was unable to carry out this task. *'Jesus, You know very well what I am'* [I said], and I started enumerating my weaknesses to the Lord, hiding behind them so that He would agree that I was unable to carry out His plans. Then I heard these words: *'Do not fear; I myself will make up for everything that is lacking in you.'* ...I understood that God demands a more perfect way of life of me. However, I kept using my incompetence as an excuse.*

(Diary, Notebook I, para. 435).

The protracted silence on the subject of the revelation, and the later very resistant and unwilling account of it indicate the desperate struggle in Sister Faustina's soul. The resistance to revealing the will of Jesus was so great that she was no longer at that point able to be as totally objective as before. From somewhere in the very depths of her being a protest welled up, which broke through all the restrictions binding on her. She did not describe that revelation.

The question of a new religious congregation came up for the first time in a conversation Sister Faustina had with Father Sopoćko on 29th June, i.e. about a month after she confessed to him during the sacrament of penance that she was avoiding the voice of the Lord.

'When I talked to my spiritual director [Father Sopoćko] *about various things that the Lord was asking of me, I thought he would tell me that I was incapable of accomplishing all those things, and that the Lord*

Jesus did not use miserable souls like me for the works He wanted done. But I heard words [to the effect] that it was just such souls that God chooses most frequently to carry out His plans. This priest is surely guided by the spirit of God; he has penetrated the... deepest secrets [of my soul] which were between me and God, about which I had not yet spoken to him, because I had not understood them myself, and the Lord had not clearly ordered me to tell him. The secret is this: God demands that there be a Congregation which will proclaim the mercy of God to the world and, by its prayers, obtain it for the world. When the priest asked me if had not had any such inspirations, I replied that I had not had any clear orders; but at that instant a light penetrated my soul, and I understood that the Lord was speaking through him.

*In vain had I defended myself by saying I had not received any clear orders, for at the end of our conversation I saw the Lord Jesus on the threshold, as He is represented in the image, and He said to me, **'I desire that there be such a Congregation.'**... Yet I did not tell him about it right away, as I was in a hurry to get back home, and I kept repeating to the Lord. "I am unable to carry out Your plans, O Lord!" But, strangely enough, Jesus paid no attention to my appeals, but gave me to see and understand how pleasing this work was to Him. He took no account of my weakness, but gave me to know how many difficulties I must overcome and I, His poor creature, could say nothing but "I am incapable of it, O my God!"*

(Diary, Notebook I, paras. 436, 437).

In the then ensuing struggle of Sister Faustina with God, the contradictions of her feelings and aims can clearly be seen: on the one hand, with all her soul she wishes to fulfill the will of God, and on the other she defends herself stubbornly against this latest wish of Jesus. According to her reasoning, it cannot be done. Her service to God up to this point opposes it, for would this not be an insult to the community of which she was a member, a community, moreover, chosen for her by Jesus Himself? His latest wish raised an incomprehensible question mark over everything. It is not surprising then, that her best intentions were as if paralysed, and she was speechless. We shall never learn either the words in which Jesus expressed His will, nor the circumstances in which this took place. Sister Faustina closed her eyes, shut her ears and even silenced her thoughts so as somehow to escape from that voice which appeared to her to be asking something impossible.

Humanly speaking, the Lord's request came at the worst possible time. For it was just a short time ago that Sister Faustina had had the opportunity to think over her vocation once more, and to appreciate what the Congregation meant to her. In the middle of February, 1935, her family had summoned her to their dying mother. Without difficulty, Sister Faustina had received permission to hurry home. Her arrival turned out to be the most efficacious remedy. Her mother became stronger and began to feel unexpectedly better. The danger of death passed.

Her family received Sister Faustina emotionally. The atmosphere at home was almost exalted, and they spent their time in prayer together and in conversations on religious themes. Sister Faustina enjoyed her apostolate to the full, and in a wider circle, for the village people, hearing that she was back, came around in crowds, and as they listened to what she had to say, were surprised and delighted to find her "as wise as a priest." This was, then, an experience full of joy and inner satisfaction. But after a day or two at home, Sister Faustina very much missed her community. Her place was with them, and not at home... She returned to Vilnius with joy and relief. She writes in her Diary:

"Oh, how happy I felt to be back in our convent! I felt as though I was entering the convent for the second time. I took unending delight in the silence and peace in which the soul can so easily immerse itself in God, helped by everyone and disturbed by no one."

(Diary, Notebook I, para. 407).

After all, it was in this Congregation that her vocation had flowered, a rich inner religious life developed in her soul, and now God wished her to leave it and found another. It was extremely difficult to understand His teaching. It had to be accepted in humility and darkness.

The next day, after she had talked with Father Sopoćko, Jesus renewed His request and very clearly defined the kind of community He wanted. This vision was a turning point in the spiritual conflict of Sister Faustina. For the first time she again opened herself interiorly to the words of the Lord. Her inhibition was overcome. A new trustingness entered her heart, a new courage with it, and at the end Sister Faustina was inclined towards fulfilling the new demands of the Lord.

"At the very beginning of Holy Mass on the following day I saw Jesus in all His unspeakable beauty. He said to me that He desired that 'such a Congregation be founded as soon as possible, and you shall live in it together with your companions. My Spirit shall be the rule of your life. Your life is to be modeled on Mine, from the crib to My death on the Cross. Penetrate My

mysteries, and you will know the abyss of My mercy towards creatures and My unfathomable goodness - and this you shall make known to the world. Through your prayers, you shall mediate between heaven and earth.'

Then came the moment to receive Holy Communion, and Jesus disappeared, and I saw a great brightness. Then I heard these words: 'We give Our blessing', and at that moment a bright ray issued from that light and pierced my heart; an extraordinary fire was enkindled in my soul - I thought I would die of joy and happiness. I felt the separation of my spirit from my body. I felt totally immersed in God, I felt I was snatched up by the Almighty, like a particle of dust, into unknown expanses. Trembling with joy in the embrace of the Creator, I felt He Himself was supporting me so that I could bear this great happiness and gaze at His Majesty. I know now that, if He himself had not first strengthened me by His grace, my soul would not have been able to bear the happiness, and I would have died in an instant. Holy Mass came to an end I know not when, for it was beyond my power to pay attention to what was going on in the chapel. But when I recovered my senses, I felt the strength and courage to do God's will; nothing seemed difficult to me; and whereas I had previously been making excuses to the Lord, I now felt the Lord's courage and strength within me, and I said to the Lord, "I am ready for every beck and call of Your will!"

(Diary, Notebook I, paras. 438-439).

The whole of the second half of the year 1935 was occupied in maturing Sister Faustina to undertake the last command of Jesus. She still wavered between resistance and acceptance, depending on which emotion prevailed at the time: fear, or courage. But Jesus acted without haste, allowing the new seed He had sown within her soul to grow. And, although He did not promise an easy task, and showed her the difficulties and obstacles, He ordered her to trust unconditionally, as He Himself would be the guarantor of this work.

And so, in the struggle with herself, Sister Faustina found herself developing a new understanding of fulfilling the will of God. This lesson continued on two paths, as was usual with her: the natural, as taught by the priest, and the supernatural, direct from Jesus. Usually, the first of the lessons was given by the confessor, and then the Lord Jesus supplemented and enriched it. Here is a characteristic example:

"On one occasion I heard these words, 'I desire that you live according to My will, in the most secret depths of your soul.' I reflected on these words, which spoke very much to my heart. This was on the day of confessions for the community. When I went to confession and had accused myself of my sins, the priest [Father Sopoćko] repeated to me the same words that the Lord had previously spoken. The priest spoke these profound words to me, 'There are three degrees in the accomplishment of God's will: in the first, the soul carries out all rules and statutes pertaining to external observance; in the second degree, the soul accepts interior inspirations and carries them out faithfully; in the third degree, the soul, abandoned to the will of God, allows Him to dispose of it freely, and God does with it as He pleases, and it is a docile tool in His hands.' And the priest said that I was at the second degree in the accomplishment of God's will and that I had not yet reached the third degree, but that I should strive to attain it."

(Diary, Notebook I, paras. 443, 444).

The above lesson from her confessor was illustrated for Sister Faustina by Jesus in a vision in which He showed her how differently people approach fulfilling the will of God, and which way is the correct one:

"Then I saw the Lord Jesus nailed to the cross. When He had hung on it for a while, I saw a multitude of souls crucified like Him. Then I saw a second multitude of souls, and a third. The second multitude were not nailed to [their] crosses, but were holding them firmly in their hands. The third were neither nailed to [their] crosses nor holding them firmly in their hands, but were dragging [their] crosses behind them and were discontent. Jesus then said to me, 'Do you see these souls? Those who are like Me in the pain and contempt they suffer will be like Me also in glory. And those who resemble Me less in pain and contempt will also bear less resemblance to Me in glory.'"

(Diary, Notebook I, para. 446).

Similar contemplations and inspirations at length weighed the scales down towards an acceptance of Jesus' last demands. Her desire to act, previously paralysed by fear, now began to grow quickly. Since Jesus had asked it, His will must be fulfilled. But Sister Faustina sought in vain for a practical solution. She simply had no idea how to begin. In her feelings of complete helplessness, she turned to the saints for aid. The feast of St. Ignatius was approaching, one of the patron saints of the Congregation.

"I prayed fervently to this Saint, reproaching him for looking on and not coming to my aid in such important matters as doing the will of God. I said to him, "You, our Patron, who were inflamed with the fire of love and

zeal for the greater glory of God, I humbly beg you to help me to carry out God's designs." This was during Holy Mass. Then I saw Saint Ignatius at the left side of the altar, with a large book in his hand. And he spoke these words to me, **"My daughter, I am not indifferent to your cause. This rule can be adapted, and it can be adapted to this Congregation."** And gesturing with his hand toward the big book, he disappeared."

(Diary, Notebook I, para. 448).

Not quite a week later came the chief patronal feast-day of the Congregation, that of Our Lady of Mercy.

"I prepared for this feast with greater zeal than in previous years. On the morning of the feast itself, I experienced an inner struggle at the thought that I must leave this Congregation which enjoys such special protection from Mary. This struggle lasted through the meditation and through the first Mass as well. During the second Mass, I turned to our Holy Mother, telling Her that it was difficult for me to separate myself from this Congregation... "which is under Your special protection, O Mary." Then I saw the Blessed Virgin, unspeakably beautiful. She came down from the altar to my kneeler, held me close to herself and said to me, **'I am Mother to you all, thanks to the unfathomable mercy of God. Most pleasing to Me is that soul which faithfully carries out the will of God... Be courageous. Do not fear apparent obstacles, but fix your gaze upon the Passion of My Son, and in this way you will be victorious.'**

(Diary, Notebook I, para. 449).

Both the supernatural promises of aid - that of St. Ignatius and that of the Blessed Virgin - gave Sister Faustina inner strength, but they gave no practical indications on how to start to act. Jesus spoke in a similar way. It was as if the entire supernatural activity of heaven was concentrated upon one task, that Sister Faustina gain in fortitude, before she attempted any action. The heavenly powers participating do not insist on haste. The right time to make a decision would come.

On one occasion, the Lord said to me, 'Why are you fearful and why do you tremble when you are united to Me? I am displeased when a soul yields to vain terrors. Who will dare to touch you when you are with Me? Most dear to Me is the soul that strongly believes in My goodness and has complete trust in Me. I heap My confidence upon it and give it all it asks.'

(Diary, Notebook I, para. 453).

During this difficult time, the two retreats that Sister Faustina attended had great significance for her. The first was in Vilnius, between 12th and 16th August, and the second was the annual retreat between 20th and 28th October, for which she went to Cracow.

The retreat in Vilnius was given this time by Rev. Emil Zyczkowski S.J., a well-educated priest of wide interests, the rector, and later the Provincial, of the Jesuit Fathers. His instruction, according to what Jesus told her, was to confirm,, by the official teaching of the Church, her private revelations. She writes:

On the evening of the introductory day of the retreat, as I listened to the points for the meditation, I heard these words: 'During this retreat I will speak to you through the mouth of this priest to strengthen you and assure you of the truth of the words which I address to you in the depths of your soul. Although this is a retreat for all the sisters, I have you especially in mind, as I want to strengthen you and make you fearless in the midst of all the adversities which lie ahead. Therefore listen intently to his words and meditate upon them in the depths of your soul.'

(Diary, Notebook I, para. 456).

The prophecy Jesus made to her was one hundred per cent true:

" Oh, how astonished I was, for everything the Father said about union with God and the obstacles to this union... about divine mercy... about the goodness of God, was exactly what Jesus had said to me concerning the Feast of Mercy... This is the first time in my life that I have made such a retreat. I understand in a special and clear way every single word that Father speaks, for I have first experienced it all in my soul.. I have now come to understand clearly what the Lord has promised me, and I have no doubt about anything; God's language is clear and distinct.'

(Diary, Notebook I, paras. 457, 458, 461).

Sister Faustina made herself open to the action of grace now in utter confidence. Her heart experienced a great wave of gratitude. Innerly prostrating herself, she humbled herself before the Lord:

'O Jesus, my heart stops beating when I think of all You are doing for me! I am amazed at You, Lord, that You would stoop so low to my wretched soul! What inconceivable means You take to convince me!'

(Diary, Notebook I, para. 460).

But interior acceptance alone is insufficient to fulfill the will of the Lord. In everything concerning the Divine Mercy, Sister Faustina was bound strictly to obedience to her confessor, Father Sopoćko, by the often-repeated and clear instructions of Jesus. Thus, the final decision was always with Him. Father Sopoćko, surprised by this new project, was awaiting further developments, which would supply him with more material on which to base a proper opinion, and he hesitated over any decision.

"In 1935 or 1936", he writes, "Sister Faustina came to me outside the confessional to say that she was to leave her Congregation on the orders of Jesus. I tried to disregard the idea, thinking that it was a temptation. But she came to me a number of times about this. I cannot say at exactly what moment Sister Faustina told me that she was to found a new community... because the communities then existing were insufficient for the difficult times that were coming upon the world... I felt that Sister Faustina, as a simple nun without any material support, could not do this; I counselled her not to leave her Congregation."

(Archives of S.F., Recollections).

From all the statements of Father Sopoćko which have been preserved, it appears that Sister Faustina's personal conviction that she should follow the voice of the Lord was arrived at independently of her confessor, and even despite him. It is an interesting and noteworthy phenomenon that confirmation in the belief that her visions and inspirations were genuine and correct, was given her indirectly rather than otherwise, from priests not involved with her, who either did not know, or knew only little, of the background to the whole affair, such as Father Zyczkowski during the retreat conferences he provided. Similar confirmations of her belief happened more than once. They were most frequently preceded by Jesus foretelling them.

Sister Faustina was not one of those who allow matters to be delayed. She sought help wherever she could, attempting to widen the sphere of those able to give her competent opinions. She even reached the highest ecclesiastical authority in her area.

About half way through August, 1935, Father Sopoćko was away from Vilnius. She used this opportunity to present her difficult problem to the Metropolitan of Vilnius, Archbishop Jałbrzykowski, during confession:

"When I revealed my soul to him, I received this reply: "My daughter, arm yourself with great patience; if these things come from God, they will be realized sooner or later. So be completely at peace. I understand you very well in this matter, my daughter. And now, as regards your leaving the Congregation and thinking of another one, do not entertain such thoughts, for this would be a serious interior temptation"... "To entreat mercy for the world is a great and beautiful idea. Pray much, Sister, pray for mercy upon sinners, but do it in your own convent." "

(Diary, Notebook I, para. 473).

This advice was not enough for Sister Faustina. After a couple of months she renewed her request. The Archbishop clearly took a less harsh view. His attitude was no longer wholly negative, and, though with caution, he held ajar the door on the possibility of answering Jesus' request positively.

"When I went to see the Archbishop, I... asked his permission for all the Lord Jesus was demanding of me. The Archbishop answered me in these words: "As for prayer, I give my permission and even encourage you,

Sister, to pray as much as possible for the world and to beg God's mercy, as mercy is what we all need; and I presume that your confessor does not forbid you to pray for this intention. But as regards this congregation, wait a while, Sister, so that all things may arrange themselves more favorably. This thing is good in itself, but there is no need to hurry. If it is God's will, it will be done, whether it be a little sooner or a little later. Why shouldn't it be? There are so many different kinds of congregations; this one will come to be if God so wills. Be completely at peace. The Lord Jesus can do all things. Strive for a close union with God and do not lose heart.

(Diary, Notebook II, para. 585).

So those who received her confession were agreed in restraining Sister Faustina from making a hasty decision.

But they were taking her new inspirations more seriously into consideration. The delay in the matter of founding a new congregation did not put a brake on the personal commitment of Sister Faustina to the work of the Divine Mercy. It had the opposite effect. Her prayers of entreaty and of reparation for the faults of sinners increased. It is from this period that a new prayer dates, dictated to her by Jesus - the chaplet to the Divine Mercy, which Sister Faustina began to put into practice at once and with enthusiasm. She has described the scene of this vision at length and in great detail:

In the evening, when I was in my cell, I saw an Angel, the executor of divine wrath. He was clothed in a dazzling robe, his face gloriously bright, a cloud beneath his feet. From the cloud, bolts of thunder and

236

flashes of lightning were springing into his hands; and from his hand they were going forth, and only then were they striking the earth. When I saw this sign of divine wrath which was about to strike the earth... I began to implore the Angel to hold off for a few moments, and the world would do penance. But my plea was a mere nothing in the face of the divine anger. Just then I saw the Most Holy Trinity. The greatness of Its majesty pierced me deeply, and I did not dare to repeat my entreaties. At that very moment I felt in my soul the power of Jesus' grace, which dwells in my soul. When I became conscious of this grace, I was instantly snatched up before the Throne of God. Oh, how great is our Lord and God and how incomprehensible His holiness! ... I found myself pleading with God for the world with words heard interiorly. As I was praying in this manner, I saw the Angel's helplessness: he could not carry out the just punishment which was rightly due for sins. Never before had I prayed with such inner power as I did then... The next morning, when I entered chapel, I heard these word interiorly: **'Every time you enter the chapel, immediately recite the prayer which I taught you yesterday.'** When I had said the prayer, in my soul I heard these words: **'This prayer will serve to appease My wrath. You will recite it for nine days, on the beads of the rosary, in the following manner: First of all, you will say one OUR FATHER and HAIL MARY and the I BELIEVE IN GOD. Then on the OUR FATHER beads you will say the following words: 'Eternal Father, I offer You the Body and Blood, Soul and Divinity of Your dearly beloved Son, Our Lord Jesus Christ in** atonement for our sins and those of the whole world.' On the HAIL MARY beads you will say the following words: 'For the sake of His sorrowful Passion have mercy on us and on the whole world.' In conclusion, three times you will recite these words 'Holy God, Holy Mighty One, Holy Immortal One, have mercy on us and on the whole world.' '

(Diary, Notebook I, paras. 474, 476).

This prayer particularly appealed to Sister Faustina's fervent soul. She learned it at once and used it ever afterwards. For her, it became the gate leading to the source of the Divine Mercy for the world. When she prayed in the words Jesus had commanded, a conviction arose in her soul that it was her task to direct that fountain of Mercy upon the world:

'O my God, I am conscious of my mission in the Holy Church It is my constant endeavor to plead for mercy for the world. I unite myself closely with Jesus and stand before Him as an atoning sacrifice on behalf of the world. God will refuse me nothing when I entreat Him with the voice of His Son. My sacrifice is nothing in itself, but when I join it to the sacrifice of Jesus Christ, it becomes all-powerful and has the power to appease divine wrath... O my Creator and Lord, I feel that I am going to remove the veil of heaven so that earth will not doubt Your goodness... an unquenchable fire of supplication for Your mercy burns within me. I know and understand that this is my task here and in eternity.'

(Diary, Notebook, I, 482, 483).

On 30th October there fell the annual eight-day retreat of the Congregation, usually organized in Cracow. Sister Faustina was sent to it by her Superior. Father Sopoćko was pleased at the opportunity. He wished to hear the opinion of the Cracow confessor of Sister Faustina who had been shown her spiritual life and her mission, namely Father J. Andrasz, S.J. Father Sopoćko wanted to compare his own views with those of a priest from another background. But Sister Faustina went away full of anxiety. The thought that she would have to explain from the beginning everything once more to a priest who knew nothing of the latest revelation exacerbated her former crisis, which had since died down. Again her interior tension rose. On the day on which confession to Father Andrasz was to take place, she wrote:

"From early morning, the turmoil in my soul was more violent than anything I had ever experienced before. Complete abandonment by God; I felt the utter weakness that I was. Thoughts bore in upon me: why should I leave this convent where I am loved by the sisters and superiors, where life is so tranquil; [where I am] bound by perpetual vows and carry out my duties without difficulty; why should I listen to the voice of my conscience; why follow an inspiration coming from who knows where; wouldn't it be better to carry on like all the other sisters? Perhaps the Lord's words could be stifled, not taken heed of; maybe God will not demand an account of them on the day of judgment. Where will this inner voice lead me? If I follow it, what tremendous difficulties, tribulations and adversities are in store for me. I fear the future, and I am agonizing in the present."

(Diary, Notebook I, para. 496).

Finally Sister Faustina did reveal her holy secret to her confessor, and in spite of all her fears Father Andrasz did offer her spiritual counsel. Convinced from the moment he had met Sister Faustina that the voice of God spoke in her soul, he now also questioned nothing, only warning her about the possibility of a mistake. Therefore, too, not only did he not remove from her the duty of obedience, but he placed yet greater emphasis on the necessity of it. The picture he painted of the scene as he saw it presents the whole problem very clearly. His was not a counsel which was decisively "yes" or "no". But his advice did give mental support by its very affirmation of the genuineness of the revelation. This is it:

'Do nothing without the consent of the superiors. One must think this matter over thoroughly and pray much. One must be very careful about these things because, in your present situation, Sister, the will of God is certain and clear, for you are in fact bound to this Congregation by vows, and perpetual vows at that; so there should be no doubt. What you are experiencing interiorly, Sister, are only the glimmerings of a project. God can make some alterations, but such things are very rare. Don't be in a hurry, Sister, until you have received more precise knowledge. The works of God proceed slowly, but if they are of Him, you will surely recognize them clearly. If they are not, they will disappear; and you, by being obedient, will not go astray. Speak frankly about everything to your confessor and obey him blindly.

For the present, Sister, there is nothing more for you to do than accept the suffering until the time when everything will become clear; that is, all things will be resolved. You are well disposed as regards these matters,

*and so continue in this simplicity and spirit of obedience;
this is a good sign. If you continue in this attitude, God
will not allow you to fall into error. Still, as much as is
possible, keep far away from these things, but if despite
that they still come your way, receive them calmly and
do not fear anything. You are in the good hands of a
very good God. In all that you have told me, I do not
see any illusion or anything contrary to faith. These are
things which are good in themselves, and it would indeed
be good if there were a group of souls pleading with God
for the world, as we are all in need of prayer.'*

(Diary, Notebook I, para. 506).

Sister Faustina returned to Vilnius quite at peace.
She understood that she should listen to the voice of
God in her soul and wait until she had a better grasp
of what God wanted. Waiting patiently, however, was
not in her nature. She had become accustomed to
reacting quickly, so she found another way of doing so.
She used her new flow of psychic energy on working
out a rule for the proposed congregation. This is tiring
work, requiring a person to concentrate and be systematic. In the conditions Sister Faustina had, the
work had to be spread over many days. But although
she did it in short bursts in moments spared from her
daily duties, the outline of the rule she worked out is
compact, well thought through, ordered and complete,
even as to details. In the main, her project is based on
the Rule of the Sisters of Our Lady of Mercy - the only
rule she knew - which she adapted in her own way for
the use of a contemplative community. It is possible to
see in it, too, the traces of her own experience of
convent life, by the greater emphasis she placed on
certain passages. Sister Faustina's rule combines her
former longings for the convent with the experience she
had gained during her actual religious life.

But here we are in for a surprise. Sister Faustina's project was worked out for a contemplative congregation, and meanwhile we also learn from Father Sopoćko that the religious family proposed by Sister Faustina was to have three branches:

"1. A penitential congregation, enclosed, situated in parishes, and composed of not many members;

2. A congregation including members of the laity with three vows or promises, without communal life (for unmarried women);

3. A congregation including lay persons, even married women, also living in the world, without communal life."

(Archives of S.F., Recoll.).

Unfortunately, Father Sopoćko did not recall either the exact time when Sister Faustina spoke of this to him, nor any details. In everything which concerns the proposed congregation we are left in the twilight, for there are in this matter, too, a number of things left unsaid: above all, it cannot be established whether the full concept developed over a period of time, or whether it was fully formed at once, and it was only that Sister Faustina did not finish working on it before being transferred to Cracow. We can find more detailed data in her diary, but not until the entry under 27th June 1937. At that date, Sister Faustina was already seriously ill, which naturally has an effect on the clarity of her text. The thoughts, expressed through a haze of suffering and the exhaustion of her illness, are unfinished and break off, and the various threads are intermingled. It is as if she is supplementing something which had already been clearly formulated earlier.

But let us return to the interior experiences of Sister Faustina. The struggle with herself was not sterile; one small victory led to another, and her spiritual attitude slowly changed. She was sufficiently intelligent to realise in what a paradoxically difficult situation she was placed. On the one hand, Jesus was more and more strongly urging her to act, and on the other He permitted her to undertake nothing without the approval of her confessor and superiors. The latter all counselled waiting, and - so far - avoided giving a final decision. So, practically speaking, the one cancelled out the other. She prayed:

"O Eternal Truth, Word Incarnate, who most faithfully fulfilled Your Father's will, today I am becoming a martyr of Your inspirations, since I cannot carry them out because I have no will of my own, though interiorly I see Your will clearly. I submit in everything to the will of my superiors and confessor. I will follow Your will insofar as You will permit me to do so through Your representative. O my Jesus, it cannot be helped, but I give priority to the voice of the Church over the voice with which You speak to me."

(Diary, Notebook I, para. 197).

Nevertheless, the thought that Jesus' wishes were as yet unfulfilled tormented her conscience and was harder and harder to bear. In the end, the longing to do something active was greater than all her other feelings:

"I understood that all striving for perfection and all sanctity consist in doing God's will... To receive God's light and recognize what God wants of us and yet not do it is a great offense against the majesty of God. Such a soul deserves to be completely forsaken by God. It resembles Lucifer, who had great light, but did not do God's will... O Jesus, grant me the grace to put Your will into practice as I have come to know it, O God."

(Diary, Notebook II, para. 666).

Another time, Sister Faustina notes:

'Today during Holy Mass I experienced a strange force and urge to start realizing God's wishes. I had such a clear understanding of the things the Lord was asking of me that truly if I were to say that I do not understand what God is demanding from me, I would be lying, because the Lord is making His will known to me so clearly and distinctly that I do not have the least shadow of a doubt about them. I realized that it would be the greatest ingratitude to delay any longer this undertaking which the Lord wishes to bring to fulfilment for His glory and the benefit of a great number of souls... Truly, how ungrateful my soul would be to resist God's will any longer. Nothing will stop me any longer, be it persecutions, sufferings, sneers, threats, entreaties, hunger, cold, flattery, friendships, adversities, friends or enemies; be it things I am experiencing now or things that will come in the future or even the hatred of hell - nothing will deter me from doing the will of God.

I am not counting on my own strength, but on His omnipotence for, as He gave, me the grace of knowing His holy will, He will also grant me the grace of fulfilling it. I cannot fail to mention how much my own lower nature resists this thing, manifesting its own desires, and there results within my soul a great struggle, like that of Jesus in the Garden of Olives. And so I too cry out to God, the Eternal Father, 'If it is possible, take this cup from me, but, nevertheless, not my will, but Yours be done, O Lord; may Your will be done.' What I am about to go through is no secret to me, but with full knowledge I accept whatever You send me, O

Lord. I trust in You, O merciful God, and I wish to be the first to manifest to You that confidence which You demand of souls.'... One thing alone holds me back, and that is holy obedience. O my Jesus, You urge me on the one hand and hold me back and restrain me on the other. In this, too my Jesus, may Your holy will be done."

(Diary, Notebook I, para. 615).

Despite her complete interior readiness. Sister Faustina was not, however, able to conquer herself sufficiently to take the step of leaving her beloved Congregation of her own free will. She was waiting for circumstances which would facilitate it for her. Her superior, though full of goodwill, felt helpless. For the problem presented difficulties not only for Sister Faustina. Her superiors, too, did not know how to find a solution to the situation. The Congregation had absolutely no reason to expel her. On the contrary, she was a very positive element within it. The matter could not be resolved at the level of the convent in Vilnius. At the end of March, 1936, the Superior General transferred her from Vilnius, and, after some weeks in Walendow and in Derdy, Sister Faustina went permanently to Cracow.

Matters now began to move fast. In the second half of June of that year Sister Faustina told Father Andrasz that she had taken a final decision without waiting for his approval: she would leave the Congregation and take the first steps towards founding a new congregation. Father Andrasz did not oppose her:

"Know that these are hard and difficult things. Your principal spiritual director is the Holy Spirit. We can only give direction to these inspirations, but your real director is the Holy Spirit. If you yourself have decided to leave, Sister, I neither prohibit nor order you to do so.

245

You take the responsibility for yourself. I say this to you, Sister: you can begin to take action. You are capable of doing so, and therefore you c a n do so. These things are indeed probable; all you have told me up to now [before perpetual vows in Cracow in 1933] *speaks in favor of taking action. Still, you have to be very careful in all this. Pray much and ask that I be given light.'*

(Diary, Notebook II, para. 658).

In mid-September, Archbishop Jałbrzykowski came to Cracow, and Sister Faustina had the opportunity to speak to him again about her affairs. His advice was much more generalised than that of Father Andrasz:

'He showed himself very favorably disposed to this cause of mercy: 'Sister, be completely at peace; if this is within the plans of divine providence, it will come about. In the meantime, Sister, pray for a clear outward sign. Let the Lord Jesus give you a clearer knowledge of this. I beg you to wait a little in such a way that everything will turn out all right.''

(Diary, Notebook II, para. 693).

Additional light is thrown on the course of events and over a wider sphere by Father Sopoćko:

"While she was in Cracow, Sister Faustina in her letters to me frequently raised this subject and asked for my advice... I counselled caution and recommended that she inform her confessor and superiors... At a certain time, Sister Faustina wrote that she had already received permission from her superior general and her confessor, with the condition that I give my permission. I wrote back that for me the permission

*alone of her superiors was not sufficient for me. I
would agree if she received a clear order to leave the
congregation, and only in those circumstances. She
never did receive such a directive; she remained in her
Congregation and died in it."*

(Archives of S.F., Recollections).

No, indeed, Sister Faustina never left her community.
Not because she did not wish to, but circumstances did
not permit. A complication arose which made it impossible to undertake any kind of further action: illness.
Her health, which had never been too strong, worsened
to the extent that the last two years of her life should
more properly be called a slow death. The tuberculosis
which had for years undermined her health finished its
ruinous assault. Sister Faustina, exhausted in the
extreme, passed her time between the hospital and the
convent. She died in the Cracow house of her congregation, brought there from the hospital some days before
her death, and said farewell to her companions and
was bidden farewell by them according to the nuns'
customs. To the end of her life Sister Faustina remained as Sister Faustina of the Blessed Sacrament
in the Congregation of Sisters of Our Lady of Mercy.

The last stages of her life pose a problem that is
difficult to solve. They place a large question mark over
the genuineness or the significance of the last appearance of Jesus. Fortunately, the answer to the
question was supplied by Sister Faustina herself, and
Father Sopoćko has given it:

*"When I saw her on her deathbed... I told her that
the demand that she leave her Congregation to found
a new one was an illusion and I asked her to pray
for that intention. I would come the next day and
request an answer.*

*On the following day I said Mass for this intention,
during which some thoughts or interior inspirations
came to me, that just as Sister Faustina herself could*

not paint the image of the Merciful Jesus, so she herself could not found a new congregation. But because of the terrible times approaching, such a congregation was needed.

When, in the evening of that day, I visited Sister Faustina again,... I asked her if she could give me an answer to the question I had asked her the day before. Sister Faustina considered for a moment, and then said: "Father, you received the answer today during Mass; I do not need to say anything more."

(Archives of S.F., Recollections).

Sister Faustina explained to Father Sopoćko not only the significance of the last revelation of Jesus, she also described exactly the place where the first convent would stand and what its beginnings would look like:

"When I visited her in the last days of her life in the hospital at Pradnik ...she told me then... that she had had a vision that I was receiving the vows of the first six members of the new congregation in a small wooden chapel. In fact, in 1944 in Vilnius on 16th November I did receive the first private vows from six women who had decided to serve God in the new congregation, and in addition to the usual three vows they made a fourth, to propagate the devotion to the Divine Mercy... And the vows were made in the wooden chapel of the Carmelite Sisters...

She also told me that she saw the first convent of the congregation, a large but poor house, with a great spirit within it and it stood beside a church... When, in 1947, I visited the house of the new congregation (Handmaids of Divine Mercy) in Mysliborz near Gorzow, I saw that everything confirmed what she had said, exactly."

(Archives of S.F., Recollections).

What her rôle was to be in the erection of a new congregation, Sister Faustina understood only in the last period of her life. This knowledge was not at all caused by resignation from it, due to illness. It was the result of a spiritual maturity attained not long before her death. As always, she ready to do everything that Jesus asked. But He did not permit her to make this greatest sacrifice - He accepted just the readiness to make it. This last gift of Jesus' love, allowing her to remain in the congregation where she had completed her lifetime's vocation, was, for Sister Faustina at the end of her life, a source of additional deep joy, which shone through even the most severe physical sufferings. The then Superior of the Cracow convent, Mother Irene Krzyżanowska, wrote movingly of this, and she stated that previously:

"...I often saw her upset that the matter of the Feast of Divine Mercy was progressing so slowly, as indeed was the whole cultus of the Divine Mercy. One could observe much uneven behaviour: sometimes she was very happy, other times sadder, which had not been the case before...

"When she come back from [the hospital in] *Pradnik,"* Mother Irene continued, *"I liked to visit her in her isolation ward, for our sick Sister was so peaceful and had such strange charm. How she had changed! She took all anxieties over the whole question of the Divine Mercy calmly, submitting to the will of God: "There will be a Feast of Divine Mercy, I see it; I want only the will of God."*

"In our conversation, when she spoke of another congregation I said to her that the Divine Mercy would not leave us. She did not disagree..."

(Archives of S.F., Recollections).

When we observers on the sidelines look at the spiritual journeys of Sister Faustina, it is hard to resist the thought that God put her to a similar test to that He had given Abraham in times of old. Both in the case in the Old Testament and in this, a gift offered by God Himself as a mark of special grace had to be given back to Him. There was a demand that one strip oneself of attachment to the greatest of God's gifts in the name of pure love for Him and of the blind obedience that such a love dictated. From Abraham God demanded the sacrifice to Him of his only son Isaac, that son of a special promise. From Sister Faustina, the leaving of the Congregation to which He had Himself directed her steps, and in which she had received all His graces and gifts.

At the last moment, with Abraham and with Sister Faustina, God withdrew His demand. For it was not the deed He desired, but the readiness to do it. In both cases, the action required was the breaking of the last links which were connected, not with God Himself, but with what He had given. A gift, for man, may not be as important and dear to the heart as the Giver Himself.It was to be only a gift. For the goal of love can only be God. And even as Sister Faustina attained that level, and God obtained what He desired, He left her in the Congregation of Sisters of Our Lady of Mercy. To remain there was her vocation.

The matter did not concern her alone. Sister Faustina never obtained anything only for herself. Besides her, her partner was the Congregation. It was also important for it, that she remain a member till the end of her life, so that her vocation should be accomplished there usque ad finem. For by the will of God, Sister Faustina was to be the source of a new grace for it, and the pattern on which its spirituality was to develop afresh. Before her death, Sister Faustina spoke quite openly with Mother Krzyżanowska of this role she was to have in the Congregation. We learn from the Mother's words that:

"to my question, whether she was happy to die in our Congregation or not, she answered, "Yes. For all the sufferings I have had because of this, dear Mother, you will have great joy here on earth."

During her last illness she said: "I am glad to have

250

this disease... Dear Mother, you will see that the congregation will be very happy because of me".

"She did not speak to the Sisters about the extraordinary grace she had received, but she only said before she died, to me: "Jesus wishes to exalt me and the Congregation will have many joys because of me." She said these words with such simplicity and so kindly and emotionally that I could not sense the slightest shade of vanity."

(Archives of S.F., Recollections).

The words of Sister Faustina quoted by Mother Krzyżanowska bring back a memory. They recall a certain experience of hers some time in the period 1929-1931, and now they have risen to the rank of a symbol of the highest union of the Congregation with God.

"One day Jesus said to me,'I am going to leave this house... because there are things here which displease Me.' And the Host came out of the tabernacle and came to rest in my hands and I, with joy, placed it back in the tabernacle. This was repeated a second time, and I did the same thing. Despite this, it happened a third time, but the Host was transformed into the living Lord Jesus, who said to me, 'I will stay here no longer!' At this, a powerful love for Jesus rose up in my soul. I answered, "And I, I will not let You leave this house, Jesus!" And again Jesus disappeared while the Host remained in my hands. Once again I put it back in the chalice and closed it up in the tabernacle. And Jesus stayed with us."

(Diary, Notebook I, para. 44).

Inter alia, the task of Sister Faustina was to ensure that Jesus was in the Congregation in the fullest possible sense. She was to show this active Congregation the "little way" of the contemplative life, one possible to adopt amid the duties of every day. For this first congregation devoted to the cultus and deeds of mercy was, by the will of God, the matrix from which the devotion to the Divine Mercy would spread to the souls of sinners and inflame sacrificial souls to offer themselves to God for the sins of mankind. This does not at all preclude the existence of other communities with similar aims, such as those desired by Jesus. Saint Francis was only one person, yet he inspired many Franciscan families. Why should Sister Faustina not inspire similarly?

SISTER FAUSTINA'S ILLNESS

Sister Faustina's great spiritual development did not go hand in hand with physical vitality. She obtained her strength from other sources, and other factors decided her fate. Physically she was rather slight, and in addition while she was young, she developed tuberculosis, which was not diagnosed for the first few years. And because her constitution was particularly sensitive and susceptible to attacks of this disease, unchecked it undermined her strength, until at last it passed into the acute form known as galloping consumption with metastases in the intestines, and this, in the last three years of her life, quickly completed the destructive action of the disease.

So this ill-health was not the decisive factor in the spiritual growth of Sister Faustina. The motive power of her religious life was her deep emotional commitment, which mobilized her will to a constant and heroic effort to extend herself in aiming for her goal, to be with God. Every situation in life was, for her, the material from which to make spiritual growth. Even her final three-year illness, which in bitter suffering brought her body to complete emaciation, could not make her will falter. She pressed on with that same iron determination toward Him whom she loved as if, in spite of her illness, she was sufficiently strong to lead to Him countless sinful souls won for Him by her prayer and sacrifice.

If one wants to understand Sister Faustina properly, it is essential to look at her in wider scope, and to see her placed in the context of her daily life. An important element of that life amidst the normal daily matters, was her illness. Chronic in nature, and for a long time not outwardly obvious, it made a significant mark, both on her physical and her spiritual life. Only in the light of the illness - which changes the proportions of everything - can one understand the heroism of her efforts and her great love of God. Therefore it is necessary to begin by looking carefully at the psychological and physical reserves Sister Faustina possessed, and how she made use of them.

This is not easy. Suffering was a very real element in the life of Sister Faustina, but it was also greatly differentiated. In her, physical, mental, and strictly spiritual sufferings all encountered each other, arising from a variety of causes and had such mutual effects that it is often difficult to disentangle what was purely physical, what had a spiritual origin, and which was the effect of what.

We know that her health was poor and that she died of tuberculosis, but we also know that many of her physical sufferings had their source in various kinds of mystical experiences; in addition, a sensitive nervous system reacted so strongly to mental stimuli that it had an adverse effect on her physical wellbeing in a way that was sometimes painful. Now it becomes necessary to place all these stimuli to Sister Faustina's person in some logically arranged picture, so that their mutual interdependence and cooperation may be shown.

Let us begin with the tuberculosis, for this was the chief illness which consumed her for almost half her religious life and finally cut it short when she was only 33 years old.

At that time, tuberculosis was so universal in Poland - in all social classes - that to combat it was one of the chief problems of public health with which the young State had to contend in its care for the nation. For it had become a social disease. The situation was the more serious because the population, though it was panic-stricken in its fear of the disease (and sick people carefully hid from others the fact they were infected with it), understood only the acute form. Few realized that tuberculosis is such a dangerous disease because it is deceptive. It attacks young persons most readily, those who are strong: thus for a long period it goes unnoticed by the sick person and by those around him, and this is due to the illusion of health given by the first stage of the disease. The patient has shining eyes, rosy cheeks and displays considerable physical vitality, and this has often misled even the medical profession. This superficial appearance of good health is due to a slightly sub-feverish state, which may go on for years, until the disease, at some dramatic moment, reveals how it has ravaged the body. When Sister Faustina was alive, the illness continued for years with the then known drugs, and only at a late stage general prostration took place. Unfortunately, by then its ravages were irreversible. The patient was lucky if the disease could be arrested. His health was lost for good.

As far as Helena Kowalska is concerned, in her childhood and early youth there seems to have been no trace of tuberculosis, in her or in any member of her immediate family. Even later, when she had left the family home, we do not find that anyone close to her had suffered from the disease. Therefore she did not take the disease from her home. From all we know, she left it healthy and sturdy. Her employer at the time she was in Lodz calls her plump, and her last employer before she entered the convent, Mrs Lipszyc, also confirms that when Helena entered her service she was a strong and healthy girl.

Nevertheless it was while she was in that post that the first symptoms of ill health in the hitherto strong constitution of Helena did first appear. We hear the description of Helena as a *"skinny little thing"* for the first time, from the lips of Mother Michael, who went to the parlour when the girl, on her arrival in Warsaw, came to ask to be allowed to enter. The word *"skinny"* alone does not mean much, and may have various meanings not connected with health alone, when placed in the context of the Mother's opinion. Mother Michael had added that she seemed *"shabby"*. At all events, it was the first warning sign, which we must note. A year later, when Helen had come to the convent, her companions also thought she looked poorly. We learn that she was always, from the beginning, weaker than her other contemporaries, and that she performed her duties with a certain difficulty. Why? we must ask. What could be the cause of this? After all, she was a country girl, used to manual work. But after just a couple of weeks of the religious life she looked so poorly that Mother Superior sent her for rest and recuperation to nearby Skolimow, where the nuns had a small house.

The first supposition that springs to mind is that the rapid exhaustion she was suffering from was in large measure of a nervous origin and arose from her entry into the convent, the total change in life-style, and Helena's hesitation as to whether she had chosen the right community for herself. It seems probably to be so. All those factors could have had a marked effect on the sensitive constitution of the young postulant, but at the same time it must be obvious that the health of Helena when she crossed the threshold of the convent was no longer of the best, if its equilibrium could be so easily shattered. Something must have seriously undermined her health already. But what?

Her nature was austere and self-denying, and to limit her food or hours of sleep, or to have some greater or smaller mortification was something she was quite used to. Throughout her religious life she was constantly inhibited by her superior and her confessor from undertaking too severe ascetic practices. Her employers stated that this asceticism was early developed in her character. The teenaged Helena amazed her employer in Lodz by rigorously observing fasts, not only one-day fasts, but throughout the whole period of Lent. She herself said that she had become used to this at home. Nevertheless, at home there was a mother to oversee everything and to make sure that a proper proportion was kept and no excesses permitted. But when Helen as a teenaged girl went to work and was responsible for herself, her youthful fervent piety seems to have propelled her at times to excessive multiplication of sacrifices for her beloved Lord. A lack of experience did not correct, with necessary commonsense, the promptings of her sacrificial love. Lent was universally kept strictly in Poland at that time, so that her employers' being struck by Helena's way of keeping Lent gives rise to the suspicion that the girl did so without a sense of proportion and to excess, which, in a short space of time, undermined her health.

An interesting observation of Sister Z., who was asked to look after Helen during her postulancy in Warsaw, confirms that she was insufficiently nourished:

"At the time, I was sitting in the refectory at the table of the postulants, and I was taking care that each ate enough. When Sister Faustina came to the refectory, she sat opposite me, and I then noticed that she took very little food onto her plate. I do not know if she always ate so little; she said she did. Seeing this, I helped her to some more, so that she had a normal portion. At first she refused it, then she wept and her tears fell on the plate, but she ate what I had put on it, and she made herself eat, so that later she ate normally."

But let us not lay too much emphasis on Helena's excessive fasts. Perhaps if this were the only factor undermining her physical strength, it would not have ended in tuberculosis. But it was a factor which weakened a still growing body, and when Helena entered the convent her strength was already to some extent impaired. Sister J. recalls that even at the time of her novitiate she was "slight and anaemic", she had problems with her work in the kitchen; "She had to gasp for breath and became weak. She lost weight." It sometimes happened that the Directress of Novices would dispense her from going for a walk, as causing her too much effort, etc.

Halfway through her novitiate, a new factor emerges, which led to her marked exhaustion. Namely, it was at that time that Sister Faustina began her mystical nights, which lasted for almost six months from the time of her first annual vows. This long-lasting spiritual experience affected her physically to such an extent that all who surrounded her were full of sympathy for the obvious change within her.

Here we have for the first time in the life of Sister Faustina such an evident connection between the spiritual and the physical factors. As her difficult vocation in life developed, the spiritual factor had increasing influence on her physique, so it becomes more difficult to estimate correctly her real state of health. The symptoms she displayed would sometimes mislead those around her, focusing their attention in the wrong direction. The severe spiritual trials during Sister Faustina's novitiate caused her additional exhaustion, and an exhausted body has insufficient resistance. so that any infection can take hold and develop. This is what now occurred. The illness did not take long to manifest itself, and because it was not immediately diagnosed, it is impossible to say when, exactly, it began.

Tuberculosis has this specific feature: it can lie dormant in someone for years, inactive or weakly active, until favourable circumstances stir it into development. In Sister Faustina, those circumstances were now operative. As she notes in the Diary:

'When I fell sick after my first vows and when, despite the kind and solicitous care of my Superiors and

*the efforts of the doctor, I felt neither better nor worse,
remarks began to reach my ears which inferred that I
was making believe.'*

(Diary, Notebook I, para. 67).

The same statement was made by her a few years
later during Sister Faustina's conversation with Sister
D., when the latter complained the doctors did not
believe in her illness.

*"For three years, they treated me, too, for nerves
and did not treat my lungs"*, she observed then.

(Archives of S.F., Recoll.)

It is a fact that the lady doctor to the community
did not diagnose anything seriously wrong with her.
She ascribed everything to anaemia, general exhaustion
and over-sensitive nerves, and accordingly she prescribed restoratives, which of course gave no results. There
is no summary treatment for tuberculosis. Treatment in
general, and particularly in those years, was very
lengthy and above all demanded absolute rest. The
treatment given to Sister Faustina was tonic medicines
and additional nourishment. This undiagnosed
commencement of the tuberculosis not only decided the
fate of Sister Faustina's future health; it also affected
her relationship with certain sisters. From this time
onward, she suffered because of the renewed suspicions
that the discomforts of which she complained were
exaggerated, and that she was trying, by taking refuge
in illness, to create conditions to give herself more time
for prayer, for which it was known she longed. A time
of hidden martyrdom began, because once the view had
become established that she was over-sensitive and
exaggerated her illness, it accompanied her from one
convent to another. These rumours persisted even when
signs of the disease were clearly evident externally.
But it is difficult to fault those sisters, since the view

mentioned originated with the physician. In particular, those periods in which the disease seemed somewhat in abeyance and her temperature fell almost to normal (when Sister Faustina, despite her lack of strength, heroically concealed, went to her normal daily work) deceived those around her. They saw her pale drawn face but merely thought it the trace of an illness which would disappear when she became stronger. Therefore the superiors tried to make her stronger and ordained additional meals for Sister Faustina. She also received certain dispensations in the convent life, when on occasion she requested them: to be allowed to go to bed earlier, to rest in the daytime, etc. But even these requests of hers caused surprise because she had previously exhibited physical endurance.

From the time of her first vows, which is officially regarded as the commencement of her illness, the tuberculosis progressed inexorably. Two years later, when Sister Faustina was in Płock, the changes in her were obvious, but the diagnosis had not yet been made. A brief circumstantial remark of Sister B. illustrates the situation very well. She noticed that when she asked Sister Faustina to run an errand for her, the latter went to do it clinging onto the handrail of the stairs. Seeing this, her companion realized *"how ill and suffering she must be"*.

Indeed, the worsening of her health was so evident that the superior transferred her for some time to healthier country surroundings and lighter work at the daughter house of Płock, in Biała. But this did not bring about the desired results. Sister Faustina had to lie down more often; it was more difficult for her to carry out her daily duties. She did not give in to weakness, however, and did not complain, trying to lead the normal community life. How difficult this was can be judged from the words of Sister S., who says she heard Sister Faustina and saw how

"when it was hard for her and she had no more strength, she would throw herself on the ground in

*the form of a cross before Jesus and say: "Jesus, are
You there or not?" And she would hear (or feel) a
voice saying, I am, and I see everything, which
filled Sister Faustina, as she said, with peace and
joy."*

Sister Faustina did not regain her normal strength
when in 1932 she travelled to Warsaw before making
her third probation prior to offering her perpetual vows.
Weakness was now a daily occurrence. For the five
months the probation lasted, she worked in the clothing
store with Sister Z., who openly complained of the
uselessness of her helper:

*"I was displeased, because I was supposed to have
a helper, but the whole weight of the duty fell upon
me alone. In addition I could not use her for any
heavier work, because she went to bed and could do
no more, because she was ill. God ordered natters so
that neither could the doctors find anything serious
nor could the analysis of her sputum show anything."*

Since several sisters recall that analysis of the
sputum revealed nothing, there seems to be an indication that she was not yet suffering from open tuberculosis, but that this was a gradual process which had
not reached the disintegrative stage. The disease had
nevertheless overtaken her body, which because of her
intensive spiritual life and hard work, had not enough
strength to resist. This state of affairs lasted for
another year. In July 1934, a sharp infection caused
several sisters in the Vilnius house to take to their
beds. Among them was Sister Faustina.

Every additional infection in a patient with tuberculosis is life-threatening. It can cause the tuberculosis
to accelerate from the chronic to the disintegrative
phase. What happened in the case of Sister Faustina?

About two weeks after she had risen from her
sick-bed, one evening Sister Faustina suddenly became

ill. The incident is clearly recalled by Sisters Ch., A., L., W., and J. This was like an attack of asthma, so the convent's physician was hastily summoned. The sick woman herself, thinking that she was dying, asked that Father Sopoćko should be sent for. Her request surprised the sisters, because there was a priest at hand, while Father Sopoćko lived at a distance. But as the state of the patient gave cause for concern, her wish was granted and Father Sopoćko came with the holy oils. Sister Faustina describes the event in detail in her Diary:

"A sudden illness - a mortal suffering. It was not death, that is to say, a passing over to real life, but a taste of the sufferings of death... Suddenly, I felt sick, I gasped for breath, there was darkness before my eyes, my limbs grew numb - and there was a terrible suffocation. Even a moment of such suffocation is extremely long... There also comes a strange fear, in spite of trust. I wanted to receive the last sacraments, but it was extremely difficult to make a confession even though I desired to do so. A person does not know what he is saying; not finishing one thing, he begins another... After I received the last sacraments there was a definite improvement. I remained alone. This lasted for half an hour and then came another attack; but this one was not so strong, as the doctor intervened... The next day, I felt very weak, but experienced no further suffering."

(Diary, Notebook I, paras. 321,323,324).

It is not quite clear what was diagnosed. It seems it was a severe sunstroke, which is likely with her work in the garden. A healthy person generally gets over this without trace, but the consequences in a patient with tuberculosis can be catastrophic. The severe symptoms of sunstroke in Sister Faustina were, happily, controlled, thanks to immediate medical aid. But she remained so weakened that she had to stay in bed for a few days. The attack took place on 12th August, but by 15th, the Feast of the Assumption of the Blessed Virgin, she was still unable even to attend Mass. But were the consequences limited only to continuing weakness?

The Sister Infirmarian was, at the time, Sister Chrysostom, a professional nurse, who regarded the statements of the patient as exaggerated and semi-imagined. She did not take this sudden weakness seriously, nor did she take care to have Sister Faustina more thoroughly examined after the attack. It was only when Sister Amelia became Infirmarian that she took Sister Faustina to be examined and to have an X-ray of the lungs. Then the whole truth came out: Dr. Zielinski, the pulmonary specialist, diagnosed advanced tuberculosis of the lungs.

So at some time in the autumn of 1934 it was already known that Sister Faustina had tuberculosis. The doctor thought it was no new process, and that the disease had been ravaging her for some considerable time. It is not possible to establish how far the sunstroke worsened her state of health.

Learning of the disease, Sister Faustina's superiors took care to fortify her with additional food. However, she was not dispensed from working in the garden; she lay down at those times she felt particularly ill, which happened fairly often, for her strength left her quickly, and work in the garden was not light. It is amazing that she could do it at all, much less achieve the good results she did. It is true that the wards given to her to help quickly realized that Sister Faustina had not much strength, and as they specially loved and respected her they voluntarily tried to help all they could. Of their own initiative, they often did some additional work, happy that they would be able to give her a surprise and save her effort.

Tuberculosis is not only a disease of the lungs, though it is primarily known as that. More rarely, and usually in secondary form, it attacks particular internal organs. In Sister Faustina it attacked the intestines.

Tuberculosis of the intestines is a frequently met form of the disease, because the patient infects himself. The infection reaches the intestines together with the saliva swallowed by the patient, and with phlegm which has not been entirely spat up. It is especially hard to bear, for it causes severe pains and quickly emaciates, making normal feeding impossible. The tuberculous foci spread thickly over the intestines, approaching the peritoneum. Even when they do not attack it directly, but only some neighbouring tissue, any touch on the peritoneum dramatically increases the already severe pains. The pains come in waves associated with the process of digestion. About two hours after a meal, when the food reaches the intestines, the patient writhes in a paroxysm of suffering, when the pains may only be controlled by the strongest painkillers.

These sufferings were the lot of Sister Faustina. It is impossible to understand how she was able, in an attack of pain of the sort described, to rise from her bed, and, in moments of relief, go to her normal duties. She sometimes swayed on her feet with weakness, and walked holding on to the walls, but in spite of this, when her condition was not noticed and she was asked for some service, she would give it as if nothing was the matter, with a cheerful smiling face. It is heroism of the sort demanded from those who are tortured, with this difference, that the torture is caused, not by human spite, but by illness. Dr Silberg, the pulmonary specialist and director of the sanatorium where Sister Faustina twice lay ill, understood the behaviour of this nun correctly. He treated her quite differently from all his other patients, although there were also some nuns among them. He applied completely different criteria and assessment to her case. He saw that the illness was the source of new values, not a disaster; that in applying physical help it was also necessary to take care not to damage this source. He himself, a recent convert to the Catholic Church, could not and did not wish to make it difficult for her to practise her faith in the way appropriate for her, which aroused in him the highest respect and wonder. He therefore took upon himself the responsibility, not only for her treatment, but for the greatness of effort permitted to her, which conflicted with the treatment.

"It is very serious and incurable," he stated, *"but Sister Faustina is an exceptional religious, so I do not pay attention. Anyone else in her state would not get up* (to attend Mass in the chapel).

I cannot forbid her to do so... Whenever I visit her, she is always smiling. It is not easy to smile amidst such sufferings", he said, shaking his head in great surprise.

Dr Silberg correctly surmised what the essential remedy was for Sister Faustina, which could not be forbidden her. This is what she herself says in the Diary:

"I find myself so weak that were it not for Holy Communion I would fall continually. One thing alone sustains me, and this is Holy Communion. From it I draw my strength; in it is all my comfort. I fear life on days when I do not receive Holy Communion. I fear my own self... From the tabernacle I draw strength, power, courage and light. Here I seek consolation in time of anguish. I would not know how to give glory to God if I did not have the Eucharist in my heart."

(Diary, Notebook III, para. 1037).

But let us not race ahead. Sister Faustina was in the sanatorium for the first time from the beginning of December 1936 until the end of April 1937, and for the second time from the end of April 1938 until mid-September of that year. Before we discuss this in detail, we should consider when it was that the tuberculosis attacked her intestines.

She had had certain digestive difficulties for a very long time. Sister K., who was with her in Vilnius during both her stays there, i.e. in 1929 and in 1933-1936, recalls that she had already noticed that Sister Faustina sometimes, for reasons of health, could not eat certain dishes *"and would then ask for something else instead."*

Also, Sister J., who ran the kitchen in the Vilnius house at the time when Sister Faustina was working in the garden there, remembers that when tuberculosis had already been diagnosed and she was therefore receiving additional food, it often happened that she would go to the kitchen herself to ask for something else to keep her strength up, *"as she felt so weak that she could not do her work"*. At another time, she asked if she could exchange a dish which did not suit her, for some other.

Sister Faustina herself gives us an additional key to the understanding of this situation. As she once confessed to Sister J. *"she had asked as a great grace from God, that Jesus should take away her sense of taste"*. Sister J. witnessed that *"the taking of food is, for her, a mortification."*

This symptom of the lack of a sense of taste is an important indication. It is evidence of a significant malfunction in digestion, since it led to a chronic loss of taste. In the circumstances of Sister Faustina, when the fortifying of her constitution depended on intensive nourishment, this was an especially unwelcome symptom. Where the digestion is impaired, no food can have the desired effect, and the absence of taste indicates that there was such malfunction.

Therefore, Sister Faustina rapidly lost strength. Eighteen months later she had great difficulty in performing her daily duties. Sister S., the superior's deputy in Derdy, where Sister Faustina in April 1936 worked for a few weeks in the kitchen, recalls that she sent Faustina for two hours daily to rest on the veranda, after the lunch-time recreation, so that she would have enough strength to continue her afternoon's work.

In mid-May 1936, Sister Faustina went to Cracow permanently. There, at the request of the superior, Sister B., the qualified nurse who was then the Infirmarian took our patient to be examined at the pulmonary clinic at the hospital in Pradnik, and later accompanied her to out-patient treatment at this clinic.

After she arrived, Sister Faustina was given work in the garden, to help Sister K.

This was work beyond her strength, but she did not complain, and she even managed to do it well, although she was obviously ravaged by the disease: so well that she often amazed Sister K. by her brave physical endurance. *"Even when she had a fever, she worked without complaint,"* said Sister K. Sister A. also describes Sister Faustina's unusual bravery. She saw how, in September 1936,

"she was making pickles for the winter, down in the cellar. It was obvious that she had a disease of the lungs. Her lips were chapped and as if swollen, and the skin was peeling off. I was full of respect for this sick sister, hidden in the cellar on that sunny day."
(Archives of S.F., Recollections).

But the most beautiful witness to the behaviour of Sister Faustina at that time is given by Sister B., who, as Infirmarian, best knew the state of her health:

"She would not submit to her illness, and whenever she was not confined to bed she went about her usual duties, trying to fulfil her obligations as best she could. Her cheerfulness, peacefulness and spiritual equilibrium in the face of the difficulties her illness

brought her, were astounding. She never complained, though she was often obviously exhausted. She did not allow those around her to know what she suffered, and even the superiors did not realize her state."
(Archives of S.F., Recollections).

Indeed, even Mother Irene Krzyżanowska, then superior of the Cracow convent, who was always so kind and helpful as regards the mission of Sister Faustina, was deceived by her patient and equable behaviour. Sister B. was amazed to hear once, how the superior said to the Mother General, *"Maybe Sister Faustina will at last begin to work on herself."* What could she have had in mind? She was inwardly puzzled.

Sister Faustina felt the lack of comprehension in her superior. This did not cause her any bitterness, though it was surprising and not easy to understand. She writes in the Diary:

"Our Mother Superior has great love of neighbour and especially great love for the sick sisters, as everybody knows. And yet, as regards me, it is extraordinary that the Lord Jesus has permitted that she not understand me and that she test me much in this respect... Once, when I was very tired and in much pain, I told Mother Superior about it and received the answer that I should get used to suffering."
(Diary, Notebook II, para. 700).

It is difficult, among the short remarks scattered in the recollections of Sister Faustina's companions, to be sure of the time when the tuberculosis had completely invaded her intestines. This disease usually develops slowly and imperceptibly. As those around her were long aware that Sister Faustina had for some time had digestive problems, the increasing severity of the disease escaped their notice. There were greater or smaller pains which could be overcome. The first description of an acute attack of pain in the abdomen is given by Sister Faustina in her Diary, under the date 24th September 1936:

"Mother Superior ordered me to say one decade of the rosary in place of all the other exercises, and to go to bed at once. As soon as I lay down I fell asleep, for I was very tired. But a while later, I was awakened by suffering. It was such a great suffering that it prevented me from making even the slightest movement; I could not even swallow my saliva. This lasted for about three hours. I thought of waking up the novice sister who shared my room, but then I thought, 'She cannot give me any help, so let her sleep. It would be a pity to wake her...' When the suffering ceased, I began to perspire. But still I could not move, as the pain would return at each attempt. In the morning, I felt very tired, though I felt no further physical pain. Still I could not get up to attend Mass.'

(Diary, Notebook II, para. 696).

This attack preceded others. They usually happened at night, a few hours after a meal, when the food left the stomach for the intestines. This night hour was an additional torment for the sick woman, who was compelled to awaken a sleeping companion, or to suffer alone and without help. As we might expect of her, Sister Faustina usually chose the latter course.

Just when her state of health had greatly worsened, there was a change of Infirmarian. In November 1936, Sister B. was transferred to Walendow, and to fill her place came Sister Chrysostom, well known to Sister Faustina from her time in Vilnius, where she had also been infirmarian. For someone so seriously ill as Sister Faustina, to be put in the care of one who for long had adopted a critical attitude, and who thought that *"Sister Faustina spoiled herself, hadn't enough energy, and was giving in to her illness"* etc. (Archives of S.F., Recollections) indicated that she would not have an easy life. It is true that at the beginning of December Sister Faustina went to hospital, but that last month of her stay in the convent was full of additional torment. This extra cross was hard to bear: at times inadequate nursing and humiliations. It was said of her that Sister Faustina was hyper-sensitive, little able to bear pain, etc. Such a judgment is fairly typical of healthy people who have had little to do with the ill and apply their own standards to them. In a qualified nurse this attitude is hard to justify. It must indicate some kind of basic lack of comprehension of the mentality of the sick, and also incompetence in the correct recognition of the symptoms of suffering. Indeed, some of the sisters who were not expert in matters of illness realized the sufferings of Sister Faustina and were angry at her treatment at the hands of the Infirmarian. She herself, however, accepted everything quietly. When once Sister O. in her presence criticized the Infirmarian, Sister Faustina cut short the conversation with the remark: *"All that I have on this earth is my suffering."* This sentence sums up her point of view on the matter.

There was to be, an unexpected great change in the circumstances of the patient. At the beginning of October the physician warned the community that Sister Faustina's illness was at the infectious stage, and recommended that she be separated from other sisters, and two months later proposed that she be taken to the sanatorium for treatment. The superiors agreed at once, and on 9th December she was taken to the hospital. She went unwillingly and anxiously. She no longer felt herself able to cope with new surroundings and conditions. Also, she was entering lay surroundings which were totally foreign to her. She had never, thus far, been inside a hospital. This all seemed to her too great a change, and therefore effort.

12. Interior of the Sanatorium chapel at Prądnik

"Today, I am leaving for Pradnik, just outside Cracow, to undergo treatment. I am to stay there for three months. I am being sent there through the great solicitude of my superiors especially that of our dear Mother General, who is so solicitous for the sisters who are ill. I have accepted the favor of this treatment" - she writes - *"but I am fully resigned to the will of God. Let God do with me as He pleases... When I was somewhat overcome by the fear that I was to be outside the community for so long a time alone, Jesus said to me,* **'You will not be alone, because I am with you always and everywhere. Near to My Heart, fear nothing."***

(Diary, Notebook II, para. 797).

Her stay in hospital proved less arduous than Sister Faustina had expected. She was put in an isolation ward not far from the chapel, which enabled her during the day to go in to say the rosary or to visit the Blessed Sacrament. Jesus in the Eucharist was there as near as He was at home, and to visit Him, though it meant effort, was possible. The effort must have been in fact very great. Patients several times came to the nurses to tell them that Sister Faustina was walking by holding on to the walls, in her weakness.

Sister Faustina unexpectedly found some kindred spirits in the hospital environment. The nursing was done by the Sacred Heart Sisters, people who were, like her, consecrated to God. Both patient and nurses were glad to make each other's acquaintance. The sisters quickly perceived Sister Faustina's unusual spiritual qualities. They looked after her with a truly sisterly affection, with that particular warmth of the community-family. Compared to other patients, she was, for them, a real oasis of the spiritual life, with an intensive atmosphere to which they responded with recognition. Being nurses, they fully understood her severe pains. She bore the worst pains patiently and even cheerfully. She almost never asked for painkillers or sleeping draughts, and when she was given them, she refused them. Her motive was simple: she was too weak to be able to concentrate, and she felt that suffering was the only form of prayer available to her. She therefore did not wish to deprive herself of it. Her prayerful attitude to suffering evoked respect filled with humility for this love and this sacrifice taken to the point of heroism. She became a moral authority for them.

As a patient she was neither difficult nor burdensome. She had no requirements of them, and for as long as she could she did almost everything for herself. The sisters could always, however, make her life pleasant for her. What they did were really trifles, but it showed their care, and that "fullness of heart" of which the Gospel speaks. Even Mother Irene Krzyżanowska, on a visit to her, remarked that it was too pretty for a nun, the private room in which she lay.

Not only the sisters at the hospital appreciated the holiness of Sister Faustina. The patients were also under her spell, for she always had a kind smile for them and an ear ready to listen to their complaints or the problems which illness brought in plenty. Sister F. says, "They admired her goodness, kindness and piety". They loved to be with her, for she did not so much give moral instruction as give them confidence in the Mercy of God for everyone who repents his sins and does penance. She became a symbol of hope to them. She was like a ray of sunshine which fell athwart the lives of troubled people, warming them with the love of God. In addition, she hastened with prayers to the dying, ready to be at their bedside day or night, because she considered this her duty, saying that as there was no priest at hand, the dying had no certain spiritual care. So the fear of death, which distressed the sick of that place with cruel ruthlessness, was lessened by the sight of her slight person, as if she were God's helmsman throwing a line to the drowning man, to draw him safely to the farther shore. There was a radiant strength about her which even the most obdurate could not resist. Who indeed is really hardened in the hour of severe trial such as that of a serious disease? At such a time, everyone has a moment of doubt and despair in the face of the cruel reality of disease and the fate it brings. Sister Faustina had found suitable soil on which to practise mercy and to teach it to others. It is true that after two months in hospital, at the beginning of February 1937, her superior forbade her to be present at death-beds. Sister Faustina then wrote in her Diary:

'I will send to the dying obedience in place of self, and it will support the souls who are dying'.

(Diary, Notebook II, para. 924).

Even the chief medical officer at the hospital, Dr Silberg, was under the God-given spell of this strange patient. The nursing Sisters tell, often repeating the story, how they themselves were full of amazement at his behaviour towards this simple uneducated nun, which was characterized by his deep respect for her personal sanctity and God-given wisdom. Whenever he had a free moment, he hurried to her side ward. Sister A., who only knew Sister Faustina during her second stay in the hospital, tells her story, but other nuns who remember her first stay speak in the same way:

"As infirmarian I paid particular attention to the behaviour of Sister Faustina in hospital, and I observed that although by nature she was serious and had little to say, in some strange way she attracted others and was loved by everybody. Often I met Dr Silberg, the Superintendent of the hospital, when I went to her. He came to Sister Faustina in free moments, as he said, for spiritual conversations: "I come to her for a conference, we talk about various

matters, and I learn a lot from her." Indeed, some-
times they were talking so seriously that when I was
visiting the patient I did not dare to interrupt."

(Archives of S.F., Recoll.)

We have no data on Sister Faustina's treatment. She herself speaks only of being on a veranda. This could not have been usual, for during the first two months she had several considerable rises in temperature, and she then had to keep to her bed. Only at the end of January 1937 was a certain improvement obvious:

"January 27, 1937. I feel considerable improvement in my health. Jesus is bringing me from the gates of death to life, because there was so little left but for me to die, and lo, the Lord grants me the fullness of life. Although I am still to remain in the sanatorium, I am almost completely well.

(Diary, Notebook II, para. 897).

The patient was deceived into thinking that there was a fundamental improvement, that the disease was cured, and that therefore only obedience was keeping her in the hospital. But half-way through February the pains returned to both lungs and intestines. Sister Faustina writes:

"February 15, 1937. Today my suffering increased somewhat: I not only feel greater pain all through my lungs, but also some strange pains in my intestines."

(Diary, Notebook II, para. 953).

Two or three days after the pains had returned, Sister Faustina described something which, although trivial from a medical point of view, does shed some necessary light on the problems of treating her. She had gone to the chapel for meditation. During this, she fell into ecstasy:

"And all of a sudden, my soul was flooded with the light of the knowledge of God... When I returned to my room, it seemed to me that I was coming from real life to death. When the doctor came to take my pulse, ho was surprised: 'Sister, what happened? You have never had a pulse like this! I would like to know what has speeded it up so much.' What could I tell him, when I myself did not know that my pulse was so rapid. I only know that I am dying of yearning for God, but this I did not tell him, for how can medicine help in this instance?"

(Diary, Notebook II, para. 970)

So certain symptoms, occurring now from time to time, cannot be placed in the pattern the doctors have envisaged up to now of the disease from which Sister Faustina is suffering. They also have a tendency to recur. A few days later, Sister Faustina notes:

"Last night I was in such pain that I thought it was the end. The doctors could not diagnose what the sickness was. I felt as if my entrails had been torn to shreds, but after a few hours of such sufferings I am all right."

(Diary, Notebook II, para. 999).

This extract from the Diary is still more astonishing. For unknown reasons the picture of the disease becomes more complicated and obscure. The doctors are at a loss to explain these incomprehensible symptoms.

The explanation for this new morbid phenomenon is given by Sister Faustina in later pages of her diary. The question of medical competence is in suspension, for spiritual factors are the explanation: these sufferings have a mystical origin. Lent had arrived, and

Sister Faustina, whose chief prayer in hospital was - as she wrote - suffering, now joined her sufferings to Christ's Passion, adding the small mortifications possible for her during her illness and in hospital conditions, such as: sleeping without a pillow, not eating enough so that she felt hungry, a daily chaplet of prayer to the Divine Mercy, with crossed arms, and, if possible, other prayers also said with crossed arms. (Diary, Notebook II, para. 934).

Jesus accepted Sister Faustina's sacrifice and allowed her to suffer with Him. Therefore, as Lent passed, her pains increased. They were most severe during Holy Week. Here are Sister Faustina's own words:

*"March 24, 1937. Wednesday of Holy Week... I have felt great suffering in my body, but I feel the Lord is upholding me, for otherwise I would not be able to bear it. March 25, 1937. Holy Thursday. During Holy Mass... the Lord... said to me, **Lean your head on My breast and rest... I shall give you a small portion of My Passion, but do not be afraid, be brave; do not seek relief, but accept everything with submission to My Will...** I earnestly desired to spend the whole night with Jesus in the dark prison cell*. I prayed until eleven o'clock. At eleven, the Lord said to me, **Lie down and take your rest. I have let you experience in three hours what I suffered during the whole night.***

And immediately I went to bed. I had no physical strength left; the suffering had deprived me of it com-

---

* Polish ciemnica, literally "dark cell", denotes both the altar of Maundy Thursday liturgy (Repository) and the prison in which Jesus spent the night of His Passion.

pletely. Throughout all this time I had been in a sort of swoon. Every beat of Jesus' Heart was reflected in my heart and pierced my soul... I was dying with Him, and yet I could not die. But I would not have exchanged that martyrdom for all the pleasures of the whole world. In the course of this suffering, my love grew immeasurably. I know that the Lord was supporting me with His omnipotence, for otherwise I would not have been able to endure it for even a moment."

(Diary, Notebook III, para. 1054).

In addition to the symptoms of suffering here described, there were hidden pains with the features of stigmata (Diary, II, para. 759, II para. 942, III para. 1054, V para. 1399, V para. 1425, VI para. 1619, VI para. 1724).

Because the symptoms of her illness appeared to have become more severe, Dr Silberg decided to keep Sister Faustina in hospital until April. I wonder if he had not at least in part realized their origin, for, despite the fact that these symptoms remained, he gave permission for Sister Faustina to leave hospital at the appointed time.

She arrived home for Easter itself. The sisters were convinced that she had been cured, but the doctor's view was probably not so optimistic. Dr Silberg evidently considered that the disintegrative process had been halted. There might be additional hidden reasons why he gave permission for Sister Faustina to leave hospital. We are compelled to speculate. The only indication is in his method of treating this patient. We know that he took seriously her spiritual needs. We can find such motives in his numerous remarks to nurses, Sister Faustina's companions and her religious superiors. She herself also described certain incidents in which two factors, religious and therapeutic, played a part.

The incidents concern Holy Communion.

A priest took It to the sick three to four times weekly. This was not enough for Sister Faustina. She so longed for Jesus in the Eucharist, to be able to go daily, that she tried to go to the chapel in the mornings. The doctor was opposed to her going out in the morning chill, sometimes in rain or snow, and to the effort involved. He agreed unwillingly, evidently under some compulsion.

'Today, when the doctor making his rounds came to see me, he somehow didn't like the way I looked. Naturally, I was suffering more, and so my temperature had gone up considerably. Consequently, he decided I must not go down for Holy Communion until my temperature dropped to normal... When the doctor left, I said to the Lord, "Jesus, now it is up to You whether I shall go or not"... In the evening I said to the Lord, "Jesus, if my Communions are pleasing to You, I beg You humbly, grant that I have not one degree of fever tomorrow morning." In the morning ... there wasn't even one degree of fever. I jumped to my feet at once and went to Holy Communion. When the doctor came and I told him that I had not had even one degree of fever, and so had gone to Holy Communion, he was surprised. I begged him not to make it difficult for me to go to Holy Communion, for it would have an adverse effect on the treatment. The doctor answered, "For peace of conscience and at the same time to avoid difficulties for yourself, Sister, let us make the following agreement: when the weather is fine, and it isn't raining, and you feel all right, then, Sister, please go; but you must weight these matters in your conscience."

(Diary, Notebook II, para. 878).

Matters of health and spiritual problems in connection with it were discussed by Sister Faustina not only with the doctor, but also with her confessor. We find a reflection of this in her Diary in a note for 22nd January, 1937:

"Today the doctor decided that I am not to go to Mass, but only to Holy Communion. I wanted very much to assist at Mass, but my confessor, in agreement with the doctor, told me to obey. 'It is God's will, Sister, that you should get well, and you must not undertake mortifications of any kind. Be obedient, Sister...' "

(Diary, Notebook II, para. 894).

From the answer of the chaplain, we may conclude that in this matter, which was difficult for him, Dr Silberg only took his final medical decision in many cases after consulting Sister Faustina's confessor.

A fortnight after she arrived home, Sister Faustina became very much worse, and again had to take to her bed. She was evidently surprised by this return of her illness. She had believed she was getting better, and had once more taken up her plan of founding the Congregation asked for by Jesus, when she was again overtaken by physical weakness:

"My spirit is eager to do God's work, but physical strength has left me... On Sunday, April 11, I suddenly became so very ill ... that I had to go to bed. The coughing racked me so much that it seemed to me that if this repeats a few more times, it will surely be the end of me. On April 14, I felt so bad that I barely managed to get up to assist at Holy Mass. I felt much worse than I did at the time they sent me for treatment. There

was wheezing, and there were rattling noises in my lungs and strange pains.'

(Diary, Notebook III, paras. 1085, 1088, 1089).

Sister Faustina was in spiritual confusion. Jesus was urging her to do His will, but when she was ready to do so, a return of her illness made it impossible. What was she to do? And then she had a sudden urge to ask Him for health:

'When I received Holy Communion... it was as if something were urging me to... pray in this manner: 'Jesus, may Your pure and healthy blood circulate in my ailing organism', and may Your pure and healthy body transform my weak body, and may a healthy and vigorous life throb within me, if it is truly Your holy will that I should set about the work in question...' As I was praying in this way, I suddenly felt as if something were jolting my whole organism and, in an instant, I felt completely well. My breath is clear, as if there had never been anything the matter with my lungs, and I feel no pain, and this is a sign for me that I should set about the work... After this return to health, I found myself united with the Lord Jesus in a purely spiritual way... Jesus infused my soul with power and courage to act... Then I heard these words: 'Go tell the superior that you are in good health.'

(Diary, Notebook III, para. 1089 et seq.).

From that moment, there were five weeks without any symptoms of the disease. Sister Faustina had

---

* For "organism" the more usual word in English would be "body" or "constitution". -Translator.

received from Jesus the gift for which she had asked, and she had the possibility of action. But as time went on, doubts began to arise as to whether she had done the right thing in asking for health, although it was for such a good reason. She was not sure whether Jesus would not rather that she served Him by her illness.

The question was of basic importance, and Sister Faustina did not want to leave it unexplained. She did not wish for her own will to be fulfilled, for she had long given that up to the Lord. So once more she confirmed to Him her consent to what His will destined her for.

The result of her prayer was immediate. As if it were only necessary for her to confirm her readiness once again, Jesus accepted the sacrifice. Towards the end of May 1937, the disease returned, and with it all the old sufferings with their former force.

Here, a word of explanation seems needed. It should not be thought that the act of offering God her health inhibited Sister Faustina from doing all that was natural to try to improve it. Her common sense is amazing, and her behaviour shows equilibrium and interior peace, nor is there hesitation one way or the other. With submission to the will of God she accepts what comes, but on her side she does not neglect anything possible in her circumstances to preserve her health. As Sister Brun assures, *"As far as concerned medical treatment or medicines, Sister Faustina did everything she was recommended to do."*

Her superior made a new attempt to help her and sent her to Rabka, a healthy spot in the Carpathian mountainside, for climatic treatment. Sister Faustina, however, was not suited by the air there. Her health grew so much worse that she was sent back to Cracow after not quite a fortnight, and in Cracow, though with obvious effort, she tried to lead a normal religious life, but with certain occasional concessions. She had so much less strength that at the beginning of September Mother Superior sent her from the garden to lighter work, at the gate, and she did this work for six months, until once more she had to enter hospital.

But even such work was beyond the strength of the sick woman. The progress of her disease was such that fulfilling the daily religious duties and the work required Sister Faustina to make a constant heroic effort of will. In her Diary, in various places she mentions how much it cost her to have constantly to overcome her lack of strength and to fight against pain:

"I must be on my guard, especially today, because I am becoming over-sensitive to everything. Things I would not pay any attention to when I am healthy bother me today."

(Diary, Notebook II, para. 783).

"I live from one hour to the next and am not able to get along in any other way. I want to make the best possible use of the present moment, faithfully accomplishing everything that it gives me. In all things, I depend on God with unwavering trust."

(Diary, Notebook V, para. 1400).

But when, two weeks after she had taken up work at the gate, her brother Stanley arrived to ask her advice as to whether he should enter a religious order and, if so, which one, Sister Faustina was so self-controlled, cheerful and smiling that, although he noticed how poorly she looked, she was able to reassure him that it was nothing serious, and that she had easy work that did not make her tired. He went away not suspecting that she had tuberculosis.

But the reality was very different. The devastating process of the disease continued inexorably, and it had all the right conditions to develop because those around her were, as before, often ignorant of the truth, and the infirmarian Sister Chrysostom was still mistrustful. As they gave no help when it was needed, they caused her, despite their intentions, much effort for her exhausted forces. Sister Faustina does not hide this in the Diary. There are some very bitter entries in it:

'It often happens when one is ill, as in the case of Job in the Old Testament, that as long as one can move about and work, everything is fine and dandy; but when God sends illness, somehow or other, there are fewer friends about. But yet, there are some. They still take interest in our suffering and all that, but if God sends a longer illness, even those faithful friends slowly begin to desert us. They visit us less frequently, and often their visits cause suffering. Instead of comforting us, they reproach us about certain things, which is an occasion of a good deal of suffering. And so the soul, like Job, is alone; but fortunately it is not alone, because Jesus - Host is with it. I wish to speak of one more thing that I have experienced: when God gives neither death nor health, and [when] this lasts for many years, people become accustomed to this and consider the person as not being ill. Then there begins a whole series of silent sufferings. Only God knows how many sacrifices the soul makes... At such times, God Himself comes to our rescue, for otherwise the soul would not be able to bear these crosses...'

(Diary, Notebook V, paras. 1509, 1511).

The disease brought ever new torments. The one which now came was especially hard for Sister Faustina to bear:

"For a month now, I have been feeling worse. Every tine I cough I feel my lungs disintegrating. It sometimes happens that I feel the complete decay of my own corpse. It is hard to express how great a suffering this is. Although I fully agree to this with my will, it is nevertheless a great suffering for nature, greater than ~wearing a hair shirt or a flagellation to the point of .ood. I have felt it especially when I was going to the refectory. It took great effort for me to eat anything because food made me sick."

(Diary, Notebook V, para. 1428).

One can imagine what this was to someone as fastidious as Sister Faustina. She shuddered all over with a feeling of disgust, and, unable to believe in it herself, tried to forget the corpse-like odour which nauseated and frightened her. But it was too strong to ignore, and that it was real was soon confirmed by one of her companions:

"One day, I began to doubt as to how it was possible to feel this continual decaying of the body and at the same time to be able to walk and work... One of the sisters came to converse with me. After a minute or two, she made a terribly wry face and said, 'Sister, I smell a corpse here, as though it were decaying. O how dreadful it is!' I said to her, 'Do not be frightened, Sister, that smell of a corpse comes from me.' She was very surprised and said she could not stand it any longer. After she had gone, I understood that God had allowed her to sense this so that I would have no doubt, but that He was no less than miraculously keeping the knowledge of this suffering from the whole community."

(Diary, Notebook V, paras. 1428, 1430).

We are not surprised by this symptom of disease. It appears when there is significant lung decay. The strong fetor of putrefaction coming from the mouth is so nauseating and unbearable for the patient that, in order at least to mask it, hospitals give a deodorant rinse which disinfects the mouth and to some extent takes away the unpleasant odour. But Sister Faustina did not know this.

Among her sufferings, the nights remained the hardest for Sister Faustina, for then the attacks of pain in the abdomen were almost regular. To eat became a real torture:

"All highly seasoned dishes caused me such immense pain that I spent many nights writhing in pain and in tears, for the sake of sinners. However, I asked my confessor what to do: whether I should continue to suffer this for the sake of sinners or ask the superiors for an exception by way of milder food. He decided that I should ask the superiors for milder food."

(Diary, Notebook V, paras. 1428, 1429).

Here we have another confirmation that for Sister Faustina the offering of her health to Jesus was still in force. Neither her fading strength, nor the almost constant pain broke her spirit. She always had this in her mind:

"When one is ill and weak, one must constantly make efforts to measure up to what others are doing as a matter of course. But even those matter-of-course things cannot always be managed. Nevertheless, thank You, Jesus, for everything, because it is not the greatness of the works, but the greatness of the effort that will be rewarded. What is done out of love is not small. I do

*not know why I feel so terribly unwell in the morning;
I have to muster all my strength to get out of bed,
sometimes even to the point of heroism. The thought of
Holy Communion gives me back a little more strength.
And so, the day starts with a struggle and ends with a
struggle. When I go to take my rest, I feel like a soldier
returning from the battlefield."*

(Diary, Notebook IV, para. 1310).

Sister Faustina harboured her strength as she could,
depending on what the day brought. Days could vary.
She limited what she ate to the minimum, not only to
avid the suffering she would afterwards endure, but
also not to disturb others in the night, for she was not
always successful in not waking those with her. So now
not just the progressive illness, but also malnutrition
was destroying her. Despite this, she tried to carry on
with her everyday life. She was now so thin and
changed by the disease that she was painful to contemplate, and she even began to cause antipathy in
certain individuals; Sister K. admits,

*"I met Sister Faustina in Cracow in 1938 in April.
It was at lunch. We were sitting at the same table.
She was already so ill and changed that I did not
know her. Her looks made a very painful impression
on me, for she was very thin and ugly. I thought to
myself that they should not put such a sick sister at
a common table."*

(Archives of S.F., Recollections).

Here it is necessary to return to what I have previously discussed when dealing with the treatment of Sister
Faustina in hospital: the variety of her ailments. They
still cannot all be ascribed to her illness. Just as in the
hospital the doctors were at a loss to explain sometimes
incomprehensible, severe symptoms of suffering, so too

these confused those around her in the convent. Even her superior, Mother Irene Krzyżanowska, very kindly disposed toward Sister Faustina, and the only one who knew of her complicated spiritual life, so different from that of all the other sisters, was mistaken in her appraisal both of the sufferings themselves and of their nature. The picture presented by Sister Faustina must have confused them, for they did not have the key to her soul. This was hidden before others who realized almost nothing of how the illness had become the raw material of her spiritual life. As her physical strength left her, her spiritual strength rose in inverse proportion. Meanwhile the disease overwhelmed her body entirely, and all her vital forces had to be mobilized to counteract the exhausting symptoms. The whole year 1938, almost from the very beginning, was concentrated solely in a constant and exhausting struggle with them. Sister Faustina's prayer underwent a change: from verbal and meditative, it became a prayer of suffering. Almost exclusively it was now the acceptance and oblation of pain suffered, brought to Jesus with the request that He would deign to include it in the total of His suffering which had redeemed the world.

The pains had various causes, and were not connected with each other. To those caused by the disease were joined others - not infrequently - of a mystical nature. Sister A. recalls one kind:

> "Sister Faustina several times had some pains which were physical and internal, the cause of which could not be determined by the doctor who was called. Sister Faustina afterwards told Sister A. who was infirmarian, that no one could cure her of these pains, because she was suffering for those mothers who destroy their unborn babies."
>
> (Archives of S.F.., Recollections).

Another kind of suffering with a mystical nature is recorded by Sister Faustina in the Diary:

'At eight o'clock I was seized with such violent pains that I had to go to bed at once. I was convulsed with pain for three hours; that is, until eleven o'clock at night. No medicine had any effect on me, and whatever I swallowed I threw up. At times, the pains caused me to lose consciousness. Jesus had me realize that in this way I took part in His Agony in the Garden, and that He himself allowed these sufferings in order to offer reparation to God for the souls murdered in the wombs of wicked mothers. I have gone through these sufferings three times now. They always start at eight o'clock in the evening and last until eleven. No medicine can lessen these sufferings. When eleven o'clock comes, they cease by themselves, and I fall asleep at that moment. The following day, I feel very weak.

This happened to me for the first time when I was at the sanatorium. The doctors couldn't get to the bottom of it, and no injection or medicine helped me at all, nor did I myself have any idea of what the sufferings were all about... But now I understand the nature of these pains, because the Lord himself has made this known to me... Yet when I think that I may perhaps suffer in this way again, I tremble. But I don't know whether I'll ever again suffer in this way; I leave that to God. What it pleases God to send, I will accept with submission and love. If only I could save even one soul from murder by means of these offerings!'

(Diary, Notebook IV, para. 1276).

As if this diseased and aching body were capable of re-creating without end new spiritual strengths ready for limitless oblation, to the suffering already described there came, more and more often, hidden stigmatic pains, of which Sister Faustina makes only brief mention in her Diary.

In similar suffering, month after month passed. The winter of 1937/38 had almost gone. Sister Faustina was now more often in bed than up. But it was hard to say to which rank of the community she was to be ascribed: the healthy or the sick. Her position was not clearly defined. She was officially still employed at the gate, but whether she did the work had to depend on her strength and how she felt, for at every request, she was dispensed. Here perhaps the fault lies. It is difficult for a sick person to estimate his own strength properly, and decide what he can and cannot do. For someone with a sensitive conscience, this kind of situation will always give the patient a sense of guilt: did he have the right not to do something? and a doubt: was he allowed to ask for a kindness or not?

Additionally, Sister Faustina had asked Jesus to give her strength only when it was necessary, so that she could take part in the spiritual life of the community: at least in the chief services and retreats, This therefore gave rise to the false impression that her reserves of strength (which no one knew had been obtained in a supernatural way) had been exhausted by excessive prayer at the cost of her work, which she later could not do. The truth was inaccessible to those around her, and so their judgment had to be mistaken. Mother Superior was still confused by the multiplication of symptoms of disease, and at one time would order Sister Faustina to take more care of herself, and at another to control herself and not give in to her sufferings.

"When Mother S. [Irene] visited me a week ago, she said, 'You catch every sickness, Sister, because your system is so weak, but that is not your fault. In fact, if any other sister had that same sickness, she would

*certainly be walking around; whereas you, Sister, must
stay in bed!!"*

(Diary, Notebook V, para. 1555).

It is also not known why and when Sister Faustina
was transferred from treatment by the pulmonary
specialist to the care of the convent visiting physician.
The sick young woman's health dramatically worsened,
and new attacks of pain accompanied by high fever
arrived, which, as Sister Faustina writes,

*are so violent and severe that they cause me to lose
consciousness. When they cause me to faint, and I am
drenched in cold sweat, then they gradually begin to go
away. Sometimes they last three hours or more.*

(Diary, Notebook VI, para. 1633).

*The help of the convent's doctor was then insufficient,
so the superiors decided to approach another doctor, and
he ascertained that my condition was serious and said to
me, "It will not be possible to return you to good health.
We can remedy your condition partially, but complete
recovery is out of the question." He prescribed a medicine
for the pains, and after I had taken it, the major attacks
did not return... The doctor very much wanted me to go
there for a treatment.*

(Diary, Notebook VI, para. 1634).

As we read her Diary with some emotion, sympathy
and a growing sense of admiration, we can observe the
struggle of Sister Faustina with a new, acute phase of
the disease. For Holy Week and the Feast of Easter, as
she had hoped, she remained in the convent. But
directly afterwards, on 27th April 1938 she was sent to
Pradnik for the second time, in a very serious condition. In hospital at first she lay on the veranda, and

dragged herself to chapel in the morning, at least to Communion, for she had insufficient strength to stay for the whole Mass. Her spiritual life, independently of her exhaustion, had an especially intensive course: till mid-June, she made a three-day retreat at the request and under the direction of Jesus Himself, and for the last time in her life she renewed her religious vows.

Completely unexpectedly, and without any comprehensible reason, in the second half of June the Diary suddenly breaks off. Nothing foretells its ending, and it lies incomplete. The text relates current matters, and awaits an entry for the next day. But the next day did not arrive. There must have been a very important reason which caused Sister Faustina to put down her pen. She always treated her writing as one of her basic duties. The last entry she made in the Diary may give us some clue:

"Right away, on the Friday after Corpus Christi, I felt so unwell that I thought the longed-for moment was approaching. I had a high fever and spat up much blood during the night. Yet, I did go to receive the Lord Jesus in the morning, but I could not stay for the Holy Mass. In the afternoon, my temperature dropped suddenly to 35.8 C. I felt so weak that it was as if everything inside me were dying. But when I steeped myself in profound prayer, I understood that it was not yet the moment of deliverance, but only a closer call from my Bridegroom. When I met with the Lord, I said to Him, "You are fooling me, Jesus; You show me the open gate of heaven, and again You leave me on earth." The Lord said to me, "When, in heaven, you see these present days, you will rejoice and will want to see as many of them as possible."

(Diary, Notebook VI, paras. 1786, 1787).

From this description, it would appear that she had probably suffered an internal haemorrhage, which in fact was arrested by a doctor or else stopped spontaneously, but the sick woman never regained enough strength to be able to write. Five weeks later, there was once again such a serious sudden deterioration that the hospital sent for her superior. But this too was overcome. Sister Faustina lived for three and a half more months. But all we know of this period is second-hand. We can only see her through the eyes of others.

THE FIRST FRUITS

"I see clearly that no one can release me from the duty of doing the known will of God. A great lack of health and physical strength is not a sufficient reason and does not release me from this work that the Lord himself is carrying out through me. I am to be just a tool in His hands."

(Diary, Notebook II, para. 787).

These were Sister Faustina's words under the date 1 December 1936, after about eight and a half years of struggling with disease. This statement expresses one of the great truths of her life. Illness never meant a dispensation for her in the performance of duty. It never dispensed her from the responsibility for the mission entrusted to her by Jesus. In her case, it was not to be thought of. She had received her mission when she had already been ill for three years. The time chosen by Jesus to reveal His will in regard to her clearly indicates that He took her illness into account in the plan of the apostolate He gave her. The vision of the image of the Merciful Jesus in Płock took place in February 1931, and the beginning of her illness is dated, according to the officially accepted version, in April 1928, though it might be put back two years still, without error. A comparison of the above dates shows that Sister Faustina's illness was, in God's plan, one of the elements for the genuine growth of the work. By nature active and practical, she would have a tendency to put the work entrusted to her into immediate action, while God's will was - as we may suppose today - not that she should actively perform something, but that through her should be revealed the full concept of the devotion to the Divine Mercy, and the groundwork for a new Congregation; but someone else was to bring that congregation to life. Thus, the illness was a natural brake, which would inhibit hasty impatience aimed at putting God's plan into action as rapidly as might be, without understanding that it had not yet been sufficiently absorbed, and clear, and that above all it was needful to concentrate on this.

The statement that Sister Faustina received her great mission as a patient with advanced tuberculosis may seem shocking to certain people. In reality, it is not such an exception. We can find similar precedents without looking far. A countryman of Sister Faustina, St. Maximillian Kolbe, slightly older than she, but active at the same time, also began his great missionary work as a tuberculous patient with advanced changes in his lungs. Similarly, the Primate of the Polish Millennium of Christianity, Cardinal Stefan Wyszyński, at the time he was being consecrated priest, was not predicted to have a long life, and he himself then prayed that God might just grant him one year as a priest before He took him to Himself.

Both the examples given also show that the process of tuberculosis runs by no means in a uniform manner, and how hard it is to give a correct prognosis. In Father Kolbe and in Cardinal Wyszyński the disease, though very advanced, fortunately became arrested, while in Sister Faustina's case it ran a dramatic course. I emphasize that it was dramatic, not tragic. God trusted her love: Sister Faustina in very difficult conditions transformed her overwhelming sufferings into a priceless constructive element, supported by which the work entrusted to her could develop. Every suffering she encountered, regardless of whether it was physical, mental or spiritual she offered to God day by day for years, as a sacrificial offering in reparation for the sins of mankind. She could therefore pray with full justification:

"Christ, give me souls. Let anything You like happen to me, but give me souls in return. I want the salvation of souls. I want souls to know Your mercy. I have nothing for myself, because I have given everything away to souls, with the result that on the day of judgment I will stand before You empty-handed since I have given everything away to souls. Thus You will have nothing on which to judge me, and we shall meet on that day: Love and mercy..."

(Diary, Notebook V, para. 1426).

This spiritual growth, the psychical changes taking place in the soul of Sister Faustina, in time increased in intensity, and can be followed with ease on the pages of her Diary. They even had their own milestones. Her departure from Vilnius ended her efforts to have the image of the Merciful Jesus placed on the altar for public veneration, and to have the Feast of Divine Mercy established. Both those matters now continued without her, left to the competence of Father Sopoćko, who, only after Sister Faustina had left Vilnius, being finally convinced of the genuine nature of her visions and the need for such a devotion, committed himself to its development and propagation with the same energy as Sister Faustina. She continued to give the necessary explanations and informed him of the further action of God upon her; she was kept up to date with what was happening; but her own attention was directed above all toward the new Congregation, the founding of which was demanded by God.

But precisely when she was on the sidelines as regards active propagation of the devotion, God allowed her to taste the first fruits of the work she had been spreading. From this standpoint, the year 1937 was happy and blessed.

It was begun by the hanging of the image in a church. The picture was placed on the Epistle side of the main altar in the church of St Michael, where Father Sopoćko was still Rector.

Before hanging the image of the Merciful Jesus for public veneration, Father Sopoćko had previously prepared priestly opinion by articles published in theological magazines, in which he gave reasons, *"intellectual and liturgical"*, for the need of a Feast of the Divine Mercy on the first Sunday after Easter. Simultaneously with the hanging of the image in the church, he published in the Vilnius "Tygodnik Katolicki, Nasz Przyjaciel" (Catholic Weekly, Our Friend) on 4 April 1937, an article on the Divine Mercy, this time intended for the wide spectrum of the faithful, illustrating it with a photograph of the image of the Merciful Jesus. That edition of the paper was passed on to Sister Faustina by her superior, Mother Irene Krzyża-nowska, shortly after it appeared.

This was the first printed word on the theme of the Divine Mercy (in the form revealed to her by the Lord) that she had seen, but it was not the first popular publication for the needs of the faithful. A pamphlet under the title "Divine Mercy", with a small picture of the Merciful Jesus on the cover, had been published by Father Sopoćko already in June 1936, and one year later a second booklet came out in Poznań, Poland, with the title "Divine Mercy in the Liturgy". Both these publications were, however, in small editions. The subject became widely known only when, at the end of August 1937, Father Sopoćko, visiting Cracow, had the opportunity to talk for some time with Sister Faustina and to look at her Diary written after she had left Vilnius. Their meeting was fruitful, as Father Sopoćko himself informs us:

"I found in her diary a novena to the Divine Mercy, which I very much liked. When I asked her where she had it from, she told me that Jesus Himself had dictated to her this novena. Prior to this, Jesus had taught her a chaplet to the Divine Mercy, and other prayers, which I decided to publish."

(Archives of S.F., Recollections).

Father Sopoćko published the chaplet and novena in a verbatim version, and a series of invocations in the diary was collected by him in the form of a litany of the Divine Mercy. All these prayers were collected in a small booklet called "Chrystus Krol Miłosierdzia" (Christ the King of Mercy) published that year in Cracow with the help of Mother Irene Krzyżanowska, simultaneously with a series of large and small pictures of the Merciful Jesus. Two months after meeting Father Sopoćko, it was with joyful emotions that Sister Faustina looked at samples of this publication. She well understood the importance of the event, and, in the first impulse of gratitude, above all to Jesus it was she turned her thoughts. She writes:

'I entered into an intimate conversation with the Lord, thanking Him for having condescended to grant me the grace of seeing how the veneration of His unfathomable mercy is spreading.'

(Diary, Notebook IV, para. 1300).

'As I was glancing through it, Jesus gave me to know interiorly: 'Already there are many souls who have been drawn to My love by this image. My mercy acts in souls through this work.'"

(Diary, Notebook V, para. 1379).

Indeed, these small publications from Cracow began an enormous series of pictures, prayers and theological works, which in the following years would embrace almost the whole world, despite the obstacles caused by the Second World War.

At the same time that the booklet with the prayers to the Divine Mercy was being published, Sister Faustina - after a long interior struggle - solved the problem of the new Congregation. Already when he met her in Cracow at the end of August 1937, Father Sopoćko had noticed much greater interior peace in her, and patience in waiting for a better understanding of the will of God. Sister Faustina noted his advice in her Diary:

> *"As concerns yourself, Sister, it is good that you are remaining in a state of holy indifference in everything that pertains to the will of God, and that you are better maintaining a state of equilibrium. Please do your best to keep this equanimity... Do nothing on your own, Sister, but in all matters take counsel from your spiritual director. I beg you to keep your level-headedness and as great a calm as possible.'*

(Diary, Notebook IV, para. 1255).

Father Sopoćko additionally explained to Sister Faustina that from the time she had been transferred from Vilnius to Cracow, her spiritual director was Father Andrasz, who also knew her spiritual life as well as did he himself, and she should tell him everything and adopt his counsel. Father Sopoćko could happily entrust the soul of Sister Faustina to Father Andrasz. Both priests were in complete agreement in their appraisal of the present situation: while well disposed to the concept of the new Congregation, they thought that the right time had not yet come to start forming it. God's plans were not yet sufficiently clear, nor did the health of Sister Faustina allow her to undertake the commencement of any action expected to last any length of time.

The conversation with Father Sopoćko was one of the milestones in the life of Sister Faustina which I have mentioned. It ended more than three years of lasting conflict between fidelity to the religious vows she had already made, and the necessity of breaking them if she wished to found a new Congregation. This conversation showed Sister Faustina the fault she had committed up to now: instead of being impatient, she should have prayed, waiting peacefully for the final crystallization of the will of God. Understanding of her fault led her to make a decision: almost directly after Father Sopoćko had left, she made - not for the first time in her life - an act of complete oblation to the will of God.

"Jesus-Host, when I have this very moment received into my heart, through this union with You I offer myself to the heavenly Father as a sacrificial host, abandoning myself totally and completely to the most merciful and holy will of my God. From today onward, Your will, Lord, is my food. Take my whole being; dispose of me as you please. Whatever Your fatherly hand gives me, I will accept with submission, peace and joy. I fear nothing, no matter in what direction You lead me; helped by Your grace I will carry out everything You demand of me. I no longer fear any of Your inspirations nor do I probe anxiously to see where they will lead me. Lead me, O God, along whatever roads You please; I have placed all my trust in Your will, which is, for me, love and mercy itself."

(Diary, Notebook IV, para. 1264).

By this act Sister Faustina agreed to accept without reservation every sacrifice demanded by God. She agreed to accept His will even without trying to understand it. She no longer makes its performance depend on the necessity of understanding why and what for, but entrusts herself to God blindly and without regard for the cost.

"I have placed all my trust in Your will which is, for me, love and mercy itself. Bid me to stay in this convent, I will stay; bid me to undertake the work, I will undertake it; leave me in uncertainty about the work until I die, be blessed; give me death when, humanly speaking, my life seems particularly necessary, be blessed. Should You take me in my youth, be blessed; should You let me live to a ripe old age, be blessed. Should You give me health and strength be blessed; should You confine me to a bed of pain for my whole life, be blessed. Should You give only failures and disappointments in life, be blessed. Should You allow my purest intentions to be condemned, be blessed. Should You enlighten my mind, be blessed. Should You leave me in darkness and all kinds of torments, be blessed.

From this moment on, I live in the deepest peace, because the Lord himself is carrying me in the hollow of His hand. He, Lord of unfathomable mercy, knows that I desire Him alone in all things, always and everywhere."

(Diary, Notebook IV, para. 1264).

So, at the end, the sacrifice was made. Sister Faustina had succeeded in conquering herself, and, having detached herself from the last earthly longing - though it was in its essence very much divine - agreed to accept without opposition every wish of the Lord. There was no more inner resistance in her. And this was not the result of the mood of the moment. The matter had been thought through, overcome and prayed over; her decision had been taken consciously and with full responsibility. Further pages of the diary confirm this. Three months later, as Advent approached, Sister Faustina writes:

> *"Yesterday I received a letter from Father Sopoćko. I learned that God's work is progressing, however slowly. I am very happy about this, and I have redoubled my prayers for this entire work. I have come to learn that, for the present, so far as my participation in the work is concerned, the Lord is asking for prayer and sacrifice. Action on my part could indeed thwart God's plans, as Father Sopoćko wrote in yesterday's letter."*

(Diary, Notebook V, para. 1401).

If we seek an additional stimulus which might have affected this decisive act of Sister Faustina's, we must look at the first successes of the newly-born work. The joy which accompanied these might have released new strengths essential before the maximum sacrifice could be attempted, if only to support and fortify the new work. How much easier it would have been to find the fortitude for that sacrifice, when the first fruits were becoming visible!

From the moment she accepted the will of God, the matter of founding the new Congregation ceased to concern her. This does not mean that Sister Faustina already knew what was to be done. When she finally understood that Jesus wished her to remain where she was, that it was not her task to set up the new Congregation, and how the process of realization occurred, we shall never know. The revelations concerning this matter have remained shrouded in secrecy. The words of Jesus to Sister Faustina when He asked for the new Congregation are not known, and the end of the matter is still more obscure. This most dramatic chapter in the spiritual life of Sister Faustina in certain parts was solely between Him and the elect soul, and has forever remained her exclusive secret.'She had every right to discretion, for the wish of Jesus concerned her own fate, and it is natural that she should feel inhibited in discussing it. I have already dealt with this theme in preceding chapters. But I shall recapitulate what we do know. Only those facts which Sister Faustina passed on to those persons engaged in the work of Mercy are known: to Mother General Michael Moraczewska, to her superior Mother Irene Krzyżanowska, and to Father Sopoćko.

'Tell the Superior General to count on you as the most faithful daughter in the Order,' were Jesus' words to Sister Faustina at the end of May 1937.

(Diary, Notebook III, para. 1130).

This astounding command was God's answer to the agreement of Mother General that Sister Faustina leave the community if she wished to found a new one. In the confirmation of the loyalty of Sister Faustina and of her devotion for her Congregation to which she still belonged at the time she was preparing to leave it, the true will of God can be understood. Sadly, Sister Faustina did not record how she fulfilled the request of Jesus, nor what was the reply of the Mother General.

Quite another kind of information on the same matter was received by Mother Irene. The information was composed of brief circumstantial remarks made when Mother Irene visited Sister Faustina during her second stay in hospital, and later in her isolation cell in the convent. Of the three persons mentioned, Mother Irene Krzyżanowska, who met Sister Faustina daily, was best able to observe the change in her. Once more Sister Faustina was peaceful and full of equanimity, and in her conversations returned to the theme that she would bring the superior and the Congregation many joys after her death, for "Jesus wished to distinguish her and make her a saint" - a saint of their Congregation. Sister Faustina was so radiant with God that her words had the natural ring of truth, so the superior accepted them without inner reservation. Their content dispelled any doubts as to which Congregation God intended to be her mother congregation. They are the logical supplement to what Sister Faustina had passed on from Jesus to the Mother General. The situation had been explained to both superiors.

The fullest information concerning the new Congregation was afforded to Father Sopoćko, when he visited Sister Faustina in hospital at the beginning of September 1938, a month before her death. I have this conversation on pages 247-249 of MS (but only insofar as it concerns the new Congregation). I add the rest of his account now:

"I had come to Cracow to the conference of Theological Institutes, and I found Sister Faustina in the hospital for infectious diseases at Prądnik, already prepared for death. I visited her during that week." Father Sopoćko received the final requests as to what he had to do: *"that I was mainly to try to have the Feast of Mercy established on the first Sunday after Easter, that I was not to concern myself too much with the new congregation, that I would recognize, by certain signs, who is to do what in this matter... and this also, that she would soon die, and everything she had had to say and write had been done."*

(Archives of S.F., Recollections).

There can be no doubt that before her death Sister Faustina was fully aware what Jesus wanted from her, and she also knew that she had fulfilled His commands. She died with a feeling of accomplishment, though her mission was unfinished. For us, there remains the still unanswered question; when did she understand? We can find some information in the Diary. For the date 10th April 1938, Sister Faustina wrote:

'I received a deep inner light which gave me to understand, in spirit, all the workings of mercy. It was like a flash of lightning, but more distinct than if I had watched it for hours with the eyes of my body.'

(Diary, Notebook VI, para. 1658).

'...my soul enjoyed... seeing the glory of God's mercy. The glory of the Divine Mercy is resounding, even now, in spite of the efforts of its enemies and of Satan himself, who has a great hatred for God's mercy. This work will snatch a great number of souls from him, and that is why the spirit of darkness sometimes tempts good people violently, so that they may hinder the work. But I have clearly seen that the will of God is already being carried out, and that it will be accomplished to the very last detail. The enemy's greatest efforts will not thwart the smallest detail of what the Lord has decreed. No matter if there are times when the work seems to be completely destroyed; it is then that the work is being all the more consolidated.

My soul was filled with a peace much deeper than anything I had experienced before... I am at peace; God Himself governs all things.

I spent the whole day in thanksgiving, and gratitude kept flooding my soul...'

(Diary, Notebook VI, paras. 1659-1661).

Here, Sister Faustina is writing only generally of the work of the Divine Mercy, but it is precisely because she does not give details that we may suppose that it was not necessary, because in this interior vision everything which had so far eluded her understanding was made clear.

In Sister Faustina's understanding of her thoughts on her life, it is obvious that she did not treat her approaching death as the natural closing of her account with God. Her mission was not to finish on this earth, but was to be continued in heaven. A correct interpretation of God's plan for her came to her relatively late in life, and this comprehension is closely connected with her interior process of maturing. Prior to this, she had to transfer her attention from any other activity toward prayer, and that prayer had a specific character, in which were equally distributed moments of intercession and the offering of reparation for the faults of sinners. The Diary is the chief witness in this process of maturing. It is even possible that the writing of it helped her to formulate the whole problem to herself more quickly and fully. The Diary gradually underwent a considerable evolution. She began to write it at the request of her confessor <u>for him,</u> to pass on to him the desires of Jesus intended for himself. As time passed, the person to whom the Divine words are addressed is more and more often <u>herself</u>. Jesus, when He speaks to her now, requires her to write everything He says to her, explaining His request by the future significance of the Diary:

'Apostle of My mercy, proclaim to the whole world My unfathomable mercy. Do not be discouraged by the difficulties you encounter in proclaiming My mercy. These difficulties that affect you so painfully are needed for your sanctification and as evidence that this work is Mine. My daughter, be diligent in writing down every sentence I tell you concerning My mercy, because this is meant for a great number of souls who will profit from it.'

(Diary, Notebook III, para. 1142).

So the aim itself of the diary has basically changed. The sphere of its eventual readers has greatly increased. Now it is no longer destined for her confessor alone, but has become one of the instruments of Sister Faustina's apostolate.

> *January 23,* [1937]. *I did not feel like writing today. Then I heard a voice in my soul:* **'My daughter, you do not live for yourself, but for souls; write for their benefit.'**

(Diary, Notebook II, para. 895).

Jesus' words of a similar import occur on more than one page of her Diary:

> *The Lord Himself moves me to write prayers and hymns about His mercy, and these hymns of praise force themselves upon my lips. I have noticed that ready-formulated words of praise of God's mercy enter my mind, and so I have resolved to write them down in so far as is within my power. I can feel God urging me to do so.*

(Diary, Notebook VI, para. 1593).

This is why, despite her failing strength, despite obvious difficulties at times in formulating her thoughts, Sister Faustina does not stop writing. The tone of her utterances takes on fresh expression. They have become one great hymn in praise of the Divine Mercy. At one moment words of adoration spring to her lips, at another she offers Jesus her sufferings in exchange for the salvation of sinners, absorbed in seeking the lost sheep of the Lord. Her adoration now more often takes the form of verses. One has the impression that in the harmony of rhyme and rhythm she can most fully express her own inner harmony, which is seeking language to be able to manifest itself.

For when the spiritual conflicts had ended, Sister Faustina - though in physical pain - mentally entered a state of happiness which was gradually establishing itself more firmly.

"My heart is drawn there where my God is hidden,
Where He dwells with us day and night,
Clothed in the white Host;
He governs the whole world, He communes with souls.

My heart is drawn there where my God is hiding,
Where His love is immolated.
But my heart senses that the living water is here;
It is my living God, though a veil hides Him,"

(Diary, Notebook VI, para. 1591).

Elsewhere, there occurs a similar ecstasy on the same theme of God concealed in the Eucharist:

"O You who are hidden, body, soul and divinity,
Under the fragile form of bread,
You are my life from Whom springs an abundance of graces
And, for me, You surpass the delights of heaven.

When You unite Yourself with me in Communion, O God,
I then feel my unspeakable greatness,
A greatness which flows from You, O Lord, I humbly confess,
And despite my misery, with Your help, I can become a saint."

(Diary, Notebook VI, para. 1718).

Those around her noticed the happiness and the unfailing smile of Sister Faustina throughout her sufferings, and rightly praise her heroism in the bearing of pain. But this is not the whole picture. The inner cheerfulness shining through the physical sufferings was so natural that it was surely reflecting the true state of her soul. She was happy in the face of all sufferings, even the most acute pain. She was simply happy.

"All things will have an end in this vale of tears,
Tears will run dry and pain will cease.
Only one thing will remain-
Love for You, O Lord.
All things will have an end in this exile,
The ordeals and wilderness of the soul.
And though she live in perpetual agony,
If God is with her, nothing can shake her."

(Diary, Notebook III, para. 1132).

Although Sister Faustina had made her peace with herself, and, to use the well-known saying of Pope John XXIII, had her bags packed, she had not finished her apostolic work, which now expressed itself through the medium of prayer and the diary-writing, for the value of the latter was still emphasized by Jesus. Her diary becomes a dialogue, in which the words of Jesus thread through her own prayerful utterances. God speaks to us through them, and Sister Faustina is the interpreter of His love.

'Write down everything that occurs to you regarding My goodness. ...do as I tell you. Your thoughts are united to My thoughts, so write whatever comes to your mind. You are the secretary of My mercy. I have chosen

you for that office in this life and the next life,' said
Jesus.

(Diary, Notebook VI, para. 1605).

Jesus' statement that Sister Faustina was not only
the apostle but also the secretary of His Mercy gives us
the additional explanation of why, exhausted in the extreme, she did not let the pen fall from her hand as
long as she could hold it. Her sudden breaking-off the
diary does not mean that she might not have had
anything more to say, but that the pen slipped from
her powerless grasp. To the end of her life there
remained to her one thing - the most important: prayer,
which had become almost exclusively the prayer of
suffering. This ended only with her death. One of her
last reflections, in the Diary, Notebook V, para. 1582,
ran like this:

*'O my Jesus, I now embrace the whole world and ask
You for mercy for it. When You tell me, O God, that it
is enough, that Your holy will has been completely
accomplished, then, my Saviour, in union with You, I
will commit my soul into the hands of the Heavenly
Father, full of trust in Your unfathomable mercy. And
when I stand at the foot of Your throne, the first hymn
that I will sing will be one to Your mercy. Poor earth,
I will not forget you. Although I feel that I will be
immediately drowned in God as in an ocean of happiness,
that will not be an obstacle to my returning to earth to
encourage souls and incite then to trust in God's mercy.
Indeed, this immersion in God will give me the possibility
of boundless action.'*

SISTER FAUSTINA HELPS THE DYING

The shadow of death was drawing ever closer to the life of Sister Faustina, but it came slowly and almost imperceptibly. She was aware that it was near, but although she recalled the fear she experienced with an attack of suffocation in 1934 in Vilnius, it was not fear that was her prevailing emotion, but a longing to be united with her beloved Lord. Her thoughts returned again and again to death and were never far from it, especially since the time of that attack. Sister Faustina had been so certain that her life was then at an end that she had asked Father Sopoćko for Confession and the Sacrament of the Sick.

Death had not, indeed, arrived, but its nearness had left a visible trace in her personality. The brutal reality of this moment in human life had been shown to her at that time in all its naked truth.

"Although it gives us eternal life, death is dreadful", she noted as she recalled that experience.

But though she was frightened by the fearfulness of the experience itself, the fact that she had escaped the claws of death did not leave her happy; rather, she was conscious of disappointment. She complained:

"Jesus, I thought You were going to take me." And Jesus answered, *"My will has not yet been fully ac-*

complished in you; you will still remain on earth, but not for long. I am well pleased with your trust, but your love should be more ardent. Pure love gives the soul strength at the very moment of dying. When I was dying on the cross, I was not thinking about Myself, but about poor sinners, and I prayed for them to My Father. I want your last moments to be completely similar to Mine on the cross... Pure love understands these words; carnal love will never understand them.'"

(Diary, Notebook I, para. 324).

So Jesus did not leave unanswered the complaint from the heart of Sister Faustina. Here we have a clear example of how, and to what degree, God respects and takes into account human feelings. He explained to her without delay His reasons for leaving her upon earth. There were, it appears, two motives: 1) she had not yet fulfilled all the task He had given to do, 2) she had not interiorly matured for the kind of death He wanted for His spouse. She had not understood that the moment of death gave her the last opportunity to offer Him a sacrifice, so that sinners whose offences weighed them down might be forgiven. This was to be a moment of great importance and it had to be carefully prepared for.

Finally, to sum up this first experience of the nearness of death, it had an educational significance in the spiritual development of Sister Faustina and her mission.

However, let us first look again at her apostolate.

Up to this point, as far as concerned the life beyond the grave of human souls, her attention had been focused on the souls of those who had died and were suffering in Purgatory, especially the souls of the religious who had died since she had entered the Congregation. She knew of their deaths from a distance: they came to ask for her prayers and explained how they were suffering. Not long after she had entered the convent, she had also had a general vision of Purgatory, to which her Guardian Angel had taken her (see Diary, Notebook I, para. 20), and from that moment, as she herself wrote, she was in close contact with "suffering" souls, and well knew their needs. She herself prayed for them and encouraged others to do so. But she had had no special interest in those who were actually dying. They need prayers even more than the "holy souls", for the holy souls, although they are in Purgatory, are souls that have been saved, while for those who are dying, this is their last chance of salvation. However, this knowledge had not yet appeared clearly in anything that Sister Faustina had written. There is no mention of such realization in her Diary, nor has anyone who knew her commented on this. This knowledge appeared only during her time in Vilnius. The ward, Hedvig O., who worked with Sister Faustina in the garden, says:

"Every hour, she gave us an ejaculatory prayer for the dying. When we asked her why she prayed so frequently for the dying, she answered that it was all too little and that one should pray constantly, because at every second some human being was dying somewhere in the world, who needed help."

(Archives of S.F., Recollections).

This account by a ward shows that Sister Faustina's personal brush with death had awakened her sensitivity to a need of the human soul of which up to now she had been unaware. From the moment she had had her own experience, it was easier for her to sympathize with what others were going through, and to use this experience of her own to help others in a practical way.

She fully realized the whole question of the seriously ill and the dying only when, at the end of 1936, she herself was in hospital at Prądnik near Cracow. The ward in which she lay was for the seriously ill, and the number of deaths among the patients was considerable. Almost every day, one of them died.

The hospital and its world, closed in upon itself, was a completely new experience for Sister Faustina. Until that time, she had encountered the sick only singly, and then sporadically. Now she had the opportunity to take part in their daily life, and this changed her standpoint. Besides, in the hospital, disease and its threat were very obvious; there was nothing to screen them from view. Above all the painful and difficult problems of hospital life, the question of death became, for her, the most prominent. Here she could observe at will the state of the human souls it approached. How they varied! She saw peaceful deaths, where the patient seemed reconciled to what was to come; but much more frequently she observed the torment of a protracted agony during which evil powers stalked the dying person, preying upon him in the hope of controlling the remains of the consciousness he might at times recover, in order to snatch him then forever from God! The sight of the soul's last deathly contest with evil compelled Sister Faustina's generous heart to help immediately to save the soul of the sinner. Heedless of her own illness and its consequences, she hastened to the bedside of the dying person day or night, and knelt in prayer until she had obtained what she was asking for, and the person sorely tried by a protracted agony was calm. In the moment of consciousness still left to him, begged for by the fervent prayer of Sister Faustina, it would be clear that in repentance and sorrow he had reached God and that at the very gates of death the grace of salvation had been poured out upon his soul. In her diary time after time can be found notes on the dying. It was one of the chief themes of this period.

The knowledge that one of the patients was dying came to Sister Faustina in a variety of ways, but usually supernaturally, through an inner voice: from her Guardian Angel, or even from Jesus Himself, though this happened most infrequently.

'The Lord Jesus makes it known to me in a special way when someone is in need of my prayer. I especially know when my prayer is needed by a dying soul. This happens more often now than it did in the past.'

(Diary, Notebook II, para. 820).

'I feel vividly and clearly that spirit who is asking me for prayer. I was not aware that souls are so closely united, and often it is my Guardian Angel who tells me.'

(Diary, Notebook II, para. 828).

'My vision is purely spiritual, by means of a sudden light that God grants me at that moment... It sometimes happens that the dying person is in the second or third building away, yet for the spirit, space does not exist. It sometimes happens that I know about a death occurring several hundred kilometres away. This has happened several times with regard to my family and relatives and also sisters in religion, and even souls whom I have not known during their lifetime... I have also discovered that if I feel constrained to pray for a longer time; that is to say, I experience interior unrest, the soul is undergoing a greater struggle and is going through a longer final agony.'

(Diary, Notebook II, para. 835).

Sister Faustina knew why she was so certain that her prayers would be heard. God Himself had assured her of it.

'At the hour of their death, I defend as My own glory every soul that will say this chaplet [to the Divine Mercy]; *or when others say it for a dying person... When this chaplet is said by the bedside of a dying person, God's anger is placated, and unfathomable mercy envelops the soul, and the very depths of My tender mercy will be moved for the sake of the sorrowful Passion of My Son.'*
(Diary, Notebook,II, para. 811).

'Oh, if only everyone realized how great the Lord's mercy is and how much we all need that mercy, especially at that crucial hour!' writes Sister Faustina

(Diary, Notebook II, para. 811).

'I always pray until I experience in my soul that the prayer has had its effect.'
(Diary, Notebook II, para. 834).

The chaplet to the Divine Mercy contains great help for the dying, as Sister Faustina could say on the basis of her own practice. She is clearly greatly affected by seeing the efficacy of the prayer recommended by Jesus. Even for her it was a discovery. Her life up to that point had not afforded her the opportunity to see how quickly it acted. This was only possible to observe in the dying. In those last hours of life, when there is no going back, the human soul's "yes" or "no" is decisive and, in the nature of things, immediate. Everything is resolved now and at once, and the resolution is simultaneously the measure of the value and efficacy of this prayer.

Although Sister Faustina's generosity really knew no bounds, her illness imposed some limitations. Rising from bed at the least suitable times and kneeling for hours with the dying was beyond her strength, and even harmful to her. Therefore, after two months her religious superiors, in conjunction with the doctor, forbade her to do this, which compelled her to change the method by which she would fulfil her apostolic mission. Being immobilized in bed was no barrier to her in giving aid to the dying. Her spiritual "ear" became so sensitive that without difficulty she could not only receive at a distance the "signals" of approaching death, but also know the state of the soul of the dying person. Prayer is not bounded by space. Lying alone in her side ward, just as before when she was kneeling by a patient, she pestered God fervently and persistently for mercy until she intuitively felt that she had achieved her aim. Now, however, she checked every time whether her intuition agreed with reality. It never failed.

Prayers for the dying would become an inseparable part of Sister Faustina's life until she died. Not in vain had she demanded Jesus to give her human souls, in exchange making an oblation of everything she had. She could hardly, therefore, abandon without helping those souls which were in a desperate situation. Hospital life opened her eyes to this basic activity of her apostolate, and she could not close them to the necessity of continuing it after her stay in hospital. The question was not one of circumstances, but fundamental, as she understood it. Once she had understood her duty, she fulfilled it. Her first four-month stay in hospital (December 1936 - March 1937) was devoted to this important matter of God's will.

A story told by the ward A.B., who worked with Sister Faustina in the garden in Cracow in the years 1936 - 1937, shows how sensitive to human needs Sister Faustina could be - it is an amazing instance:

"In the morning Sister Faustina quite unexpectedly spoke to us girls who were weeding. She said, "Let us pray for someone who is being hanged." And her face, which, a moment before, had been happy, took on

such a terrible expression that we were frightened and terrified."

Sister Faustina herself, in May 1938, i.e. a month before she finally ceased writing, wrote in her diary,

'I often attend upon the dying and through entreaties obtain for them trust in God's mercy... God's mercy sometimes touches the sinner at the last moment in a wondrous and mysterious way. Outwardly, it seems as if everything were lost, but it is not so. The soul, illumined by a ray of God's powerful final grace, turns to God in the last moment with such a power of love that, in an instant, it receives from God forgiveness of sin and punishment, while outwardly it shows no sign either of repentance or of contrition, because souls [at that stage] no longer react to external things.'

(Diary, Notebook VI, para. 1698).

It is certain that Sister Faustina did not cease from that form of her apostolate until death closed her own eyes, and then she took it with her to intercede into eternity - as she had foretold - before the throne of the Merciful Lord.

MATURING TOWARDS SANCTITY

The words of Jesus to Sister Faustina directly after the attack of suffocation in Vilnius, when He told her that she had not yet fulfilled the task entrusted to her on earth, stimulated her to still greater concentration on the mission she had received. Her attitude of watchfulness and care, which directed all her free thinking-time to the problems which faced the work of Divine Mercy, did not lessen her longing for eternity, for the meeting with God face to face, without the veil hiding Him here on earth. She did, however, with all the strength of her will, make the longing subordinate to active love, for Sister Faustina wished just as much as to fulfil the wishes of her beloved Lord, as to see Him in heaven. Her desire to please Him was stronger than all others. This is why, in her meditations and prayers, the theme of her own death does not appear until the end of 1936, when she went to hospital, and even then death is a peripheral matter.

Nevertheless her loving heart wanted, sometimes, to dream. It is too hard to give this up, and Sister Faustina, amidst her apostolic activity in the hospital, sometimes sighed:

"We know each other mutually, O Lord, in the dwelling of my heart. Yes, now it is I who am receiving You as a Guest in the little home of my heart, but the time is coming when You will call me to Your dwelling

place, which You have prepared for me from the beginning of the world."

(Diary, Notebook II, para. 909).

"O bright and clear day on which all my dreams will be fulfilled; O day so eagerly desired, the last day of my life! I look forward with joy to the last stroke the Divine Artist will trace on my soul, which will give my soul a unique beauty that will distinguish me from the beauty of other souls... O great day, on which divine love will be confirmed in me. On that day, for the first time I shall sing before heaven and earth the song of the Lord's fathomless mercy... That the song of my soul may be pleasing to the Holy Trinity, do You, O Spirit of God, direct and form my soul yourself. I arm myself with patience and await Your coming, O merciful God, and as to the terrible pains and fear of death, at this moment more than at any other time, I trust in the abyss of Your mercy and am reminding You, O merciful Jesus, sweet Saviour, of all the promises You have made to me."

(Diary, Notebook II, para. 825).

It is true that the problem of death entered Sister Faustina's thoughts and interests through wide gates when she found herself in hospital - as I have already written in an earlier chapter. But it was both by the will of Jesus, and in her own anxiety over souls which might escape the merciful love of Jesus, that Sister Faustina at this period did not look at death from her personal viewpoint but objectively, assisting at death-beds when death took others. With Christ at her side, she had come to know and become used to the death of others, before she began to contemplate her own. The hospital gave her more than enough opportunity. Death there was a daily occurrence.

Having met the reality, Sister Faustina found that her idea of death was transformed. From being a general idea, imprecisely imagined, it became a real picture in which particularly clear elements, for her, were the connection of the soul with the body, the problem of sin and forgiveness in all the variety and unique nature of the deaths which she observed. Each death was different, each brought a new knowledge of the human soul, and all this increased her understanding of the intercession she had been charged with by Jesus.

So, then, her meditations on death did not take Sister Faustina in the direction of the concept that, with death, life is extinct. As regards the question of approaching death, what interested her was that to the very last moment of life there exists the possibility of asking God for forgiveness of sins, and receiving it. Seeing the death of others, Sister Faustina learned the practical needs of that moment, and her thoughts were taken up with seeking ways to help; she avoided that passivity which, in the majority of people, is the natural result of reflection on the approaching end of life.

God so created the world, that in giving to others, we make ourselves rich. Our own souls grow in proportion to the greatness of our love of our neighbours. So, too, Sister Faustina, in becoming absorbed with the problems of saving people at this final stage of their lives, at the same time developed and was interiorly enriched. Her love of neighbour took on more of the character of universal love, unlimited by any ties or loyalties. As far as she could, she mirrored in herself something of the love of Jesus.

However, to learn Christ-like love in these circumstances does not come easy. It is only possible to attain it by a heroic act of the will.

'O merciful Jesus... I give You my whole being. Transform me into Yourself and make me capable of doing

*Your holy will in all things and of returning Your love...
grant me Your divine life. Let Your pure and noble blood
throb with all its might in my heart,"* prayed Sister
Faustina with her whole heart.

(Diary, Notebook II, para. 832).

*"Transform me into Yourself, O Jesus, that I may be
a living sacrifice and pleasing to You. I desire to atone
at each moment for poor sinners. The sacrifice of my
spirit is hidden under the veil of the body; the human
eye does not perceive it, and for that reason it is pure
and pleasing to You."*

(Diary, Notebook II, para. 908).

Sister Faustina well understood that she would never
obtain the salvation necessary for souls on her own.
However great her love, it would always be too small.
For that, the redemptive love of the Saviour was
needed. She would attain what she wanted by as much
as she allowed Him to act through her. It was not for
nothing that she had loved Him in His Passion,
streaming with blood. If she wished to obtain mercy for
sinners, she must permit just such a suffering Redeemer to grow in her own soul, and act through Him. The
whole content of Sister Faustina's communion with God
was in meditating on His sorrowful mysteries and
applying them to the everchanging circumstances of her
life. She spent every day in close union with Him, and
His "interests" were of prime importance in her soul, in
a way that was becoming more decisive and exclusive.
She knew that she was united with Him, and the
spiritual climate in which her soul breathed was as
natural to her as breathing air for her lungs. She was
therefore surprised and awed, when, during her stay in
hospital, some time at the beginning of February 1937,
at a moment of ecstatic union with the Holy Trinity,

she suddenly heard that Jesus "wanted her to be His spouse" (Diary, Notebook II, para. 912)

Several times, Sister Faustina had not understood, at first, the wishes of Jesus. She gradually came to know them, in laborious meditation and with the help - as sometimes occurred - of additional explanations from the Lord. Usually, however, the unclear commands concerned matters she was to act upon. This time, what Jesus had said referred to herself.

What could it mean? - she reflected, full of surprise. As far as she understood it, she was already vowed to Him for more than five years, since she had taken her perpetual vows, which in her case had been confirmed by a mystical union with the Holy Trinity. God had then introduced her to His divine love, sharing His supernatural Being. From then on, through daily communion with Him she had gradually entered new realms of spiritual growth. Through active participation in His redemptive love, she had transformed herself into love, making herself more like God. At the time of her vows, she had once called herself a novice beginning her "novitiate with Jesus". This novitiate was now, it seemed, to end with the total outpouring of God into her soul.

We now come to a period in the spiritual life of Sister Faustina in which it is difficult to present her mystical experiences without the possibility of error. It is the time in which Jesus permeates her to the extent that any tangible boundary between what is Faustina, and what is God, disappears, as He is in her. She herself sometimes writes that her intimacy with God has its secrets, known only to Jesus and to her. In such a situation it seems best to refrain from commentary, presenting only what Sister Faustina herself says.

The mystical espousal of Sister Faustina took place on Good Friday 1937, and was the crowning point of the Passion she had been experiencing with Jesus throughout the whole of Holy Week. She has recorded this in her Diary, but, sadly, in only a few sentences.

'I had no physical strength left; the suffering had deprived me of it completely. Throughout all this time, I had been in a sort of swoon. Every beat of Jesus' Heart was reflected in my heart and pierced my soul. If these tortures had concerned me only, I would have suffered less; but as I looked at the One whom my heart has loved with all its might and saw that He was suffering, and that I could not bring Him any relief, my heart dissolved in love and bitterness. I was dying with Him, and yet I could not die. But I would not have exchanged that martyrdom for all the pleasure in the whole world. In the course of this suffering, my love grew immeasurably. I know that the Lord was supporting me with His omnipotence, for otherwise I would not have been able to endure it for even a moment... Together with Him, I underwent, in a special way, all the tortures... I accompanied Him to the Garden of Gethsemane; I stayed with Him in the prison; I went with Him before the judges; I underwent with Him each of the tortures. Not a single one of His movements or looks escaped my notice. I came to know all the omnipotence of His love and of His mercy toward souls.'

(Diary, Notebook III, para. 1054).

And then came the culmination - union with God:

'At eleven o'clock... He brought me into such close intimacy with Himself that my heart was espoused to His Heart in a loving union, and I could feel the faintest stir of His heart and He, of mine. The fire of my created love was joined to the ardor of His eternal love... I am immersed in incomprehensible love and

incomprehensible torture because of His Passion. All that concerns His Being is imparted to me also."

(Diary, Notebook III, para. 1056).

In these few words, Sister Faustina has nevertheless been able to communicate to us the essence of her experience; a drowning of the soul in God in a total consummatum fuit. Now it was not she who lived, but Christ in her. He filled her totally and without reserve. She had left nothing in her soul for herself.

To the reservations and doubts of her prudent confessor, Jesus told Sister Faustina:

'Tell your confessor that I commune with your soul in such an intimate manner because you do not steal my gifts, and this is why I pour all these graces upon your soul, because I know that you will not hoard them for yourself.'

(Diary, Notebook III, para. 1069).

His words, intended for Father Andrasz, are also a valuable guide for us. They confirm, with Divine authority, the role of Sister Faustina as a co-worker of Jesus in His work of the salvation of human souls.

Hidden deep in the Heart of Jesus, Sister Faustina trustingly confides to Him now her most secret personal dream:

"My Jesus, penetrate me through and through so that I might be able to reflect You in my whole life. Divinize me so that my deeds may have supernatural value. Grant that I may have love, compassion and mercy for every soul without exception. O my Jesus, each of Your saints reflects one of Your virtues; I desire to reflect Your compassionate heart, full of mercy; I want to glorify it.

Let Your mercy, O Jesus, be impressed upon my heart and soul like a seal, and this will be my badge in this and the future life.'

(Diary, Notebook IV, para. 1242).

Ecstatic declarations of love, to have real meaning, must be put into practice in real life. In Sister Faustina's situation, this meant that she was to accept, not only witout resisting, but willingly, adversities caused by others, and also all sufferings of her progressive disease, which indeed at this time gave almost constant occasion for such sacrifice. The tuberculosis of the intestines had developed fully, bringing almost daily attacks of searing pain. For readers not familiar with this disease. one might compare the pain to another more widely known - that occurring in cancer. Although of another type, her pains were no less in severity than those in the most acute stages of cancer. Sister Faustina's oblation was of heroic proportions and Jesus aided her in every effort with supernatural food, without which her human strength would have failed her. With Divine patience He taught her time and again how to profit from it.

'Know, my daughter, that your silent day-to-day martyrdom in complete submission to My will ushers many souls into heaven. And when it seems to you that your suffering exceeds your strength, contemplate My wounds.'

(Diary, Notebook III, para. 1184).

'Meditate frequently on the sufferings which I have undergone for your sake, and then nothing of what you suffer for Me will seem great to You... Join your little sufferings to My Sorrowful Passion, so that they may have infinite value before My Majesty...Do not forget,

My disciple, that you are a disciple of a crucified Master.'

(Diary, Notebook V, paras. 1512,1513).

Sister Faustina obediently followed the path indicated to her by Jesus. Similar words, often heard now, are, each time, an injection of supernatural strength - they break down the resistance in her caused by pain overwhelming her body,the bitterness caused by misunderstanding and false appraisal, and the sometimes inadequate care during her illness. Everything she experiences, everything she meets, is compared to His life, and the comparison is the most effective antidote for all kinds of suffering, whether physical or mental. The Lord's Passion was absorbed by her to such a degree that it was ever-present to her senses, and accompanied her daily life at every moment. Even her past life comes back to her only from the point of view of how well she fulfilled the will of God in it. As she recalled it in this way, she saw that not only was God present at every moment, but also He had put his seal on its course. By God's help and grace Sister Faustina had come to such a union and intimacy with Him that she could confidently say:

"My Jesus, I see that I have gone through all the stages of my life following You; childhood, youth, vocation, apostolic work, Tabor, Gethsemane, and now I am already with You on Calvary. I have willingly allowed myself to be crucified, and I am indeed already crucified; although I can still walk a little, I am stretched out on the cross, and I feel distinctly that strength is flowing to me from Your Cross, that You and You alone are my perseverance. Although I often hear the voice of temptation calling to me, "Come down from the cross!" the power of God strengthens me. Although

329

loneliness and darkness and sufferings of all kinds beat against my heart, the mysterious power of God supports and strengthens me. I want to drink the cup to the last drop. I trust firmly that Your grace, which has sustained me in the Garden of Olives, will sustain me also now that I am on Calvary.'

(Diary, Notebook V, para. 1580).

'There are no indifferent moments in my life, since every moment of my life is filled with prayer, suffering and work. If not in one way, then in another, I glorify God; and if God were to give me a second life, I do not know whether I would make better use of it...'

(Diary, Notebook V, para. 1545).

Jesus was not sparing of ever new words of love for His spouse, as if their loving intimacy were, at the present stage of communion, one of His aims. It is precisely from this touching intimacy with God that Sister Faustina's deep commitment to His interests stems. The mystical espousal is not the end of the spiritual maturing of Sister Faustina, but it opens a new chapter: everything in her is focused, at that present, around one thing - the transformation of natural love into supernatural. The maturing in her of the love of God is directed closely by Jesus. It is He who decides on its direction and kind, and He corrected every wandering from the path. Two retreats - the last in her life - have fundamental significance. The first was an eight-day retreat of the community in October 1937, and the second was an individual retreat made at the desire of Jesus in June 1938 in the hospital in Prądnik.

During the October retreat, Sister Faustina considered the question of her own sanctity.

The thought of aiming for sanctity, of course, was not new to her. It must have shown itself in a form which was conspicuous to those around her, often irritating, since her companions had given her the spiteful and ironic nickname of "Saint". Her thought had not gone beyond general conventions, which assume that sanctity is the sum of virtues attained. In her diary for preceding years, there are several visions reported of her being raised to the altar, scenes which are half real, half symbolic, and which are not always clear.

Only now, as she is so deeply united with God, sanctity as the natural result of this relationship enters her thoughts in the form of more thorough meditations, and this affects the character of the retreat. Sister Faustina began with a detailed analysis of herself. She examined her soul with care, but she did so in an atmosphere of deep interior peace. Nothing spoiled the sweetness of her communion with God. Under His watchful eye, she knew that she would not fall into error, and that she would achieve her goal.

"My daughter, this retreat will be an uninterrupted contemplation... Close to My merciful Heart, you will meditate upon all the graces your heart has received".

(Diary, Notebook V, para. 1327).

With precise detail, Sister Faustina records the course of those eight days, and this alone indicates how important they were to her.

"Profound silence engulfs my soul. Not a single cloud hides the sun from me. I lay myself entirely open to its rays, that His love may effect a complete transformation in me."

(Diary, Notebook V, para. 1333).

"May Your Spirit guide me, O God, into the most profound depth of knowledge of Yourself, and of my own

331

self as well, For I shall love You only as much as I shall come to know You. And I shall despise myself only as much as I shall come to know my misery."

(Diary, Notebook V, para. 1326).

"In this profound silence, I am better able to judge the condition of my soul. My soul is like clear water in which I can see everything: both my misery and the vastness of God's graces. And owing to this true knowledge of itself, my spirit is strengthened in deep humility."

(Diary, Notebook V, para. 1336).

"I want to come out of this retreat a saint... in spite of my wretchedness, I want to become a saint, and I trust that God's mercy cam make a saint even out of such misery as I am, because I am utterly in good will. In spite of all my defects, I want to go on fighting like a holy soul and to comport myself like a holy soul. I will not be discouraged by anything, just as nothing can discourage a soul who is holy. I want to live and die like a holy soul, with my eyes fixed on You, Jesus, stretched out on the Cross, as the model for my actions."

(Diary, Notebook V, para. 1333).

The motif of sanctity in those retreats is the chief theme of Sister Faustina's meditations. She tries to understand everything which is essential for the attainment of holiness, and also what might hinder it. However, in order to understand her, we must break off for a moment these retreat contemplations and clarify for ourselves which elements Sister Faustina at present thought were the most important in sanctity, and which picture of sanctity looked most convincing to her. It is such a vital question that even insufficient discussion could cause a false interpretation. Happily, in her diary a few pages further on, we have her own statement on the subject of interest to us:

"My Jesus, You know that from my earliest years I have wanted to become a great saint; that is to say, I have wanted to love You with a love so great that there would be no soul who has hitherto loved You so."

(Diary, Notebook V, para. 1372).

"Once, when I was seven years old, at a Vesper Service, conducted before the Lord Jesus in the monstrance, the love of God was imparted to me for the first time and filled my little heart... From that day until this, my love for the hidden God has been growing constantly to the point of closest intimacy. All the strength of my soul flows from the Blessed Sacrament."

(Diary, Notebook V, para. 1404).

"At first these desires of mine were kept secret, and only Jesus knew of them. But today I cannot contain then within my heart; I would like to cry out to the whole world, "Love God, because He is good and great is His mercy!""

(Diary, Notebook V, para. 1372).

Sanctity, as Sister Faustina understood it, depends therefore on limitless love of God. The greater the love, the greater the sanctity. Love is the basic feature, to which all others are subordinate. Only from it, springs full and willing acceptance of the will of God. This is the conclusion she reaches:

"Neither graces, nor revelations, nor raptures, nor gifts granted to a soul make it perfect, but rather the intimate

union of the soul with God... My sanctity and perfection consist in the close union of my will with the will of God.

(Diary, Notebook III, para. 1107).

Nevertheless, the development in oneself of the love of God meets considerable obstacles. God is possessive, He want our total commitment. But in us there is a multitude of different attachments greater or lesser, easier or more difficult to break. They conceal God, they push Him into the distance. They grow in us like weeds, as strong as weeds are, and only when we try to root them out do we realize how many they are and what an attraction they represent. Sister Faustina knew their rapacity, and she began her retreat meditations by examining herself for these weedy patches of earthly attachments in her soul. As a result of this examination, she realized that if not for the special help of God, she would never have been able to root them out.

"Jesus, You yourself have deigned to lay the foundations of sanctity, as my cooperation has not amounted to much. You have taught me to set no store on the use and choice of created things, because my heart is, of itself, so weak. And this is why I have asked You, O my Master, to take no heed of the pain of my heart, but to cut away whatever might hold me back from the path of love. I did not understand You, Lord in times of sorrow, when You were effecting Your work in my soul; but today I understand You and rejoice in my freedom of spirit. Jesus himself has seen to it that my heart has not been caught in the snares of any passion. I have come to know well from what dangers He has delivered me, and therefore my gratitude to my God knows no bounds."

(Diary, Notebook V, para. 1331).

A positive reckoning of that which has been achieved is in itself no guarantee of safety in the future. The conquering of past faults gives no automatic surety that they will never return. In the place of former faults, new ones may appear which are equally hard to overcome. It is always needful, therefore, to have a watchful eye on the inclinations of one's nature which can hold us back on the chosen path to perfection. Sister Faustina observed:

"My Jesus, despite these graces which You send upon me, I feel that my nature, ennobled though it be, is not completely stilled; and so I keep a constant watch. I must struggle with many faults, knowing well that it is not the struggle which debases one, but cowardice and failure."

(Diary, Notebook V, para. 1340).

So Sister Faustina, in the eight days of this retreat, moves systematically forward in thinking through the problems of sanctity. Jesus fortifies her efforts, fully approving her attitude:

'This firm resolution to become a saint is extremely pleasing to Me. I bless your efforts and will give you opportunities to sanctify yourself. Be watchful that you lose no opportunity that My providence offers you for sanctification. If you do not succeed in taking advantage of an opportunity, do not lose your peace, but humble yourself profoundly before Me and, with great trust, immerse yourself completely in My mercy. In this way, you gain more than you have lost, because more favour is granted to a humble soul than the soul itself asks for...'

(Diary, Notebook V, para. 1361).

'Bear in mind that when you come out of this retreat, I shall be dealing with you as with a perfect soul. I want to hold you in My hand as a pliant tool, perfectly adapted to the completion of My works.'

(Diary, Notebook V, para. 1359).

Gratitude fills the soul of Sister Faustina at the thought of what she has received, and how God helps a heart which sincerely loves Him. She had obtained so much from Him that her "cup runneth over", as the Psalmist says.

At the end of the retreat and her meditations she sums up once more what she has obtained. It is as follows:

"I have come to a knowledge of my destiny; that is, an inward certainty that I will attain sanctity."

(Diary, Notebook V, para. 1362).

She confides in Jesus:

"In profound silence, close to Your merciful Heart, my soul is maturing during this retreat... [It] has lost its tartness and has become a sweet ripe fruit.

Now I can be wholly useful to the Church by my personal sanctity, which throbs with life in the whole Church, for we all make up one organism in Jesus. That is why I endeavour to make the soil of my heart bear good fruit."

(Diary, Notebook V, para. 1364).

Assured by Jesus that she has properly understood her road to sanctity, Sister Faustina finishes the retreat with the decision that she will do everything to love Him to a heroic degree, and to reflect in herself His love for mankind.

'I am coming out of this retreat thoroughly transformed by God's love. My soul is beginning a new life, earnestly and courageously... I feel that I have been totally imbued with God and with this God, I am going back to my everyday life, so drab, so tiresome and wearying, trusting that He whom I feel in my heart will change this drabness into my personal sanctity.'

(Diary, Notebook V, para. 1362).

It would be difficult to overestimate the significance of this retreat. It gave Sister Faustina a solid foundation for further work upon herself. And only one more year of life was left to her. For someone fit and strong, this is not a long time, but for someone so sick as she it stretches into infinity. Joy shortens time, suffering draws it out. Sister Faustina did not yet know when her death would occur. She had only the general assurance of Jesus, that eternity was not far off. But although He repeated this more often, thereby making it easier for her to make her daily sacrifice, at the same time He did not lessen His emphasis on fulfilling the mission with which He had entrusted her.

Approaching death, and the task facing Sister Faustina during her life, are not in contradiction. Nothing has freed her from anything - she is to carry out her work to the end. Sister Faustina closely followed Jesus' indications, went through life with the blind trust of a child, and concentrated all her attention on what He demanded of her.

A little time later, at the beginning of 1938, she formulates in her diary, one more time, her "programme" of sanctity. And although she herself does not hint at it, similarities with the "Little Way" of St Thérèse of Lisieux are too obvious to need pointing out. Sister Faustina was completing the mission of Thérèse Martin, finding a practical application of her concept of attaining holiness in ordinary everyday life. She showed its unobtrusive heroism, so hard to achieve because it is demanded so frequently.

"I am striving for sanctity, because in this way I shall be useful to the Church. I make constant efforts in practising virtue. I try faithfully to follow Jesus. And I deposit this whole series of daily virtues - silent, hidden, almost imperceptible, but made with great love - in the treasury of God's Church for the common benefit of souls. I feel interiorly as if I were responsible for all souls. I know very well that I do not live for myself alone, but for the entire Church."

(Diary, Notebook V, para. 1505).

This heroism necessary in each successive day now absorbed all the slender strength Sister Faustina had left. Although she was in severe and overwhelming physical pain, she gladly gave Jesus her daily offering of suffering undergone. But it was an effort so great that it left no space for other reflections. The time had now come for putting into practice the decisions she had made during the retreat. Close attention had to be paid, so as not for a moment to lose her goal from sight. In reality, her thoughts of sanctity confined themselves to thoughts of love, because that active love of God was what was important: to love God, and out of love for Him to love souls. In the brain of Sister Faustina, weakened and battered by suffering, this single thought was retained, clearly, precisely and obstinately. She had no strength to reflect on other problems of sanctity. She was wholly consumed in what she was giving, neither weighing nor pricing the greatness of her gift. So we are not surprised by the incident which took place on the First Friday of April 1938, five months after her last retreat - an incident which demonstrates how much real humility there was in Sister Faustina's soul.

"When I took the _Messenger of the Sacred Heart_ into my hand and read the account of the canonization of Saint Andrew Bobola, my soul was instantly filled with a great longing that our Congregation, too, might have a saint, and I wept like a child that there was no saint in our midst. And I said to the Lord, 'I know Your generosity, and yet it seems to me that You are less generous toward us.' And I began again to weep... And the Lord Jesus said to me, 'Don't cry. You are that saint'. Then the light of God inundated my soul, and I was given to know how much I was to suffer, and I said to the Lord, 'How will that come about? You have been speaking to me about another Congregation.' And the Lord answered, 'It is not for you to know how this will come about. Your duty is to be faithful to My grace and to do always what is within your power and what obedience allows you to do.'

(Diary, Notebook VI, para. 1650).

OUR LADY IN THE LIFE
OF SISTER FAUSTINA

It would be an incomplete picture of the spiritual life of Sister Faustina that did not include the role that Our Lady played in it.

Everyone who met Sister Faustina was struck by the fact that her faith was so very Christocentric. The Incarnate God - from cradle to Cross - occupied her whole heart and left no room for other thoughts. Connected with Him by her vows, like some careful housewife she fervently minded His business.

But precisely because the Incarnate God was the focus of her fascination, Mary the Mother who brought Him into this world was also included. True love embraces everything connected with the beloved. So, therefore, Sister Faustina loved the Mother of Jesus very much. In her heart, Our Lady had her own place and express honour; she accompanied Sister Faustina throughout her whole life, from the cradle to her deathbed.

As a child, Helenka became used to the figure of Our Lady in the daily religious practices of her home, taking an active part in the "Little Office" sung by her father, and in the rosary the family said together. So the Mother of God had an honoured place in her prayers from babyhood. Although her greatest longing was always to belong only to the Lord Jesus, at the same time she perfectly understood that if He were to dwell fully in her heart, she needed the helping hand of His Mother. No one could prepare souls as she could, to become the dwelling place of Her Son, no one but she could make sure that everything necessary for that step was accomplished - so thought Sister Faustina in her heart, and her love and gratitude to the Blessed Virgin grew. She had never avoided close spiritual contact with her, and as her spiritual life developed the contact became closer, taking on a more intimate and strictly personal character. It is even possible to pinpoint accurately the time at which this occurred. In her Diary for the day of her perpetual vows, Sister Faustina reminds Our Lady that she has acquired new "rights" in relation to her:

> *Mother of God, Most Holy Mary, my Mother, You are my Mother in a special way now because Your beloved Son is my Bridegroom, and thus we are both Your children. For Your Son's sake, You have to love me. O Mary, my dearest Mother, guide my spiritual life in such a way that it will please Your Son.*

(Diary, Notebook I, para. 240).

The whole format of this invocation, as well as the insistent tone, "You have to love me", shows that Sister Faustina already had a deep devotion to Our Lady and that she connected it with her inner life; the Mother of God was an integral part of it.

If we take a chronological view of the role of Our Lady in the life of Sister Faustina, we can find the first clear trace at the time when Helenka commended herself to the Mother of God, when her entry into religious life seemed hopeless. Helenka trusted the Blessed Virgin as the only one who could lead her to the service of Christ. In the light of this, the fact that the convent she actually entered was under the patronage of the Blessed Virgin, and the Mother of Mercy at that, has its own significance.

In the Congregation, whose Patron is Our Lady, by the nature of things her cultus is at the heart of the spirituality of its members. Their piety has its expression not only in the form officially recognized by the Congregation, in the prayers recommended and the Feast-days observed, but can further be seen in the personal predilection of the various sisters for one of the attributes of the Blessed Virgin, or in their favourite prayers to her. Sister Faustina was one of the latter. Her devotion to Our Lady, in the liturgically-ordered life of the Congregation, took on new depth. It was only now that she fully understood the role of the Mother of God in the work of the Redemption, and the need for her constant intercession, which must have had an influence on the choice of her personal devotion. This is recalled by two of her former companions, Sister Justine and Sister Louise for whom Sister Faustina acted as "guardian angel":

"Sister Faustina particularly prayed to Our Lady of Perpetual Succour, and while still in the novitiate she taught us the following prayer, advising us to say it for all our needs: Mother of Perpetual Succour, I approach You as my Mother in all the sufferings that assail me and in every need of my life. Therefore at any time of day or night come to the aid of my helplessness, and in the hour of my death come to my aid, my Only Mother."

(Archives of S.F., Recollections).

It is Mother Borgia, her Superior in Vilnius, who has shed most light on the Marian elements in Sister Faustina's spirituality. In Vilnius, the most orientated towards Mary of any Polish city, the nuns of the Congregation of Sisters of Our Lady of Mercy had an especially favourable spiritual climate for their devotion to the Mother of God. The devotion of their Congregation here met with, and was supported by, the local devotion to Our Lady of Mercy in the Dawn Gate.

Mother Borgia, witnessing to the great devotion of Sister Faustina to the Blessed Virgin, recounts how

> *"she always took part with visible joy in all the devotion and feast days of Our Lady... Whenever she had the opportunity, she would go to Ostra Brama, although it was more than three miles from the convent."*

(Archives of S.F., Recollections).

The devotion to the Blessed Virgin which can be so clearly seen in the spiritual life of Sister Faustina is a feature which must give rise to an understandable interest. Because we know that she always took everything that concerned her to the Lord Jesus hidden in the Blessed Sacrament, we must ask ourselves what matters she brought before Our Lady.

Sister Faustina made no clear division between the sphere of Jesus and the sphere of His Mother. Rather can it be said that every matter had a Marian foundation. In her religious life, the two devotions augmented and supplemented each other. She regarded the Mother of Jesus as the most trustworthy Guide to her Son. It was her presence that took away the fear of erring or of neglecting something. She therefore consecrated to Our Lady all her concerns, desiring the Mother of God to put her stamp on her whole interior life. Among all the requests she brought to Our Lady one was foremost: that the Immaculate Mother would protect her from the temptations of the flesh. In her Diary, almost at the beginning, can be found the prayer:

> *"O Mary, my Mother and my Lady, I offer You my soul, my body, my life and my death, and all that will follow it. I place everything in Your hands. O my Mother, cover my soul with Your virginal mantle and*

grant me the grace of purity of heart, soul and body. Defend me with Your power against all enemies..."

(Diary, Notebook I, para. 79).

We find a mention that this fervent prayer, which was often repeated in various forms, had been answered in the diary entry where Sister Faustina recalls the renewal of the annual vows in 1929. In describing the events of that day, she states that from then on

"I have never experienced any attacks against this virtue, either in my heart or in my mind. I later understood that this was one of the greatest graces which the Most Holy Virgin had obtained for me, as for many years I had been asking this grace of Her. She has taught me how to love God interiorly and also how to carry out His holy will in all things."

(Diary, Notebook I, para. 40).

Sister Faustina returned once more to the theme of her own virginal life in her diary a year and a half before her death. In April 1937, she wrote:

"When, one day, God gave me the inner knowledge that I had never lost my innocence, and that despite all dangers in which I had found myself, He Himself had been guarding me so that the virginity of my soul and heart would remain intact. I spent the day in fervent interior thanksgiving. I thanked God that He had been pleased to protect me from evil, and also for this: that I had found favor in His eyes... And a few years later, He deigned to confirm me in this grace, and since that time I have not experienced the rebellion of the senses

against the soul... Since that time, I have been living under the virginal cloak of the Mother of God. She has been guarding and instructing me. I am quite at peace, close to Her Immaculate Heart.'

(Diary, Notebook III, paras. 1095, 1096).

In the light of the above admissions, it is hardly surprising to learn that Sister Faustina's favourite Feast of Our Lady was the Feast of the Immaculate Conception. She prepared for it annually with great scrupulousness. Always prayerful, she still further increased her religious practices at this time, in order in some way to honour this attribute of Our Lady which particularly attracted her soul, and to which she felt personally attached. In her Diary for 8th December 1937 we find an exact description of what she did, which is the more significant for us as this was to be the last Feast of the Immaculate Conception during Sister Faustina's life:

"It is with great zeal that I have prepared for the celebration of the Feast of the Immaculate Conception of the Mother of God. I have made an extra effort to keep recollected in spirit and have meditated on that unique privilege of Our Lady...

I prepared not only by means of the novena said in common by the whole community, but I also made a personal effort to salute Her a thousand times each day, saying a thousand 'Hail Marys' for nine days in Her praise. This is now the third time I have said such a novena to the Mother of God... Although I have done this now three times in my life, and two of these while in the course of my duties... carrying out my tasks with the greatest exactitude, I have always said the novena outside the time of my exercises: that is to say, I have

not said the Aves during Holy Mass or Benediction.
Once, I made the novena while lying in the hospital.
Where there's a will, there's a way. Apart from
recreation, I have only prayed and worked. I have not
said a single unnecessary word during these days.
Although I must admit that such a matter requires a
good deal of attention and effort, nothing is too much
when it comes to honoring the Immaculate Virgin.'

(Diary, Notebook V, paras,1412,1413).

It is not possible to establish in which year the first
novena of nine thousand Hail Marys took place. The
second such novena probably took place in 1936, for it
was at this time that Sister Faustina was in hospital.
She must already then have had serious difficulty in
making such an exhausting novena. The last, which fell
in December 1937, was a positively heroic feat. By
then, Sister Faustina was very seriously ill, tormented
with pain and exhausted by the constant repetition of
attacks of fever, although, as far as she could, she still
worked. In these conditions, when she often had not
the strength to attend Mass, a novena which required
nine days of total daytime concentration was beyond
her physical capabilities, and humanly speaking,
impossible to complete. But great love shows that it can
do wonders, and only such love could have provided the
motivation.

Great love in the spiritual sphere always brings love
in reward. Our Lady replied to the veneration of Sister
Faustina with a special grace; she revealed herself in
all her glory, confirming her motherly care over Sister
Faustina and showing her how she must continue to
work on herself:

'My daughter, at God's command I am to be, in a
special and exclusive way your Mother; but I desire that

you, too, in a special way, be My child. I desire, My dearly beloved daughter, that you practice the three virtues that are dearest to Me - and most pleasing to God. The first is humility, humility, and once again humility; the second virtue, purity; the third virtue, love of God. As My daughter, you must especially radiate with these virtues.'

(Diary, Notebook V, paras.1414,1415).

Sister Faustina received the instructions of Our Lady with joyful readiness. She confesses in her Diary that her heart

'became so wonderful attracted to these virtues' that they are *'as though engraved'*, and that *'I practice them faithfully.'*

(Diary, Notebook V, para. 1415).

It can easily be seen that Sister Faustina's attitude to Our Lady had all the marks of the familiarity which daily intimacy gives. Further, we are aware that it was her usual practice to ask Her for help in preparing for Holy Communion. An especially intensive period of prayer for Faustina was Advent, the liturgical period serving to make ready the soul for the birth of the Infant Jesus. Sister Faustina took this duty very seriously so that even more than usual she would ask the Holy Mother of God to help her and direct her in accomplishing this duty.

The prayers mentioned above were part of her daily programme and were constant. There were others, according to the need of the moment or the particular stage in spiritual development. For Sister Faustina's spiritual needs found immediate expression in her prayers. Thus, for example, in 1933, when, after her perpetual vows she left Cracow for Vilnius, on her way she visited Jasna Gora (the "Mountain of Light"), in Czestochowa. To get there, she had to go out of her way, because Czestochowa does not lie on the railway link between Cracow and Vilnius. Sister Faustina had her own serious reasons for wishing to pray at the feet of Our Lady of Czestochowa. She was frightened. She was compelled to leave the place where her spiritual life had, for the first time, begun to take on equilibrium and order, and go once more into the unknown. She was leaving behind a spiritual director, Father Andrasz, who so clearly understood her soul, and the house, of all the convents of her Congregation, which she perhaps loved the most. Alone again, she would have to struggle with the demands of Jesus, and find a confessor to whom she could entrust the difficult problems of her interior life.

She spent six hours in prayer before the image of Our Lady in the shrine at Czestochowa. In her diary she noted:

'The Mother of God told me many things. I entrusted my perpetual vows to Her. I felt that I was Her child and that She was my Mother. She did not refuse any of my requests'.

(Diary, Notebook I, para. 260).

More than a year later, in Vilnius, when a particularly great number of difficulties had piled up in her life - the mistrust of Father Sopoćko, the hardship and burdensome nature of her work, the weight of the mission entrusted to her by Jesus now pressing hard upon her, together with a mass of painful experiences and humiliations from all sides - Sister Faustina summoned the Mother of God to her aid, counting upon her understanding over suffering.

'Mother of God, Your soul was plunged into a sea of bitterness; look upon Your child and teach her to suffer

and to love while suffering. Fortify my soul that pain will not break it.'

(Diary, Notebook I, para. 315).

In answer, the Most Holy Mother taught her

'to accept all that God asked of me like a little child, without questioning; otherwise it would not be pleasing to God.'

(Diary, Notebook II, para. 529).

In 1937, when physical pain and exhaustion through disease were so intense that they dominated all her thoughts and feelings, and Sister Faustina taught herself to transform them into an oblation for sinners, her prayers to Our Lady took on a completely different tone. Sister Faustina realized that in order to withstand this trial of suffering given her by God she would need heroism, and that this was attainable only in close union with Him. In boundless torment, as usual she approached the Mother of God, for comfort:

'O Mary, your soul does not break; it is brave, because it is with Jesus. Sweet Mother, unite my soul to Jesus, because it is only then that I will be able to endure all trials and tribulations, and only in union with Jesus will my little sacrifices be pleasing to God. Sweetest Mother, continue to teach me about the interior life. May the sword of suffering never break me.'

(Diary, Notebook II, para. 915).

Thus, we see throughout the life of Sister Faustina what an absolutely essential help the Mother of God is for her, and that such help was never lacking at any critical moment. It was natural that Sister Faustina felt herself to be Our Lady's child and quite natural that she hastened to her in her need. She receive the

Holy Mother's help sometimes in visions, during which the Most Holy Mother, while comforting her and explaining, at the same time strengthened and supported her failing forces. These visions were not frequent - they only gave an essential dose of spiritual strength in moments of especial crisis.

Sister Faustina's spiritual communion with Our Lady was so intimate and personal that it excluded other types of devotion to the Blessed Virgin. We search in vain among Sister Faustina's writings for some other of the many titles of Mary, than Most Holy Mother. Even the calling of the Mother of God by the title "Queen of Poland", so popular in Poland, does not appear, although Sister Faustina very much loved her country. In the Diary, many pages have prayers for the intention of Poland, where it might seem that invoking the Queen of Poland would be the obvious thing to do. Nevertheless, this title does not appear. This is even more obvious where Sister Faustina is describing her visit to Jasna Gora, the shrine of Czestochowa, the very centre of the Polish devotion to the Madonna. It does not seem to occur to her to call her "Queen", though she considered Poland to be the Kingdom of the Mother of God. For Sister Faustina, there too she was simply "Mother". The only exception is her use of the title The Immaculate Conception.

To clarify why the invocation "Queen of Poland" is never found in Sister Faustina's writings, I shall quote one or two of her most typical prayers for her country.

The first, which begins the entry of them in her Diary, probably comes from the year 1934, as it is near the beginning. We learn that Jesus had told her to say a novena for the intentions of her country, which was to be composed of the Stations of the Cross and a hour's adoration, during which she was to join her prayers with the Mother of God:

'Pray with your heart in union with Mary... ' *'On the seventh day of the novena I saw, between heaven and*

earth, the Mother of God, clothed in a bright robe. She was praying with Her hands folded on Her bosom, Her eyes fixed on Heaven. From Her Heart issued forth fiery rays, some of which were turned toward Heaven while the others were covering our country."

(Diary, Notebook I, para. 33).

In 1936 there occurred the first dramatic vision of the punishment awaiting Poland, which was prevented only - as we would say - by the intervention of the "Queen of Poland". But Sister Faustina writes:

"In the evening, I saw the Mother of God, with Her breast bared and pierced with a sword. She was shedding bitter tears and shielding us against God's terrible punishment. God wants to inflict terrible punishment on us, but He cannot because the Mother of God is shielding us... I kept praying incessantly for Poland, for my dear Poland, which is so lacking in gratitude for the Mother of God... I intensified my prayers and sacrifices for our dear native land, but I see that I am a drop before the wave of evil. How can a drop stop a wave?"

(Diary, Notebook II, para. 686).

It is obvious that the Mother of God was, for Sister Faustina, not only her Mistress in the art of personal perfection, but to the same degree her Guide in the great mission left to her by Jesus. It was Our Lady who made her realize that *"the graces God was granting me were not for me alone, but for other souls as well"* (Diary, Notebook II, para. 561). This was later repeated to her many times by Jesus. The warning was once more repeated in 1936, when the Mother of God finally defined the mission of Sister Faustina:

'... you have to speak to the world about His great mercy and prepare the world for the Second Coming... Speak to souls about this great mercy while it is still the time for [granting] mercy. If you keep silent now, you will be answering for a great number of souls on that terrible day. Fear nothing. Be faithful to the end.'

(Diary, Notebook II, para. 634).

It would indeed be difficult to over-estimate the role of the Most Holy Mother in the life of Sister Faustina. As she felt it, Jesus was inextricably linked with His Mother. In order to fulfil His will, therefore, one should stay as close to her as possible. This is what in fact she did. This is confirmed by these verses from her Diary:

'O sweet Mother of God,
I model my life on You;
You are for me the bright dawn;
In You I lose myself, enraptured.
O Mother, Immaculate Virgin,
In You the divine ray is reflected,
Midst storms, 'tis You who teach me to love the Lord,
O my shield and defence from the foe.'

(Diary, Notebook IV, para. 1232).

LIFE DOES NOT END WITH DEATH

The year 1938, that is the last nine months in the life of Sister Faustina, showed a change from all other forms of her apostolic work towards intercession. Thus, the oblation of her own suffering was the chief component of her prayer. On several pages of her Diary, we find its expression in the requests she makes with imploring persistence: "Give me suffering if You wish, but in exchange give me souls".

Sister Faustina did not wish to choose the souls, nor did she define which souls she wanted. The souls of any sinners - both those within her sphere of influence and those which Jesus told her of - were all the object of her intercession. Jesus not only did not inhibit her fervour, but, as if it were insufficient for Him, encouraged her to greater efforts, placing before her the highest standard as a pattern:

'My daughter, look into My Merciful Heart and reflect its compassion in your own heart and in your deeds, so that you, who proclaim My mercy to the world, may yourself be aflame with it.'

(Diary, Notebook VI, para. 1688).

This speedily increasing enormous love of souls gave Sister Faustina strength to make a daily oblation of suffering. Meanwhile, the knowledge that her prayers were being answered - for Jesus was generous in His

355

assurances of this - gave joy which overwhelmed all her pains, and Sister Faustina on her deathbed, her "bed of pain" was cheerful and smiling, though thin and altered to such a degree that "it was painful to look at her", as some of the sisters who visited her said.

The Diary also reflects the image of someone equable and full of inner happiness. We can find a great number of verses with a lyrical character, which show in full the mood she was then in. The Diary is a uniform song of praise to the Divine Mercy.

The circumstances in which this poetic creativity arose reminds us of another troubadour of God's love -St. Francis of Assisi. With both of these two, a body destroyed by disease had no effect on the basic equilibrium of their souls, which to the contrary - as if independently - blossomed in the rays of God's love and grace in a maturity full of harmony, making energetic attempts to express in words what was filling the heart, and finding an appropriate outlet in a poetic use of rhyme and rhythm. St. Francis, in his poetry, sings of God's Creation about him, glorifying both the light and the dark side of it, while Sister Faustina sings the praises of that Divine Mercy which supports the world.

Sister Faustina's poetry is such an important part of her witness, especially in the last stage of her life, that it deserves at least a superficial discussion.

Verses began to appear in her Diary at the end of her stay in Vilnius, but those attempts, as yet timid and clumsy in form, were short and infrequent. Their number increased in the last two years of her life with greater rapidity, which would indicate that she had found the most appropriate form for her to express what she felt and thought. The last several score pages of her Diary are mainly filled with verses.

Sister Faustina's poetry strikes one above all for the precision of her thought and the clarity of its expression. Clumsiness, in places very noticeable, is present only in the forms she used. There are mistakes in the rhythm, or poor rhymes, but not in the content. That is crystal clear.If we take into account that her intellect was clouded with suffering and fever, and that her verses were only a first attempt, for none of them was ever in any way revised, our first impression must be corrected. The verses are a spontaneous witness and as such form a special kind of mirror of the sick young woman's emotions. According to the skill with which the form is used, it becomes easy to guess when she was feeling better, and also when it was with difficulty that she could find the words to express the inner content of her soul. It is then that the text seems rough and clumsy.

There are three themes in Sister Faustina's verses: approaching death, the bearing of the suffering which is her lot, and adoration of the Divine Mercy.

On the subject of death, Sister Faustina slides over the moment of death itself, not so much concerned with the threshold she must cross as with the eternity which waits upon the other side.

I hasten on to the other world, to God alone,
Into the incomprehensible light, the very fire of love,
For my soul and my heart are created for Him,
And my heart has loved Him from my tender youth.
                    (Diary, Notebook VI, para. 1653).

My day is drawing to a close,
Even now I glimpse the refulgence of Your light,
O my God,
No one shall learn of what my heart is feeling;
My lips shall fall silent in great humility.
  Even now, I draw nigh to the eternal nuptials,
  To heaven unending, to spaces without limit.
  I long for no repose or reward;
  The pure love of God draws me to heaven.

Even now, I go to meet You, eternal Love
With a heart languishing in its desire for You,
I feel that Your pure love, Lord, dwells in my
heart,
And I sense my eternal destiny in heaven.
   I go, O my Bridegroom, I go to see Your glory,
   Which even now fills my soul with joy
   There where all heaven is plunged in Your
   adoration,
   I feel that my worship is pleasing to You,
   nothingness though I am.
In these last moments I know not how to converse
with others.
In silence I await only You, O Lord,
I know the time will come when all will understand
the work of God in my soul.
I know that such is Your will. · So be it.

(Diary, Notebook VI, from 1653).

The suffering she was undergoing was also a frequent subject in Sister Faustina's verse. The genuine nature and honesty of her oblation comes through and moves us with its force. The verses are written as she was in actual pain, so they come from within the pain itself. The physical and mental endurance of Sister Faustina is absolutely astounding, for she is able not only to conquer the most fierce pain, but even to sing a paean in honour of the Divine content of that pain. It is contemplation of suffering during suffering, as f drilling into the nucleus of the pain itself. Sister Faustina transformed meditation upon suffering into a song which celebrates the spiritual content of the pain because it is connected with Christ the Lord.

I would not know how to suffer without You,
O Christ.
Of myself I would not be able to brave adversities.
Alone, I would not have the courage to drink from Your
cup;
But You, Lord, are always with me, and You lead me
along mysterious paths.

(Diary, Notebook VI, para. 1654).

It seems that the redemptive work of Jesus was most strongly felt by Sister Faustina in the Sacrament of the Altar. She always sought Him there constantly available under the humble appearance of bread. This is why, when she tries to join her sacrifice with the redemptive sacrifice of her Lord, she often compares it to the symbol of the Host. Fascinated by this theme, she repeats it in a new version each time.

I am a host in your hand, O Divine Priest,
Do with me as You please;
I am totally dependent on Your will, O Lord
Because it is the delight and adornment of my soul.
  I am like a host in Your hand, O Eternal Priest,
  May the wafer of my body hide me from human eye;
  My Your eye alone measure my love and devotion,
  Because my heart is always united with Your
  Divine Heart.
I am like a sacrificial host in Your hand, O Divine
Mediator
Am I burn on the altar of holocaust,
Crushed and ground by suffering like grains of
wheat,
And all this for the sake of Your glory, for the
salvation of souls.

*I am a host abiding in the tabernacle of Your
Heart,
I go through life drowned in Your love,
And I fear nothing in the world,
For You Yourself are my shield, my strength, and
my defence.
I am a host in Your hand, O Judge and Savior.
In the last hour of my life,
May the omnipotence of Your grace lead me to my
goal,
May Your compassion on the vessel of mercy become
famous.*

(Diary, Notebook VI, para. 1629).

Sister Faustina's third theme has two variants;
adoration for the Divine Mercy raining down upon the
world, and adoration of the Mercy which is always
awaiting man in the Eucharist.

*Be adored, O our Creator and Lord.
O universe, humbly glorify your God;
Thank your Creator to the best of your powers
And praise God's incomprehensible mercy.
   Come, O earth in all your fine greenery;
   Come, you too, O fathomless sea,
   Let your gratitude become a loving song
   And sing the greatness of God's mercy.
Come, beautiful, radiant sun.
Come, bright dawn which precedes it.
Join in one hymn, and let your clear voices
Sing in one accord God's great mercy.
   Come, hills and valleys, sighing woods and
   thickets,*

Come, lovely flowers of morningtide;
Let your unique scent
Adore and glorify God's mercy.
Come, all you lovely things of earth,
Which man does not cease to wonder at.
Come, adore God in your harmony,
Glorifying God's inconceivable mercy.
Come, indelible beauty of all the earth,
and, with great humility, adore your Creator,
For all things are locked in His mercy,
With one mighty voice all things cry out; how great is
the mercy of God.

(Diary, Notebook VI, para. 1750).

Sister Faustina's verses on the theme of the Eucharist have already been quoted in a preceding chapter on page 295 of MS.

Her verses say astonishingly little of the conflicts with which her life abounded. They are the expression of her positive attitude, quite approving whatever life brings, though they do not hide the presence of suffering and the essential task of transforming sufferings so that they have a divine value.

The patterns for Sister Faustina's poetic creativity are, to speak very generally, the Bible and those Polish liturgical and paraliturgical texts she was able to obtain. Her method of constructing sentences, certain archaisms and grandiloquence, indicate that she had absorbed a Biblical style. For it was not only what the Church said, but how it said it, that was, for her, the highest index of what was of value. She therefore did not seek other models not only most probably out of ignorance, as some have frequently suggested, because we do know that she was at least familiar with Polish poetry even if only in the narrow confines of the school programme; but she chose her models most likely in the conviction that the form used by the Church (in which we must include the psalms and canticles she would know, hymns, and even the method of composing a prayer) was the proper form, and even the only way to express this type of content. Hence, of the literary models other than ecclesiastical, there is merely an echo of one in her verses: Kochanowski, and that is only because she knew some of the psalms in his translation.

An equally strong influence upon Sister Faustina was that of hymns. Sister Faustina loved to sing. She sang a great deal, until her illness made it impossible, although she did not have a good voice. When she felt too ill to sing, she would beat the rhythm of a given hymn with her fingers on the table. When she had become seriously ill, she would often ask someone to sing her favourite hymns. She had her favourites, a different one at each stage of her life. They were often something that gave the impetus to one of her own poems. In her diary (Diary, Notebook II, para. 994) she mentions that when she once heard the hymn, Good night, Holy Head of my Jesus, on the radio, it inspired her to express her own feelings for Him. This note illustrates well how the melody of a hymn at once translated itself, for her, into the rhythm of words ready to express the mood which that hymn had evoked in her.

If we were to seek them out, it would be possible to illustrate Sister Faustina's spiritual path with hymns. For example, we know that before she entered the convent, when she was in her last place of service with Mrs Lipszyc, her favourite hymn was I must honour Jesus hidden in the Eucharist. In 1937, when she was still working in the garden, the ward Helen Skowroń- ska often sang, at her request, I long for You, merciful Lord. The hymn she most gladly listened to in the last days of her life was I am Yours, Jesus, for which she would ask Sister A., her nurse.

As a creative talent, Sister Faustina is an interesting phenomenon. She undoubtedly possessed great artistic sensitivity. Beauty was no mean element in her piety. But it was always the beauty of God's creation, and not beauty created by man. The latter did not interest her at all. The most beautiful churches were resplendent with the beauty of God present within them, and not in their exterior appearance. This child of the country-side never took the least notice of even the most splendid churches of God in cities so rich in them as are Cracow and Vilnius. The beauty which attracted her soul was that with which God has Himself surround us. She was, and remained uniformly to the end of her life, enchanted with Creation.

But let us return to the mental state which gave rise to her poetry. This mood of inner cheerfulness and harmony which most particularly characterizes the last months of Sister Faustina's life was something so extraordinary that it must have been noticed by those around her, the more so that when she had last been working, and struggling with the work she had been given by Jesus, she was sometimes seen to be in a state of nervous tension. This had now totally vanished. Her behaviour became equable and a deep peace entered that soul which was now drowned in God. Eternity was fast approaching, and she went to meet it with open arms. This is confirmed by Sister D., who in the spring of 1938 went to see Sister Faustina, who told her, For six months I have been feeling as if I were in eternity.

Those who surrounded Sister Faustina did not know of her preceding spiritual difficulties, but the sufferings resulting from her progressing illness were highly visible to all. The change in the attitude of the sick woman was all the more obvious to everyone about her, and they began to say, while she was still alive, that she was a saint.

"I liked to visit Sister Faustina", says her then superior, Mother Irene Krzyżanowska. *"These visits gave me spiritual joy. Our conversations were always saturated with the atmosphere of the divine. Whenever I spent a longer time with her, I felt the presence of God."*

(Archives of S.F., Recollections).

Sister Bozena still more emphatically describes the spiritual atmosphere which Sister Faustina radiated:

"When in 1938 I lived in close contact with her for two months and I observed Sister Faustina at close hand, I simply thought she was a saint... When I returned from Cracow to Walendow to my usual duties, I felt as cheered up after two months' familiarity with Sister Faustina, as if I had made a successful retreat."

(Archives of S.F., Recollections).

More than one of the sisters came to Sister Faustina to ask that she intercede for them at the throne of the Eternal Father after her death. Among those who asked were not only companions from her own Congregation, but the Sacred Heart Sisters from the hospital at Prądnik. When she was approached, Sister Faustina attentively but silently listened to those intimate matters of human souls, entrusted to her to straighten out as if they were the last errands before she set out on a voyage. In general she simply smiled in affirmation, but if the mental condition of her client required the giving of a promise, she did not hesitate to give one. In her diary, she has noted two such requests:

'Today, one on the sisters came to see me and said, Sister, I have a strange feeling, as though something were telling me to come to you and commend to you certain problems of mine before you die, and that perhaps you

will be able to beseech the Lord Jesus and arrange these things for me. Something keeps telling me that you will be able to obtain this for me." I answered her with equal frankness that, yes, I felt in my soul that after my death I would be able to obtain more from the Lord Jesus than at the present time. *"I will remember you Sister, before His throne."* "

(Diary, Notebook VI, para. 1614).

The second request was of a different nature:

"When I entered the neighbouring dormitory to visit the sisters who were ill, one of them said to me, "Sister, when you die I will not fear you at all. Come to see me after you die, because I want to confide to you a secret concerning my soul, something I want you to settle for me with the Lord Jesus. I know you can obtain this from Him." "

(Diary, Notebook VI, para. 1615).

There were similar requests from other sisters, so there is no need to linger over these. Those which I have cited supply sufficient of the atmosphere which had grown around the invalid Sister Faustina.

It is not sufficient for us to observe the spiritual portrait of Sister Faustina towards the end of her life only from the exterior, on the basis of her companions' impressions. After all, we have accompanied her through her successive spiritual transformations, so that we wish to remain in close contact with her until death itself. Let us therefore come back to the problems of her interior life and the final maturing before her death.

As I have already written in a preceding chapter, the retreats she had in October 1937 and in 1938 before the Feast of Pentecost - the latter being the last in her life - had a decisive effect upon her.

During the first retreat Sister Faustina took the decision to attain holiness above all through prayer and the offering of her own sufferings for sinners. The question had been thoroughly thought through, and, as Jesus had accepted her decision with approval, Sister Faustina lost no time in putting it into action. Unfortunately the state of her health now no longer allowed her either to lead a normal life in her community, or even to use her now freer time to the full for more prayer. She could do only one thing, but this, in order to practise it daily, required constant heroism. The aim was to accept all the sufferings of her illness and all adversities as gifts from Providence and to transform them into intercession for sinful souls. This "prayer" was to be said daily, regularly and without a break.

Sister Faustina undertook her planned task at once, straight after the first retreat, but obviously not on a heroic scale as yet, because more or less six months later as Lent was beginning in 1938, Jesus said that **"He would take her to His school, to teach her how to suffer."**

This last stage in Jesus's school, which ended the programme of her life's spiritual education, had a similar course to that in the Gospels with the Apostles: it began with the Passion of Christ and lasted until Pentecost. She accompanied Christ to Golgotha, experiencing His Passion both spiritually and physically. Her final and definitive joining in His redemptive grace and activity as an apostle of the Divine Mercy fell on the Feast of the Sending of the Holy Spirit, Pentecost, after previous preparation in a three-day retreat.

This retreat was undertaken at the desire of Jesus. Sister Faustina already lay in hospital in a hopeless state, barely able to drag herself from her bed, but she still had strength for the retreat. She therefore received the permission of her superior to undertake it.

Jesus Himself led the retreat. Sister Faustina had become used to God taking part in one of her retreats. Jesus had many times already, in various ways, enriched their content or taught her to understand them more deeply and fully. Up to now, this had always been help by augmenting the retreat given by a priest. This time, He was leading the retreat. He decided on the programme, gave out the texts to read, the themes for meditation, and Himself gave the instructions. For each day of the retreat there was a Scriptural reading, two meditations and an instruction, which summed up the theme previously given for meditation and contained practical directions on how to introduce the requirements of behaviour into her daily life.Sister Faustina has given a detailed account of this retreat in her Diary, (Notebook VI, paras. 1753-1779). The plan of the retreat was as follows: on the first day of the retreat the Lord gave her the following order:

'Today you will read chapter fifteen of the Gospel of Saint John. I want you to read it very slowly.' The chapter contains the following texts: - Jesus is the true Vine. - His command to love one another. - The hatred of the world for Him and His disciples. For the first meditation Jesus gave: *'Consider... Who it is to whom your heart is so closely united by the vows...'* and for the second meditation: *'Consider the life of God which is found in the Church for the salvation and the sanctification of your soul. Consider the use that you make of these treasures of grace.'*

The teaching of Jesus, summing up the whole day's meditation, discussed in a very particular way how Sister Faustina was to carry on the spiritual struggle to preserve the virtues meditated upon. Among other matters Jesus recommended:

'Never trust in yourself, but abandon yourself totally to My will, In desolation, darkness and various doubts, have recourse to Me and to your spiritual director... Do not bargain with any temptation; lock yourself immediately in My Heart and, at the first opportunity, reveal the temptation to the confessor. Put your self-love in the last place, so that it does not taint your deeds. Bear with yourself with great patience. Do not neglect interior mortifications... Shun murmurers like a plague... Observe the rule as faithfully as you can. If someone causes you trouble, think what good you can do for the person who causes you to suffer... Be silent when you are rebuked. Do not ask everyone's opinion, but only the opinion of your confessor... Do not become discouraged by ingratitude. Do not examine with curiosity the roads down which I lead you. When boredom and discouragement beat against your heart, run away from yourself and hide in My heart. Do not fear struggle,' - Jesus fortified Sister Faustina, finishing His instruction - *'courage itself often intimidates temptations, and they dare not attack us. Always fight with the deep conviction that I am with you... I will not delude you with prospects of peace and consolations; on the contrary, prepare for great battles...'*

(Diary, Notebook VI, para. 1760).

On the second day of the retreat Jesus recommended:

'... for your reading you shall take chapter nineteen of Saint John's Gospel, and read it, not only with your lips, but with your heart.'.

368

This chapter contains the description of the Passion of Christ, from the scourging, through the sentencing to death, to the last words and death, the opening of Jesus' side, the taking down from the cross and burial.

As meditation, Jesus suggested:

'Consider My Sorrowful Passion in all its immensity. Consider it as if it had been undertaken for your sake alone.'

For the second meditation:

'Consider the rule and the vows which you have offered to Me.'

The teaching of Jesus, in summing up the whole day's meditation, instructed her how Faustina was to save souls.

'You will save more souls through prayer and suffering than will a missionary through his teachings and sermon alone. I want to see you as a sacrifice of living love, which only then carries weight before Me. You must be annihilated, destroyed, living as if you were dead in the most secret depths of your being. You must be destroyed in that secret depth where the human eye has never penetrated; then will I find in you a pleasing sacrifice, a holocaust... And great will be your power for whomever you intercede. Outwardly, your sacrifice must look like this: silent, hidden, permeated with love, imbued with prayer... I will not spare My grace, that you may be able to fulfill what I demand of you.

I will now instruct you on what your holocaust shall consist of, in everyday life, so as to preserve you from

369

*illusions. You shall accept all sufferings with love. Do
not be afflicted if your heart often experiences repugnance
and dislike for sacrifice. All its power rests in the will,
and so these contrary feelings, far from lowering the
value of the sacrifice in My eyes, will enhance it.'*

(Diary, Notebook VI, para. 1767).

On the third day of the retreat, Jesus recommended:

*'Today, for your spiritual reading, you will take the
Gospel of Saint John, chapter twenty-one. Let it feed
your heart more than your mind.'*

The chapter contains three texts from the period
when Jesus appeared to His disciples after His
Resurrection: Jesus shows Himself at the Sea of
Tiberias, and His two discourses: Peter as the supreme
Shepherd, and a prophecy of the deaths of Peter and
John.

On this day of the retreat, Jesus' teaching concerned
His Mercy:

*'My daughter, know that My Heart is mercy itself.
From this sea of mercy, graces flow out upon the whole
world. No soul that has approached Me has ever gone
away unconsoled. All misery gets buried in the depths of
My mercy, and every saving and sanctifying grace flows
from this fountain. My daughter, I desire that your heart
be an abiding place of My mercy. Let no one who
approaches you go away without that trust in My mercy
which I so ardently desire for souls. Pray as much as you
can for the dying. By your entreaties, obtain for them
trust in My mercy, because they have most need of trust,
and have it the least... You know the whole abyss of My*

mercy, so draw upon it for yourself and especially for poor sinners.'

At the end of the retreat, Jesus, in a short summary, emphasized what He desired from Sister Faustina:

'My daughter, let three virtues adorn you in a particular way: humility, purity of intention and love. Do nothing beyond what I demand of you, and accept everything that My hand gives you. Strive for a life of recollection so that you can hear My voice, which is so soft that only recollected souls can hear it.'

(Diary, Notebook VI, para. 1779).

This retreat was closely connected with all the others which Sister Faustina, with the help of Jesus, had made before. It forms a crowning point among them all. These three days sum up finally that which for all these years, He had been preparing her. In content, they connect daily life with the Gospel and with the Church. Against this huge panorama of the spiritual, Sister Faustina is once more to examine her life and in this context she is to take a decision. Only then will she see, in the true light, her inner truth and the purity of her own intentions. This will be a final decision, which, verifying all the preceding ones, will give them their final form, that with which she will enter eternity. The retreat is therefore a focus which links her temporal life with eternal life. In the programme He had planned Himself, Jesus gradually leads Sister Faustina along in the three days set aside. As they pass by, He gradually emphasizes her personal commitment. Sister Faustina is to experience them rather than think them through.

It is a feature of this retreat that Jesus insists that Sister Faustina should take part with her whole self, with all her faculties, and not only her intellect.This type of approach is usual in Ignatian retreats, with which Sister Faustina was familiar, so that in this case we have a new proof of how grace builds upon nature. Sister Faustina had been prepared for this retreat also in a natural manner, by the style of those retreats she had become used to making in the Congregation.

Summarising what Sister Faustina received to think about in this last retreat, we can sea that Jesus began his conference, or teaching, with instructions on how she was to act in the difficulties of everyday life, and He then discussed the way in which she was to save souls. He ended His teaching with a general definition once more of Sister Faustina's life's mission. That this retreat was a preparation for her mission in eternity can be seen from what next befell her. She made this retreat between 2nd and 5th June, and not quite two weeks later the state of her health suddenly worsened considerably. From the description in her diary, it appears that she suffered an internal haemorrhage, which was, indeed, controlled, but the sick young woman became so very weak that she was not able to continue her notes. The Diary breaks off shortly afterwards, with no explanation, and with no exact date, somewhere in the middle of the second half of June 1938. She closes it with a fervent prayer:

"May Your grace, which flows down upon me from Your Compassionate Heart, strengthen me for the struggle and sufferings, that I may remain faithful to You. And, although I am such misery, I do not fear You, because I know Your mercy well.'

(Diary, Notebook VI, para. 1803).

Sister Faustina had no more strength to write the Diary, or at least she had too little to be able to undertake both the effort of writing and the enduring of exhausting pain, the more so as, despite her suffering and lack of strength, she did not break off her decision made in the retreat: to become a saint. Many recollections of her Sisters in religion, from the period at the end of her life, bear witness to this. In their recollections, she appeared remarkably self-controlled in the midst of pain, although she would not agree to take painkillers; for everyone she had a smile on her face, as if to smile in those circumstances gave her no effort; she awaited death not only with confidence, but with longing.

Sister Crescentia, who saw her a few days before she died, remembers:

"She was very ugly, very worn out, a real
skeleton. She was breathing heavily.
- Sister dear, you are not afraid of death?
-Why should I be? - she answered and moved
strongly on her bed, becoming lively.
- All my sins and imperfections will be consumed
like straw in the fire of the Divine Mercy."

Sister S. has a similar story:

"During her last illness when I asked her if she knew she was seriously ill and would not get better, she said very peacefully, "I hasten on to the other world, to God alone,"I know." When I asked her if she were not afraid of death, she answered with a smile, as if she was looking into eternity, "I only trust in the Divine Mercy"."

Sister R. adds:

"A few days before she died, she wrote me a few words of farewell: "I feel that the end of my life is near, I do not fear death, I am going to meet my Bridegroom"."

(Archives of S.F., Recollections).

All the recollections of the sisters agree in their assessment of the attitude and behaviour of Sister

Faustina in the face of approaching death. From Mother Irene Krzyżanowska and Father Michael Sopoćko, we know that she knew the date of her death. Her departure was like a greater and greater falling towards God. Father Sopoćko said that when he saw her for the last time on 26th September, i.e., ten days before she died, she did not want to talk to him. She told him that she had said everything she had to say, and now "she was busy communing with her Heavenly Father". Father Sopoćko said that she gave him the "impression of a supernatural being." Holiness radiated so powerfully from her that it broke down the opposition even of those who had been most mistrustful of her.

Sister Faustina died in her convent, among her own. On 17th September they brought her from the hospital to her home, the convent, where she lived for two and a half weeks more. She had put all her earthly affairs in order some months earlier in the retreats she had made at the end of 1937 and in 1938.

In her Diary, under the date 22nd October 1937, we find the following:

> *In the meditation on death, I prepared myself as if for real death. I examined my conscience and searched all my affairs at the approach of death and, thanks be to grace, my affairs were directed toward that ultimate goal.*

(Diary, Notebook V, para. 1343).

Three months later, she was repeating:

> *In the meditation on death, I asked the Lord to deign to fill my heart with those sentiments which I will have at the moment of my death. And through God's grace I received an interior reply that I had done what was within my power and so could be at peace.*

(Diary, Notebook V, para. 1551).

Now she had to make her farewells to the Congregation. Sister W. recalls this moment graphically:

"After her last return from hospital, when she realized that she was dying, thorough Sister Superior she asked all the sisters to come to her, to say farewell to them, to thank them for their kindnesses to her and to apologize for her transgressions. At that time, she was lively and smiling. When I expressed surprise that at such a moment she was not weeping, she said that she must put her affairs in order in the way that the rule of the Congregation prescribed, for she was dying."

(Archives of S.F., Recollections).

She really did not feel like weeping. She was waiting impatiently for the moment of uniting herself with her beloved Master. On the day of her death, 5th October, she whispered to Sister to Sister Felicia with obvious emotion: *"Today the Lord is taking me."* (Archives of S.F., Recollections).

The sisters gathered at the bedside of the sick nun on the day of her death, 5th October, for one more time. She was dying having received the Sacraments. In the afternoon, her spiritual director in Cracow, Father Andrasz, came and she made her last confession to him. In the evening it seemed that the end was near, so the Superior gathered the sisters, who with the convent chaplain, Father Czaputa, offered prayers for the dying. She was conscious, and the presence of those in the Congregation who were nearest to her was soothing, and made it easier for her dimming mind to understand the ceremony they were carrying out. She knew what the Mother Superior, Irene Krzyżanowska, was praying for - that Superior who was a faithful witness to her revelations, she who first introduced certain forms of the devotion to Divine Mercy into the Congregation during her own lifetime; and Father Czaputa, who gave encouragement to her soul during

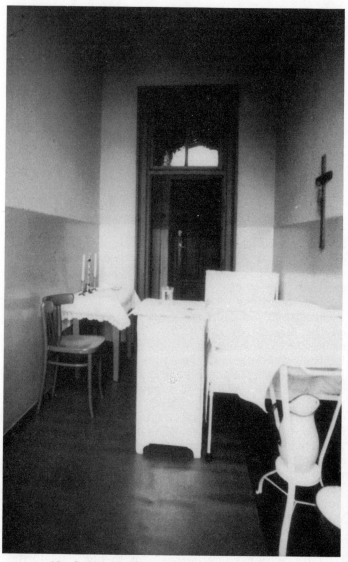

13. Isolation cell in which Sister Faustina died

14. Cementery of the Congregation of Sisters of Our Lady of Mercy at Łagiewniki near Cracow

15. Hyla's painting of the Merciful Jesus, 1943

her dark mystical night when she was a novice; her companions, some of whom she had known since the beginning of her religious life. Their prayers in common surrounded her soul like a warm, snug cloak, which protected her against her long journey. It was not hard to join spiritually in that flow of prayers and be carried along on its current toward God, Who was waiting for her any moment now...

But as her death agony did not approach, the sisters, having said prayers for the dying, left, and one of the infirmarians, Sister L., remained with her. Sister Faustina died in her presence shortly afterwards, at 10.45 p.m. She crossed the threshold into eternity so quietly and peacefu and so quickly, that Sister L. did not even have time to call back the Superior.

The funeral took place on 7th October, on the Feast of Our Lady of the Rosary. The Mother of God, who had led her to this Congregation - as her best Guide in making her first steps in eternal life - said farewell to her temporal remains on this earth. She was buried in the convent cemetery which was in the garden of the convent, and she lay there for twenty-eight years. On 25th November 1966, at the end of the informative process, with regard to the absence of a public veneration, she was exhumed and transferred to the Sisters' chapel, where she rests today.

Sister Faustina's apostolate after her death began almost at once. It increased slowly, first within the Congregation, and gradually spreading to the outer world. When, at the outbreak of the Second World war, the Sisters' chapel was opened to the faithful, the devotion increased enormously. From then on, her tomb was rarely without someone praying by it, asking for her intercession, or thanking her.

What of the devotion to the Divine Mercy? It was no particular surprise to anyone. The Sisters and their wards had become used to it even during the lifetime of Sister Faustina. Mercy as such was always a particular feature of this Congregation, so that when Sister Faustina spoke of it, no one was amazed; people only thought that she concentrated her piety and attention on it more closely. Father Sopoćko published the Novena and Litany during her lifetime, and also a little picture of the Merciful Jesus. Mother Irene Krzyżanowska is our most authoritative witness on the history of the devotion:

"When I became superior in Cracow, I obtained a little picture of the Merciful Jesus and placed it on the altar of St. Joseph (at the end of 1937 or in 1938). Seeing that both our Sisters and the wards of our institution had great reverence for this image, I decided to order a large picture to hang in our chapel. On Low Sunday, which according to the revelations of Sister Faustina was the day Jesus had chosen as the Feast of His Mercy, we placed this picture at the side altar of the Sacred Heart of Jesus. On Low Sunday a Mass was said at this altar and there was a special sermon on the Divine Mercy."

(Archives of S.F., Recollections).

In March 1943, Father Andrasz blessed a larger picture of the Merciful Jesus, painted by the artist Adolf Hyla as a votive offering for the safety of himself and his family during the war. The image was placed at a side altar. To what degree it became popular can be seen from the many votive offerings around it.

At Lagiewniki near Cracow the devotion to the Divine Mercy is especially closely connected with the person of Sister Faustina. Here it would be impossible to forget the person who made the public accustomed to the devotion. Those who come to pray in the presence of the image always visit the tomb of Sister Faustina. A great variety of people can be seen: largely, crowds of simple people come, but among them is a considerable number of representative members of the intelligentsia, such as priests, nuns, etc. Cardinal Sapieha prayed here, as did the then Ordinary of Czestochowa, Bishop Barela, when, as a priest, he still lived in Cracow. When he was the Rector of the Seminary, the present

Metropolitan Bishop of Cracow, Cardinal Francis Macharski came regularly.

During the last war, devotion to the Divine Mercy spread throughout almost the whole of Poland with an extraordinary speed. Undoubtedly, the dominant reason for its dynamic growth was the need of the moment. Sister Faustina's help was particularly consoling, but the circumstances in which this intercession came down to the people should also be taken into consideration.

Sister Faustina loved her country very much. Patriotism is one of her special characteristics. When it was that love of her country arose within her cannot be established - one might confidently say, "it was always there". It appeared in various circumstances, always in a prayerful form, as has been reported by the wards and her sister-companions. She herself in the Diary writes about it, where it is worthy of note that Jesus Himself very much encouraged love of her country. For instance, in 1933 Sister Faustina records:

"On one occasion I heard these words in my soul, 'Make a novena for your country. This novena will consist of the recitation of the litany of the Saints.'"

(Diary, Notebook I, para. 59).

In 1936 she had a vision, in which Jesus said:

'... I want all the sisters and wards to say the chaplet which I have taught you. They are to say it for nine days in the chapel in order to propitiate My Father and to entreat God's mercy for Poland.'

(Diary, Notebook II, para. 714).

In 1937, she states:

'I often pray for Poland, but I see that God is very angry with it because of its ingratitude. I exert all the

strength of my soul to defend it. I constantly remind God of the promises of His mercy. When I see His anger, I throw myself trustingly into the abyss of His mercy, and I plunge all Poland in it, and then He cannot use His justice. My Country, how much you cost me! There is no day in which I do not pray for you.'

(Diary, Notebook III, para. 1188).

Once more, she writes:

"My beloved native land, Poland, if you only knew how many sacrifices and prayers I offer to God for you! But be watchful and give glory to God, who lifts you up and singles you out in a special way. But know how to be grateful.'

(Diary, Notebook III, para. 1038).

In 1938, a year before the outbreak of the Second World War. Sister Faustina was more and more frequently asking her sisters in religion and their wards to pray for Poland, saying that a long and dreadful war was coming. Undiscouraged by their general disbelief, she repeated stubbornly, with un-shaken conviction and sometimes dramatica horrified by her vision ,"There will be a war... a terrible, terrible war." Father Sopoćko recalls:

"She pitied the fate of Poland, which she very much loved and for which she frequently prayed. Following the advice of St. John of the Cross, I almost always treated what Sister Faustina foretold in a neutral fashion, and asked for no details. In this case also, I did not ask what the fate of Poland was to be that distressed her. She herself did not say, but only sighed and put a hand her face to shut out the threatening picture."

(Archives of S.S.F., Recollections).

Sister Faustina foretold several things, including details of what would happen when the war came. For example, Mother Krzyżanowska writes:

"Sister Faustina told Sister A. the following; "There will be a terrible war, but the sisters will not leave this House"... When the war broke out, we were threatened with resettlement, at any moment, like the other religious orders. On three occasions there was a direct danger of being thrown out by the Germans. All the sisters went to the grave of Sister Faustina to pray for her intercession to the Divine Mercy that we be left in peace. Each time the danger passed, and we did not leave our house throughout the war."

(Archives of S.F., Recollections).

The facts quickly confirmed the truth of her prophecy. In any case, many heard this from the lips of Sister Faustina herself during her last illness. So, when war broke out, the parish dispersed this information more widely among those who came to visit the convent at Lagiewniki near Cracow, and this helped at the same time to propagate intercession for the Divine Mercy.

The same necessity propagated the devotion to the Divine Mercy in its new form far beyond the frontiers of Poland. As Polish emigrés dispersed, so the devotion spread almost over the globe. Particularly dynamic centres of devotion, radiating over wide areas, arose in France, Britain, and the United States of America.

The story of the growth of the devotion to the Divine Mercy is dramatic, just as Sister Faustina had foretold. It appears at present, however, that the main difficulties have been overcome, and that we have now entered a phase in which the devotion will be able to spread without obstacle to the wide mass of God's people, wherever it is most needed, and in fact at the moment when humanity is at the brink of a precipice. Divine Mercy will be the last hope of rescue. The message of Sister Faustina is the hand of God stretched out to help in these present times. It has been given to us that we should remember that there is no situation that is hopeless, and that only human paths lead nowhere. God always watches over us, and finds a solution where the human intellect cannot see one. Every human being, even the weak, fallen, without a will of his own, can be saved. The only condition is that he repent his sins and trust, deeply trust, in the Divine Mercy.

16. Ślendziński's painting of the Merciful Jesus, 1954

17. Styka's painting of the Merciful Jesus, 1957

PART II

THE SPIRIT AND AIMS
OF THE CONGREGATION
OF SISTERS OF OUR LADY OF MERCY
IN THE LIFE OF SISTER FAUSTINA

THE CONGREGATION OF SISTERS OF OUR LADY OF MERCY

The Congregation of Sisters of Our Lady of Mercy is not an old Congregation. It arose at the beginning of the nineteenth century as a Christian response to a long-standing social evil, which was then greatly increasing: prostitution and its pitiable victims, the girls of easy virtue.

The Congregation was founded in France - divine irony! - that very country which, as a result of the Revolution of 1789, had become the most dechristianized state of the Europe of those days. The Foundress was a young lady from a prosperous bourgeois family, Thérèse Rondeau /1793-1866/, who, encouraged by the Jesuits, in 1818 opened a "House of Mercy" in her home town of Laval in the Department of Mayenne in Brittany. The House was intended as a refuge for those girls who, having "fallen", wanted to rehabilitate themselves, but were now social outcasts, condemned and thrust aside with contempt by society and with little hope of freeing themselves from the kind of life into which they had sunk. These "fallen" girls, whose number was constantly increasing, were of interest to the State only from the point of view of public health and safety. Society, particularly provincial society still guided by the old moral rigour, was disposed only to treat them with unbending ostracism and contempt. The barriers of conduct having once been crossed, there was no way back, so that such girls and women of necessity went on the streets and became professional prostitutes.

Misfortune, however, calls forth sympathy. The self-sacrificing and magnanimous hasten to offer help. Such were the beginnings of the Congregation of Sisters of Our Lady of Mercy, who set themselves to draw such girls out of the moral swamp, and having offered them the material conditions for survival, enable them to return to an honest way of life.

Their task was by no means easy: at the beginning it was like struggling through thick mud. Society was mistrustful of this new religio-social initiative, frequently inimical, and in any case definitely wanted no part in such charitable action. This in turn inhibited the growth of the young Congregation, which earned its keep by needlework, yet, despite the high professional qualifications of its members, did not receive sufficient orders of work from the surrounding town. This social boycott took many forms, and obstinately persisted. For many years the "House of Mercy" suffered extreme poverty.

These circumstances explain the rather unusual beginnings of the Congregation, for independently two "Houses of Mercy" arose in France, each with an identical purpose. The first to be founded was that in Bordeaux, set up and run by Mademoiselle Thérèse de Lamourous. It was already established when Thérèse Rondeau founded her "House of Mercy" in Laval. Having neither the experience nor the training for this type of work, the young, twenty-five-year-old Thérèse decided to join forces with Mlle. de Lamourous. She spent an eight-month novitiate in Bordeaux and decided to put her own house under the Rule of Mlle. de Lamourous. Putting this into practice, however, soon proved impossible. Both Houses had such huge problems of accommodation that it was necessary to give up their first plan and run them independently of each other, adapting to the local possibilities, getting each town used to the new initiatives separately, and teaching their societies the advantages that would spring from this new form of social action. In consequence a strange situation arose; although the Congregation in Laval accepted the founding and Rule of Mlle. de Lamourous and even from time to time received financial assistance from her, formally speaking it was a separate and independent community. Nevertheless, Mlle. de Lamourous had considerable influence upon it. The first elementary propositions, which were later the basis of the Constitutions, were the work of her hand and introduced by her. The cooperation between the two Houses speaks highly of the character of both Foundresses. The twin foundations were never rivals. In fact, the reverse was true, for the experience of the one invariably supported the work of the other, and at specially difficult times Mlle. de Lamourous, as the older and more experienced, hastened to offer help and counsel.

The Congregation of Sisters of Our Lady of Mercy, fighting for its life, had grasped a serious social evil and had done so unerringly. As to how very necessary this type of Christian action was, the facts showed: although at first there were few vocations to the Congregation, for women were frightened by the need to live alongside "social pariahs" and by the extreme severity of the life, the number of penitents applying grew and grew. When it was observed how many of the "fallen" girls had much good will, and in how many cases they were the victims of misfortune, vocations began to arrive. Thus the first difficulties proved to be a blessing, because the Congregation blossomed in adversity, consolidated, and formed its own spirituality. There was only one problem to be resolved, apart from exterior circumstances dictated by local opposition, but it was serious: what form of conventual life to adopt, so that constant contact with the antisocial and frequently destructive wards should not harm the spirit of the cloister? How was it to be made possible, living among those "of this world" and even familiar with its murky depths, to preserve a spotless soul "not of this world"? For this and other reasons, these Sisters had a penitential outlook, a permanent sense of recollection in their work with errant and sometimes deeply sinful souls, so that by their own penance they night make reparation to God for their wards' offences - until wards were able to do this themselves - and then the Sisters continued the spirit of penance together with the girls when the latter began to understand the meaning of life. In such a way, the Sisters not only cared for their wards but included them in their own adoration of God.

Nevertheless, there was a barrier between the nuns and their wards: the wards might not enter the Congregation, no matter what the degree of their personal sanctity.

But before the Congregation had worked out its own spiritual formation, and in connection with this its organizational form, many years of life and work as a community elapsed. Circumstances in their lifestyle and experience gradually gave shape to both formation and organization. The Constitutions were only finalised after the death of the Foundress, in 1878, i.e., sixty years after the establishment of the "House of Mercy" in Laval.

This, however, had had no effect on the fruitfulness of their work. When Mother Thérèse Rondeau died in 1866, her life's work included the saving of 1500 souls; 1100 had died meanwhile, and there were at the time more than 400 girls in the care of the Congregation in two houses. The girls came to the House of Mercy of their own free will and could leave at any time. The only condition for acceptance was to promise to break with their former lifestyle. To help them, their real names and complicated life-stories were kept absolutely secret. The whole impedimenta of their lives remained on the other side of the convent door. In the House they received new Christian names while they were in the care of the community. Thus they were as if new-born, and only penance connected them with their former lives, as well as the newly-regenerative conscience and wish to make reparation to God for their sins. They were generally known as "penitents". Let us not however deceive ourselves. Even the utmost good will could not always make up for defects of character. The will could not keep pace with feelings of remorse or even the most fervent desire for change, where there had been a total lack of grounding in principles and of training in perseverance at putting into practice those same principles. The wards had to be taught everything from the beginning: many had to be shown the most elementary Christian concepts, and respect for work, a sense of duty, discipline and obedience. They were difficult to guide, emotional and without self-control. Therefore work with them required enormous patience and understanding, combined with firmness and refusal to compromise. The basis of dealing with them, in other words the spiritual, was to behave with the deepest sympathy, understanding and love, which must not be oppressive while remaining watchful. The system the Congregation operated to re-educate them did not depend on punishment but rather on stimulating good will and not allowing the wards to be discouraged by failures; they were constantly to be encouraged.

The girls were divided up into small groups, completely independent so-called "classes", each of which had its own life and was not in contact with the others. This system not only facilitated better control of the more unruly and difficult elements, but permitted an institution of more than two hundred wards to have a family atmosphere. Under the eye of the head of each class, a religious known as the "class mother", "the children" were not lost in the general mass, which was rather too numerous; but in the individual freedom afforded by their small group they gradually became accustomed to their new life with its different style and requirements. Complete friendliness and a quasi-family bond on the Sisters' part, and on the wards' side the knowledge that at any time when life in the House ceased to hold them, they might leave, created appropriate conditions for these errant and injured souls to return to mental equilibrium, and a considerable percentage not only returned to such equilibrium but reached a high scholastic standard and great piety. Such girls gave great joy and pride to the Congregation, as visible evidence of the appropriate nature of the work they had undertaken and the sacrifices they had made.

Perhaps the best illustration of the atmosphere and aims of the community is given by the words of the Foundress:

"My dear Sisters," Mother Thérèse would say, *"let us be real mothers and not stepmothers to our girls. Let us find our own happiness in surrounding them with love, and care for their good. Let us not seek our own diversions and recreation away from them. We must show them that it is our pleasure to be among them. God looks at us with more loving eyes if we are with our class, busy in watching over souls for love of Him, than if we are in the raptures of contemplation."*
"We must know how to leave God for God's sake", she reminded, when some Sister had sat too long in chapel, neglecting her duties. *"We must not try to make our girls into nuns, or, as the world sees it, bigots, but we must bring them up to be good Christians. Otherwise we would turn our girls into hypocrites. Let us try to inculcate real piety, which will lead them to God in the greatest simplicity."*

"We must know how to win them over, and let us not be discouraged if it is necessary to convert them. If there are among them some who are stubborn and faulty, falling at every step, let us try to get them as far as Purgatory at least."

"Mercy is the essence of our congregation. If we remove mercy, we cease to be ourselves."

The wards formed the nucleus of the community. It is therefore not surprising that the community worked out a rule and regulations for them more quickly than it did its own Constitutions. Such regulations arose according to *"the merciful intentions of the Saviour"*, Who came "not to call the just, but sinners", and Who sought "mercy and not sacrifice". So the community's method was the same: Jesus'. The sisters understood their apostolic tasks as a vocation given them by God *"in order to join with Him in the work of converting and sanctifying souls"*. They believed they should become an extension of the loving arms of God. So, taking Christ as their model, they lived alongside the "penitents", educating them and instructing them in the virtues, and simultaneously employing all possible methods open to them to make reparation to God for the sins formerly committed by their wards. Thus it was also a penitential congregation, and this factor played a role as important as their apostolate, since only by combining the two were they participating in a fully Christ-like activity. For these purposes, the Congregation lived in permanent contemplation of the life of Christ, and in particular of His Passion.

The Constitutions state that

"the degree of commitment to the love of God and the imitation of His desire to save sinners decides the degree of commitment to the spirit of the Congregation and also of the greatness of the personal sanctity of each of the Sisters".

Further, they state:

"In accordance with the spirit of their vocation [the sisters] *will offer for the intentions of the souls*

*entrusted to them prayers, mortifications and work, in
other words everything, even efforts made for their
personal sanctity, without which it would be impossible for them to work effectively for the improvement
of others."*

We should here add that the Congregation was
dedicated, as its name indicates, to Our Lady, a
dedication which offered a certain guarantee that
Christ's Mercy, with Her help, would be properly
interpreted, and their life appropriately directed.

The organization of the community was as follows: it
wad divided into two choirs. The first choir was formed
of educator-directresses, whose work was with the
wards; the second choir was formed of the sisters
coadjutrices who did the household tasks in the kitchen,
the bakery, garden etc. This formal division should not,
however, confuse us: all the sisters had a part to play
in the apostolic work with the girls, through prayer,
penance and mortification, and because the girls in
helping with the house-work and gardening alongside
the coadjutrix sisters were then under the authority of
the coadjutrices.

In Poland there were four congregations working with
"fallen" girls, but only the Sisters of Our Lady of Mercy
were entirely devoting their labour to this form of
activity. Because the problem of "fallen" girls was not
so widespread in Poland as in France, their institutions
quickly took the form, not of penitential but rehabilita-
tive and educational establishments. Increasingly there
came to them girls who were difficult to bring up,
disturbed and requiring special efforts, but not "fallen"
in the usual meaning of the term.

The Congregation was brought to Poland from France
by Mother Teresa Potocka and by the mother and
daughter Kunegunda and Rose Kłobukowska in the
year 1862. They had been suitably prepared, for in the
previous year they had spent an eight-month novitiate

in Laval under the eye of the Foundress. The first House of the Congregation was erected in Warsaw at Żytnia Street, nos.3/9, where it still is, at the request of Archbishop Szczęsny Feliński. It was opened on 1st November 1862, not long before the January Insurrection of 1863, as a result of which the archbishop was exiled to Russia. The Congregation thus had a very difficult start. They were poor and often hungry, but this did not diminish the sacrificial life of the nuns. Their needs were great. Vocations were numerous, so that in 1868 they were able to open another house, in Cracow. Local difficulties of the Cracow house caused the sisters to have to move several times, and it was only in 1890 that they found a permanent home in Łgiewniki, founded by Prince Lubomirski. The two Houses, in Warsaw and Cracow, formed the axis of the Congregation. The superiors of the Congregation and the formation of the novices were established there, the formation consisting of the postulancy and novitiate before the annual vows, and the so-called probation before final profession.

The turn of the century found the Congregation well established. It exhibited immense and dynamic vitality, opening house after house. Up to 1939 it had houses in Derdy, Płock, Częstochowa, Vilnius, Walendow, Radom, Kalisz, a second house in Warsaw in the Grochów district, in Kiekrz near Poznań, and in Rabka.

The Congregation of Sisters of Our Lady of Mercy brought in from France to Poland was for sixty years a vicariate of the French mother house. But the expansive activity of the Polish branch of the Congregation, while suffering impeded contact with the Mother House in Laval, and working in quite different social conditions and for other social needs, led to the Polish Houses becoming independent. A situation arose similar to that when the Congregation was founded in France and it was necessary to separate the House at Laval from the House at Bordeaux. Here, too, there were different social conditions and hence other needs, so it was necessary to separate. The decision came from France, from the Mother House, so in 19 the Polish Congregation of Sisters of Our Lady of Mercy separated from the mother house as an independent organization. The Sisters in Poland received the decision of the General Chapter in Laval sadly. The Polish Constitutions, based strictly upon the French, were written after separation, and in 1927 they received their first approbation from the Holy See, while in 1935 they received final approbation.

After the Second World War, the activity of the Congregation moved to the west of Poland. The Houses in Lwów, Vilnius and Płock ceased to exist. However, new Houses arose in Zakopane, Wrocław and Gdańsk. Adapting to newer possibilities and needs, at present the Sisters of Our Lady of Mercy in Poland run, among other activities: homes for the old; homes for the incurably sick, handicapped children, the mentally handicapped and crippled; centres for maladjusted young people; various pastoral centres; retreat centres for youth, catechism classes and sodalities.

WORK AND PRAYER

Work was an important factor in the spiritual life of Sister Faustina because she had entered an active congregation, not a contemplative. It was thus one of the basic elements in the realisation of her vocation. But it was not easy for Sister Faustina to accept this. As we recall, three weeks after entering she wanted to leave, as she felt that work took up too much time at the expense of prayer. However, as Jesus had decided otherwise, she remained, but this meant that she had to find a balance between the need for prayer and the demands of work. She had the difficult task of working out a repertoire of prayer suitable for the everyday household chores she did, so that the work itself could be transformed into prayer, and contemplation could be united with activity in harmonious symbiosis. The Congregation had a collection of lovely and well-chosen prayers for their style of convent life, but the demands of household chores often meant that their use was limited. Sister Faustina could not agree with this state of affairs. Prayer, she thought, is as much a duty as work. Work has a tendency to absorb a human being completely, without regard for other duties; this must not be submitted to. Work cannot be privileged at the expense of prayer and must not be allowed to dictate the conditions under which one prays.

'I will not allow myself', she writes, *'to be so absorbed in the whirlwind of work as to forget about*

*God. I will spend all my free moments at the feet of the
Master hidden in the Blessed Sacrament.'*

(Diary, Notebook I, para. 82).

On the other hand, prayer must not lead to the
neglect of other duties. It was necessary to find the
mutual link between work and prayer and to harmonise
the co-existence of the one with the other.

Sister Faustina knew how to perceive and interpret
her daily occupation in the light of the aims of her
Congregation. As a proud and joyful mumber she
emphasises that

> *"the Congregation has a special part in the Redemp-
> tion, because just as Jesus came to look for that
> which was lost, so we in our work to save difficult
> and fallen girls continue His work of seeking and
> saving souls."*

(Archives of S.F., Recoll. S.Louise G.).

Work, then, was an essential feature of the Congregation and was closely connected with the very aim of its
existence. This meant that it often interfered with its
second aim, prayer. In theory prayer pervaded every
activity of the Sisters, but for Sister Faustina this was
not yet sufficiently clear in practice. The intensity of
work prevented constant thought of God. Of course
there were quieter hours which even permitted the
recital of the rosary or the Office, but they were
succeeded by others when the whole attention was
concentrated on work, and recollection of God escaped
a mind too engaged with the needs of the moment.
Sister Faustina asked herself: how is it possible practically to pray through work and at work? She might
never have learned how, if it were not for that hunger
for prayer she experienced so sharply. Her spiritual
instinct told her that it ought to be otherwise, that it
is necessary not only to offer the intention of the work
to God, but to saturate the work with prayer.

Sister Faustina at all times, easy or difficult, preserved her inner peace. It did not scare her when she had too much work or when she had insufficient assistance, which frequently happened, because the houses of the Congregation contained up to 200 or more wards, and there were too few sisters for all the duties. Sister Faustina was not one of those who persistently complain. She would ask for help, but not insist, waiting patiently for her superiors' decision, for her superiors to her represented the will of God. What usually happens is that the person who is less forceful receives less, because superiors tend to think that because she is silent it must mean that she can manage. It therefore indeed happened that she received less help than other nuns in a similar situation. But she did not complain. She had found her own method of dealing with a difficult situation. If she did not feel capable of performing her duties, she "went for advice" to Jesus in the Blessed Sacrament, after which, having prayed, she started work. She worked handily and peacefully.

Sister Faustina did not make a division into serious and trivial when discussing matters with God. Her life was an ideal practical application of the Little Way of St. Thérèse of the Child Jesus. She included prayer in the most trivial occurrence, especially if it was anything causing her some difficulty, We learn from her own words the details of one of the "trivial" daily matters about which she applied to Jesus, and of the lesson He taught her:

"One time during the novitiate, when Mother Directress sent me to work in the wards' kitchen, I was very upset because I could not manage the pots, which were very large. The most difficult task for me was draining the potatoes, and sometimes I spilt half of them with the water. When I told this to Mother Directress, she said that with time I would get used to it and gain the

necessary skill. Yet the task was not getting any easier, as I was growing weaker every day. So I would move away when it was time to drain the potatoes. The sisters noticed that I avoided this task and were very much surprised. They did not know that I could not help in spite of all my willingness to do this and not spare myself. At noon, during the examination of conscience, I complained to God about my weakness. Then I heard the following words in my soul, *From today on you will do this easily; I shall strengthen you.*

'That evening, when the time came to drain off the water from the potatoes, I hurried to be the first to do it, trusting in the Lord's words. I took up the pot with ease and poured off the water perfectly. But when I took off the cover to let the potatoes steam off, I saw there in the pot, in the place of the potatoes, whole bunches of red roses, beautiful beyond description. I had never seen such roses before. Greatly astonished and unable to understand the meaning of this I heard a voice within me saying, *I change such hard work of yours into bouquets of most beautiful flowers, and their perfume rises up to My throne.* From then on I have tried to drain the potatoes myself, not only during my week when it was my turn to cook, but also in replacement of other sisters when it was their turn. And not only do I do this, but I try to be the first to help in any other burdensome task, because I have experienced how much this pleases God.'

(Diary, Notebook I, para. 65).

The above incident did not pass unnoticed by others. Sister R., a novice like Sister Faustina, and a companion in the kitchen, tells of it too:

"Near the end of the novitiate, Sister Faustina came to work in the kitchen. One time when the potatoes had to be drained, I wanted to help her, because I feared that she had neither the strength nor the skill. But she began with enthusiasm and did it herself. When she put down the pot with the steaming potatoes, I noticed that she was staring into the pot with some surprise. I wondered what she was seeing there, but when I asked her, she replied, "Nothing, nothing, Sister." When her Diary was read after her death, among other things there was a mention of this incident."

(Archives of S.F., Recollections).

Going to Jesus "for advice" was done once and again and became a habit, and in this way prayer came into the very basis of her work: it included not only the meaning but the organization of it. Sister Faustina learned in every case first to agree the work with God and only after looking at it from the point of view of His requirements did she start work. The Divine point of view was an essential in whatever she did, because she did everything for Him. She would not compromise on that.

To begin a task with God does not mean automatically that He will always remain in our thoughts while we do it. Remembering Him all the time certainly does not come easily, as we all know, but it is not impossible. There is only one indispensable condition needed to achieve this: one has to love. When someone loves, the thoughts automatically turn to the beloved, and she finds all kinds of ways to show her love. God was ever-present in the thoughts of Sister Faustina. Keeping contact with Him was possible many times during the day by visiting the Blessed Sacrament. She let no chance go by to drop in to the chapel for a moment. If she was passing, and in a great hurry, she would genuflect before the door of the chapel without entering, and throw a smile to the Lord. Even this was enough. Her thoughts turned constantly to the God she loved above all, whatever she was doing. Even at the busiest moments at work, when her hands were flying about her tasks, she would unexpectedly propose to her fellow workers that they say a prayer. People's impatience at such moments was not unfounded. The request to pray at times of haste seemed to be an obvious interference with duties, so sometimes her companions reacted with annoyance, thinking it unsuitable. But Sister Faustina quickly put an end to such misunderstanding. A typical example is related by Sister L.

"We were working in the kitchen in Warsaw. It was already eleven o'clock, lunch had to be ready soon and we had plenty to do. At a certain moment Sister Faustina said, "Sister, let us pray." Thinking that she wanted to recite the Office, I said there was no time for prayer, for they might be annoyed with us if lunch was not ready on time. Sister Faustina then said the ejaculation, "Most Holy Trinity, I adore You." When I had repeated the prayer, Sister Faustina asked me if it had taken too much of my time. I was amazed that, while doing hard work requiring great effort, she could so easily unite herself with God."

(Archives of S.F., Recollections).

Mother Xavier Olszanowska, then superior at Kiekrz, had a similar story:

"Other sisters, who had more to do with Sister Faustina, also emphasised her constant union with God. They would say, "Little Faustina is always talking to God."

(Archives of S.F., Recollections).

"At work she was always praying and she encouraged us wards to pray with her", said one of the wards, Leokadia. *"We were always reciting the rosary, the Office, or various chaplets. Sometimes we were not pleased to have to pray so much. Sister Faustina knew this, but by her goodness and her explanations she encouraged us to pray."* Another ward, Maria M., adds, *"Even at work she prayed and was wrapped up in God. Often at a free moment she would tell me that she was going to Jesus in the chapel, because Jesus was calling her. After a short time she would return to work."* And Maria M. gives the interesting detail that Sister Faustina often held her rosary in one hand while weeding the beds with the other."

(Archives of S.F., Recollections).

A nun with a large rosary hanging by her side is a common sight, but in the case of Sister Faustina the still-life is given movement and life: the rosary changes its character, instead of a symbol, becoming the visible sign of prayer.

Sister Faustina was not afraid of any kind of work. Whenever there was any special difficulty, she would say, *"Let us do this for Jesus"*. Even when the work was particularly hard and unpleasant, she did not evade it. She accepted it in the spirit of penance and offered it as reparation to God not only for the sins committed by the wards, but for human sin in general or with the intention *"that people should know God better and love Him more."*

Little by little Sister Faustina created her own style of work. She had found the key to including God in the whole of her everyday life. Nothing distracted her, because everything became a prayer: *"No work distracts me during a retreat"*, she said, when some sisters complained that duties done during a retreat prevented them from concentrating. *"I saw that indeed she was always close to God,"* confirmed Sister E. Mother Irene Krzyżanowska, Sister Faustina's superior in Vilnius and Cracow, adds her opinion to that of the other sisters:

"Sister Faustina knew how to reconcile her daily duties with spiritual exercises, and stated that no work distracted her from uniting herself with Jesus."
(Archives of S.F., Recollections).

There was yet another problem in connection with work. Sister Faustina took great care that it should be done in the time foreseen by God's law. She would not compromise over this. She was capable of taking this up with the highest authority in the convent.

"How seriously she treated the laws of God and His Church can be seen from the following example", says Sister D., who worked with her in the garden in Cracow in 1936. *"It was the custom of the House in Cracow, that the vegetables intended for the market on Monday were packed on the preceding day, on Sunday. Sister Faustina did not like this. She told me that she had asked one of the priests for an explanation, and he had said that such work for the good of the Congregation, even on Sunday, was permissible. She did not agree with this, for she said that the commandments of God and the Church are equally binding on everyone. She said so to Sister Superior, and with her permission we introduced the custom of rising on Mondays at three in the morning, so as to be able to prepare the goods for the market in time. This custom has persisted till today."*
(Archives of S.F., Recollections).

Sister Faustina's style of work had a social effect, as the sisters did not work alone but in small groups and together with the wards. Her behaviour could not pass unnoticed, and she herself in many cases gave it a communal character by including her fellow-nuns, who had earlier had the opportunity of checking that in no way did it interfere with work. Besides, her problem, how to cope with too heavy a load of duties, was one which the other sisters also had to face. They often spoke of this, and Sister Faustina shared with them the knowledge she had obtained at the foot of the Blessed Sacrament; in its way, it was a discreet form of apostolate. It once happened, for example, that

> "one of the younger Sisters came weeping, saying that the Sister in charge of the garden had gone to the town and left her with orders to do such a mass of work that she did not know where to begin. Sister Faustina told her, "Sister, pray for a moment, then think which is the most important job and do that without thinking about anything else. When you have done it, think what is the next most urgent and do that."

> (Archives of S.F., Recollections s.D.).

Another time Sister Faustina asked Sister P. during recreation what work she had to do today. She answered,

> "I have the hard task of watering the young trees and my hands are painful because of it." She encouraged me to do it in the spirit of penance and to offer my labour for the sins of humanity. Later in the evening, she asked me if I remembered what she had said during recreation."

Work faced Sister Faustina with serious problems other than spiritual. It was also the source of many misunderstandings with those around her. There were two conflicting and completely opposed standpoints. Some of the Sisters, having seen that her method of combining prayer with work in no way interfered with their duties, were attracted to her ways. Others thought she was insufficiently productive, the more so as she had poor health, which made them distrustful of her ability to do enough. In addition, "she wanted only to pray all the time", was the accusation of those who supervised her in the household. Such an opinion, once established, affected the reprimands, often unjust, which she received, for Sister Faustina was a conscientious and qualified worker. In the community she worked mainly in two areas, the kitchen or the garden. In both she had been trained in the convent and had attained great skills in the work. She was considered a consummate and exquisite cook and a clever and productive gardener. She liked both tasks; she could find in each an outlet for her apostolic temperament. She cooked tasty meals because she felt that care over food would be more likely to draw the stubborn and unruly wards towards God. For the same reason she took care that fruit and vegetables in the convent garden should give large crops. The flowers she grew so beautifully went to the altar in the chapel. When Sister Faustina was asked how she managed her duties, she said happily that "Jesus gives so much of everything." (Arch. S.F., Recoll.).

Her skills did not come at once. She acquired them gradually as she performed her duties. This "further training" had its thorny moments at times: it was sometimes associated with painful experiences. This was no school adapted specially to teach. The work had its specific requirements, and deadlines had to be met. So the instructions given to Sister Faustina were often abrupt and impatient, though she was sensitive and anxious to do well. The humility she learned in the convent was unable to suppress these traits. While indeed she received reproofs without discussion and with the words, "I'm sorry, I shall try to do better next time", she was painfully hurt and shed many tears, especially if the reproofs were abrupt or unjust. She did not know how to control her resentment, though she did not grumble either to her superiors or other sisters. She went to complain to Jesus.